An Introduction to Data Types

J. Craig Cleaveland

AT&T BELL LABORATORIES

Addison-Wesley Publishing Company

Reading, Massachusetts • Menlo Park, California • Don Mills, Ontario
Wokingham, England • Amsterdam • Sydney • Singapore • Tokyo
Madrid • Bogotá • Santiago • San Juan

Library of Congress Cataloging in Publication Data

Cleaveland, J. Craig
  An introduction to data types,

  Bibliography: p.
  1. Data structures (Computer science) I. Title.
QA76.9.D35C57 1986   001.64′2   85-6002
ISBN 0-201-11940-4

ABCDEFGHIJ-DO-89876

In memory of Kathleen Regina Callaghan (1905–1983)

*P*reface

While writing this book, I have been asked what is the difference between data types and data structures. I explain by analogy:

data types are to data structures
as
programming languages are to programs.

Data types are specific programming language constructs used to describe and define data structures. This helps a little, but still some people wander off shaking their heads. This is a book that explores and surveys programming language issues: design, implementation, and specification. It does not discuss data structure issues, algorithms, or performance tradeoffs, although it discusses some novel data structures such as procedural data structures. While there are many books on data structures and many books on programming languages which may contain chapters on data types, this is among the first books exclusively devoted to data types.

Since a data type is a programming language facility, this book can be safely classified as a specialized book on programming languages. It can be used as a supplementary book for courses on principles of programming languages, design of programming languages, data structures, or the semantics of programming languages. It can be used as the primary book for courses on data types. The book is suitable for upper-level undergraduates and graduate students. It is also useful as a programming language reference book.

Chapter 1 should be read before any other chapter to set the stage for overall viewpoint, definitions, and notation. The rest of the book is organized into four parts of three chapters each:

I.   A Survey of Data Types
II. Data Type Issues
III. Data Abstractions
IV. Specifications

The chapters of the last two parts (Chapters 8-10 and 11-13) probably should be read in order. The remaining chapters can be read in any order without finding too much material out of context. Part II (Chapters 2-4) contains a lot of survey material about specific programming languages and type systems and does not contain a lot of conceptual material. Rather, it gives a historical perspective on the evolution of data types as they are found in many languages. Consequently, it must occasionally refer to the concepts described in detail in later chapters. Although this material is not necessary to understand subsequent chapters, it does put everything into a historical and practical context.

Many programming languages have contributed to the myriad of ideas in this book. Many ideas and examples used in this book come from a large number of sources, some of which are the following:

Ada	Habermann and Perry (1983), Ichbiah et al. (1979)
ALGOL 60	Naur (1963)
ALGOL 68	van Wijngaarden et al. (1975), Tanenbaum (1976)
Alphard	Wulf et al. (1976)
APL	Falkoff and Iverson (1973, 1978)
BASIC	Harle (1983)
BCPL	Richards (1969)
Bliss	Wulf et al. (1971)
C	Kernighan and Ritchie (1978)
CLU	Liskov et al. (1977)
COBOL	Jackson (1977)
EL1	Wegbreit (1974)
Euclid	Lampson et al. (1977), Popek et al. (1977)
FORTRAN	Brainerd (1978)
FP	Backus (1978)
HOPE	Burstall et al. (1980)
ICON	Griswold (1982, 1983), Wampler and Griswold (1983)
LISP	McCarthy (1960), McCarthy and Levin (1965), Allen (1978)
Mesa	Geschke et al. (1977)
ML	Gordon et al. (1979)
Modula	Wirth (1977)
Modula-2	Wirth (1980)
Pascal	Wirth (1971), Hoare and Wirth (1973), Jensen and Wirth (1974), Welsh et al. (1977), Addyman (1980)
PL/I	Beech (1970)
Russell	Demers et al. (1978, 1980)
SETL	Schonberg et al. (1981)
SIMULA	Dahl et al. (1968)
Smalltalk	Goldberg et al. (1983)
SNOBOL	Griswold et al. (1971)

Various parts of this book have been tested in classes both in academia and industry. I thank my students who helped me try out the material in a classroom setting, particularly Chuck Bullis, John Sherman, and Tom Wetmore. I also thank the reviewers who provided many useful suggestions that have been incorporated into this book: Paul Eggert, Samuel Kamin of the University of Illinois, Henry Ledgard, Nancy Leveson of the University of California at Irvine, and Jon Shultis of the University of Colorado at Boulder. And I thank my wife Tina who has spent many evening hours helping me improve our book in small and large ways.

North Andover, Mass.

JCC

Contents

1

Introduction 1

Part I: A Survey of Data Types

2

Primitive Types 13

3

Aggregate Types 29

4

More Types 43

Part II: Data Type Issues

5

Type Checking 67

6

Examples of Type Checking 87

7

Values, Variables, and Storage 95

Part III: Data Abstractions

Abstract Data Types   113

Examples of Abstract Data Types   137

Polymorphism   155

Part IV: Data Type Specifications

11

Specifications   177

12

Mathematics of Data Types   189

13

Algebraic Specifications   199

Bibliography   219

Index   231

Introduction

1.1 What is a Type?

A peculiarity of the human species is the desire to classify things into different categories, which we shall call *types*. In many cases, a *type* is simply a set of items; a *type system* is a scheme for organizing a collection of types. We develop such schemes to help us understand complicated relationships. In particular, programming languages provide *data types* to classify data and help prevent errors. We can gain some insight into the use of types in programming languages by first examining type systems outside of computer science.

Words are the most familiar example of types. We use nouns, for example, to organize the objects of this complex world into smaller and more understandable sets of things. Most nouns define some type of object. Thus the word *table* defines the set of all objects we perceive as tables. Similarly, verbs, adjectives, and other parts of speech define classes of actions, properties, and other kinds of namable things.

Taxonomy is a classification scheme used in biology. That scheme is a hierarchical classification with various levels (from kingdom at the broadest level, down to species). Biologists classify each organism as a member of some species, and each species as a member of some genus, and so on. Unlike the words of everyday language, where many different words may describe the same object, each organism belongs to just one species.

A common scheme for organizing books is by subject. A general topic area is divided into smaller subtopics that can be further subdivided. This is also a hierarchical structure. We might have, for example, the progression: nonfiction, science, physics, particle physics, quantum chromodynamics. Unlike the biology taxonomy, this system can place an object in a general class rather than any specific class. An animal will always belong to some particular species, whereas an introductory book in physics may not be properly classified under any specific field of physics. Some books can be especially troublesome. Should a book on the history of mathematics be classified as history or mathematics? Should books about computers be classified under mathematics or engineering or perhaps a new subject called computer science? And multidisciplinary books, those that span several areas, may be very frustrating to classify under a rigid classification scheme.

The classification of quantities in physics is a simple matter by comparison with the classification of books. Each quantity belongs to exactly one dimension, such as time, area, energy, density, pressure. There is no hierarchy, but rather an elegant algebraic structure, called an *abelian group*.

Mathematicians classify abstract objects into different types that include sets, functions, numbers, and relations. However, the relationship between these different types depends on the point of view. A set theorist can represent everything with sets. But functions, relations, and even numbers can be used to represent sets. We could thus create an arbitrary hierarchy out of these types. Despite all these viewpoints, each of the types is distinct. Every object belongs to exactly one type; however, objects of one type can represent objects of other types.

Finally, consider the numeric types used in FORTRAN, such as INTEGER, REAL, and DOUBLE PRECISION. Each of these types specifies a set of numbers. Any numeric value used in a FORTRAN program can belong to only one of these types. This restriction presents a problem similar to those met in the classification of books. Which numeric type contains the number two? To answer this question, we must realize first that the values of a numeric type are not numbers. The values of a numeric type *represent* numbers. Every numeric type has its own representation of a number. Thus there is an INTEGER two, a REAL two, and a DOUBLE PRECISION two. We can tell the difference between them syntactically. For example, the string "2" represents the integer value and the string "2.0" represents the floating-point value two.

1.2 Motivation for the Use of Types

There are three basic motives for using types:

1. Types help us understand and organize our ideas about objects.
2. A type scheme helps us to see and discuss unique properties of specific types.
3. Types help us detect errors.

Not all of these motives are necessary for the creation of a type system, but all are important in programming languages. Let us look at them more closely.

First, types allow the programmer to organize and express a solution to a problem by naming and identifying specific ideas about data. The use of types is thus an important link between the real world and the data elements manipulated by a program. A type system allows us to restrict attention to a particular kind of object. For example, the statement

"x is of type y"

gives information about x (and sometimes about y). Consider also the following examples:

1. That is a chair.
2. Mark Twain is a member of *Homo sapiens*.
3. *Tom Sawyer* is a novel.
4. A foot is a unit of length.
5. Let S be a set.
6. INTEGER X

Item 6 is written in FORTRAN and means "let X be an integer variable." Note that all of the above statements say something about the type of an object, but not its *value* or *content*. The statements merely classify objects. By contrast, consider another kind of statement, "x is y", which specifies that x is the same thing as y. Here are six examples:

1. That is the chair.
2. Mark Twain is the person who wrote *Tom Sawyer*.
3. *Tom Sawyer* is the book written by Mark Twain.
4. A foot is 12 inches.
5. Let S be the set of all even integers.
6. X .EQ. 5

Again, item 6 is written in FORTRAN and asks "Is the value of X equal to 5?"

Second, typing helps us see the properties of what we are dealing with, for specific types have unique properties. "Number of legs" is a property of tables and animals, but not houses or plants. Relations might be reflexive, but "reflexive number" does not have a common mathematical meaning. Size is a property of arrays and strings but not a property of truth values. Sometimes the properties of a type are so important that the properties define the type. This situation occurs frequently in biology and mathematics. Mammals have hair, are warm blooded, and give milk to their young. An equivalence relation is a relation that is reflexive, symmetric, and transitive.

Finally, error detection is a powerful reason for using types. A type system can enable us to detect the improper use of an object. If an object of type x is used in a context that is not appropriate for an object of type x, there is a type error. The properties of a type often give clues to type errors. The following statements have type errors:

1. That table has two doors and four windows.
2. Mark Twain has four branches.
3. That biography is a fictional account of quarks.
4. (4 feet / 6 seconds) * 3 seconds = 2 seconds
5. $(A \subset B) \cup A$
6. X = 3 + "HI"

Type checking is one of the most powerful error detection capabilities of a compiler.

To summarize, a *type system* is a method of organizing a collection of objects into different categories called types. We often use unique properties to define a type. We use type systems to understand ideas, to communicate them, and to detect errors. In this section we looked at type systems in general and at some examples. We saw that type systems can be identified by their algebraic properties or hierarchical structure. So the classification of type systems is, in itself, yet another type system. The remainder of this book discusses the data type systems of programming languages.

1.3 What is a Data Type?

A type is a set of values. This was an early view of data types and is still commonly used because of its simplicity and elegance. The definition captures the essence of any classification scheme. To define a type, one merely specifies a set of values. This specification may be accomplished by enumeration or by properties. As a working model, this definition can take us far, but because of its very simplicity it does not and cannot capture the modern notion of data types.

Types are not sets. This was the title of a paper written by Jim Morris (1973). It succinctly expressed the on-going debate on data types. Our view of the nature of data types has in fact been evolving since the emergence of computer languages and will continue to change and expand. The process often erupts in debates that encompass a number of related issues and problems. Many of these questions involve the nature of values, variables, symbols, and objects.

The *abstract data type* revolution began in the early 1970s. The concept of abstract data types is the most important concept in the field of data types, and from it there has crystallized a definition that most people now accept:

> **Data Type.** A *data type* is a set of values and a set of operations on the set of values.

This definition is the same as the one used for the mathematical structure called an *algebra*. There are however some important differences between data types and algebras; we shall discuss them in Chapter 12.

Other significant views of data types have also been developed—for example, the Smalltalk, Russell, and SETL views. Yet another important alternative view is the *universal domain* view. In this view, there is only one underlying domain of values. Types specify how to interpret the values. This approach closely models the implementation of data types in programming languages. That is, memory is a sequence of bits, and the values of a data type are represented by certain bit patterns. The underlying universal domain is the set of all bit patterns, and types specify how to interpret those bit patterns. Thus the bit pattern 01000001 can be interpreted either as the ASCII character "A" or as the integer 65. The interpretation of the bit pattern is determined by the type discipline. In general, an interpretation of a bit pattern is determined by the operations applied to it. By restricting the operations, one can restrict the interpretation of a bit pattern to a particular "type." Thus a data type provides a consistent way of interpreting values in the universal domain. Although this viewpoint and other viewpoints are useful and applicable for certain situations, the standard viewpoint that is adopted by this book is the algebraic point of view.

Debates about data types are often obscured because of confusing terminology—a situation common in computer science and programming. One person's *object* is another's *value*. One programming language's *union* is another programming language's *record*. In the 1960s a new language, ALGOL 68, was designed and its definition included many new words rather than use the common well-worn words. The intent was to impart very specific meanings, rather than use the standard but vague words with all their built-in connotations. This approach was ideal for the formalist intent on providing a precise definition, but it was a formidable obstacle to the average layman. Although the literature on data types does not yet consistently use the same vocabulary, we can define what certain terms will mean as used in this book. The definitions below explain the common words used by computer scientists in regard to data types.

Value. A *value* is a mathematical abstraction. *Values* do not have temporal or spatial characteristics. They cannot be stored or changed in a computer memory. They can be represented (by some encoding) in computer memory.

Operation. An *operation* is a mathematical function on values.

Object. An *object* has time and space characteristics and may have values. To say an *object* has a value means that a representation of the value is encoded within the object. Typically objects exist at some location for some length of time. The value of an object may change over time.

Variable. A *variable* is an object.

Symbol. In the context of programming languages, a *symbol* is a textual entity. Programs are sequences of *symbols* that express algorithms and computer instructions.

Literal. A *literal* is a symbol used to denote some value. It cannot be redefined to mean something else. Numeric and string literals are the most commonly used literals.

Constant. The term *constant* is sometimes used to mean literals, but unlike literals, constants usually refer to the values denoted by a literal.

Identifier. An *identifier* is a symbol used to denote values, variables, operations, procedures or other things. Typically an identifier is a sequence of alphanumeric characters, beginning with an alphabetic character.

Operator Symbol. An *operator symbol* is a symbol that is used to denote an operation or procedure. Operator symbols have no inherent meaning. However, most programming languages use the conventional meaning associated with an operator symbol. For example, "+" usually denotes the addition operation.

Data Type Issues

A thought-provoking and influential description of data types that was written before the abstract data type revolution is a monograph entitled "Notes on Data Structuring" by C. A. R. Hoare (1972a). Hoare gives a summary of some of the important points:

1. A type determines the class of values which may be assumed by a variable or expression.

2. Every value belongs to one and only one type.

3. The type of a value denoted by any constant, variable, or expression may be deduced from its form or context, without any knowledge of its value as computed at run-time.

4. Each operator expects operands of some fixed type, and delivers a result of some fixed type . . . Where the same symbol is applied to several different types . . . this symbol may be regarded as ambiguous, denoting several different actual operators. The resolution of such systematic ambiguity can always be made at compile-time.

5. The properties of the values of a type and of the primitive operations defined over them are specified by means of a set of axioms.

6. Type information is used in a high-level language both to prevent or detect meaningless construction in a program, and to determine the method of representing and manipulating data on a computer.

7. The types in which we are interested are those already familiar to mathematicians; namely Cartesian Products, Discriminated Unions, Sets, Functions, Sequences, and Recursive Structures.*

---

* From O.J.Dahl, C.A.R.Hoare, and E.W.Dijkstra, *Structured Programming,* Academic Press, New York, 1972, pp. 92–93.

This description of data types may give the impression of being the final word on data types, but it should instead be viewed as posing a challenge. Do data types in fact conform to this description? *Should* data types conform to this description? These questions introduce some of the major issues in data types. For example, Hoare's first item, although not a complete definition, suggests that a data type is a set of values. As we have already discussed, this assertion is a central part of a data type definition, but the other six points expand the definition and role of data types. The first item also pointedly reminds us that these values and types do not arise out of a vacuum, but are derived from the variables and expressions of a real programming language.

The second item on Hoare's list presents a controversial issue. Should two different types be allowed to share common values? In practice, most types do not share common values. However, there do exist many important and interesting developments that employ a hierarchy of types based on subtypes and supertypes. As a simple example, consider the integers and the reals. As mathematical abstractions, all integers are reals. Just as there are many notations for expressing numbers, such as Arabic, Roman, and scientific, there are many ways of representing numbers in a computer. In PL/I, the number two can be encoded in many different ways—for example, as a floating decimal or a fixed binary. To the mathematician, the number two is a common value shared between the integers and reals. To the programmer, there is a different representation of the number two for each numeric type.

The third and fourth items of Hoare's list introduce the notion of compile-time type checking. A major debate in data types concerns compile-time type checking versus run-time type checking. At the heart of this debate is a disagreement over exactly what things should be type checked. In one view, values and not variables should be type checked. This kind of type checking must be performed at run-time in the presence of variables, since the value of a variable is not always known at compile-time. More sophisticated type checking at compile-time can be accomplished by assuming that all variables are *typed*. The value of a *typed* variable must always be of one specific type. Type-checking issues are covered in Chapters 5 and 6.

The fifth item of Hoare's list provides a means of defining data types. Like algebras, data types can be defined with axioms. An axiom is a statement about the properties and characteristics of values and operations. One result of the abstract data type revolution is the attention paid to data type specifications and in particular axiomatic specification. One popular form of this method is described in Chapters 12 and 13.

The sixth item describes a major purpose of data types. Interestingly, the abstract data type issue can be seen in this item. It states that there are two major purposes: (1) type checking and (2) representation and implementation.

Representation. The *representation* specifies how the values of a data type are to be encoded.

Implementation. Given the representation, the *implementation* of a data type is the set of algorithms that implement the operations of the data type.

Abstract Data Types. The major conceptual idea of *abstract data types* is to separate the use of a type from the representation and implementation of a type. The use of a type should depend only on the set of values and operations. It should not depend on either its representation or its implementation.

Abstract data types were probably the most important advance in programming languages during the 1970s. Abstract data types are discussed in Chapters 8 and 9.

The last item on Hoare's list is an explicit reference to the mathematical structures that are employed as the basic data types of computer science. A survey of types given in Chapters 2, 3, and 4 will show the historical developments that naturally led to such a statement.

Other topics not explicitly mentioned by Hoare are discussed in other chapters of this book. Storage issues play an important role in data types; these are described in Chapter 7. Chapter 7 also describes the relationship between values and variables, and between imperative and applicative programming. Finally, the recurring issues of polymorphism are discussed in Chapter 10.

1.4 Programming Language Syntax

A major problem faced by any author wishing to discuss programming language issues is the choice of a programming language for illustrative examples. In this book it is important to discuss examples from a wide variety of programming languages that have influenced data types. The actual syntax of the language is not important, but rather the ideas and concepts that the language introduced or extended. Programming languages are notoriously inconsistent about syntactic conventions. The use of many programming languages in this book could at times become confusing. To reduce this potential confusion, we shall adopt a consistent syntax based on Ada*. When appropriate, we will translate examples from other languages to this standard language. At times, this device will require changing the semantics of the chosen language.

The choice of a standard programming language was a difficult one. There is a wide variety of styles, each one having its advantages and disad-

---

* Ada is a trademark of the Department of Defense.

vantages. There is the ALGOL tradition versus the Pascal tradition of declarations:

```
int X;                              ALGOL tradition
X: integer;                         Pascal tradition
```

The ALGOL syntax has the advantage of a simple and intuitive initialization syntax by just adding the phrase ':= 3', whereas the Pascal syntax is similar to standard mathematical notation. In terms of record types or union types, the variety is sometimes surprising even to those who are used to such variety. For example, here is a short list of the possible ways to declare a record of two integers.

```
struct ( int x,y)                   ALGOL 68
record x,y: integer end             Pascal
1 ITEM, 2 (X,Y) FIXED BINARY(15)    PL/I
DATA("ITEM(X,Y)")                   SNOBOL
struct { int x,y; }                 C
int#int                             Hope
```

No single language can provide all the mechanisms and subtleties of data types that should be described in this book. So no matter what language is chosen for the standard syntax, there will be shortcomings that must be made up by arbitrarily choosing syntactic modifications or extensions. Both Pascal and Ada provide a rich syntax for expressing data types and abstract data types. It is the hope of many that Ada will become a major language of the 80s. It is thus reasonable to use Pascal/Ada-like notation to express ideas, since most readers will not be burdened with learning a new syntax. However, like any other programming language, Ada is not able to express all of the ideas we wish to examine in this book.

Exercises

1. Describe another example of a type system used by society or science and give examples of its use and misuse.

2. Investigate the structural differences between library classification schemes. The two best known are the Dewey decimal system and Library of Congress.

3. Some types are defined by properties. Other types are explicitly constructed without regard to properties. Explore this difference with the type systems given in this chapter.

4. What difference does it make whether a data type is defined as a set of values or as a set of values and operations? Give specific examples.

Further Reading

The use of data types in computer science has its roots in mathematics. Bertrand Russell provided a rigorous type system for mathematical systems in the 1908 paper, "Mathematical logic based on the theory of types," to avoid paradoxes such as *Russell's Paradox*. The study of types has continued along with developments in the formalization of mathematics and logic in this century. The lambda calculus developed by Alonzo Church in the 1930s, has been used as a simple but nontrivial language for developing type systems and theories, most of which directly relate to programming languages. Both Hoare (1972) and the introduction to Part IV in Gries (1978) were inspirational sources for the material in Section 1.2. Scott (1976) provides an elegant mathematical formulation of the universal domain viewpoint. The programming language Russell embraces the universal domain viewpoint; see Demers et al. (1978, 1980).

A Survey of Data Types

*P*rimitive *T*ypes 2

Data types in programming languages are sometimes simple to understand and sometimes difficult. Sometimes we think we understand a programming language well, only to discover unexpected behavior. Even seemingly simple types like numbers can be complicated. Types in different languages, even when given the same name, are often different in subtle but significant ways. The complexity of many types and many languages presents challenging work to the taxonomist of data types. Not everyone even agrees on a basic definition of data types.

Before pursuing detailed accounts of generalized properties of data types it will be helpful to examine the wide variety of data types found in programming languages. Therefore next three chapters survey data types that have appeared from before FORTRAN to Ada. We start in this chapter with the simplest data types, sometimes referred to as *primitive types*. The primitive types consist of those types that do not build upon other types and include Boolean, character, enumerated, and numeric types. The non-primitive types, sometimes called *constructor types*, build upon other types and will be considered in Chapters 3 and 4.

2.1 Boolean Types

The simplest data type is the Boolean data type. The name comes from the English mathematician George Boole, who first investigated algebras of two elements. The Boolean data type has two values, traditionally called true and false. Boolean values are the most common method of controlling the flow of computation through conditional and looping statements. Boolean types are not explicitly needed for the flow of control constructs, since the syntax of the flow of control constructs can allow expressions the form

  expression   comparison-operator   expression

Many languages use Boolean as the name of the type, and the identifiers *true* and *false* as the constants. Some languages shorten Boolean to Bool, but others have completely different names; for example, FORTRAN has the LOGICAL type and PL/I has the BIT type. In these languages, the constants for true and false differ. In FORTRAN, true is represented by .TRUE. and in PL/I as '1'B. Some languages do not even have a distinct Boolean type, but rather use some other type. LISP for example uses the value NULL to represent false and all other values to represent true. The C language uses zero to represent false and all other integers to represent true. It is a common practice in these languages to define constants or macros *true* and *false* to make programs more readable.

There are exactly four unary Boolean functions and 16 binary Boolean functions. The four unary functions are the two constants, the identity function, and the negation function. The negation function returns the other value. Most languages provide this unary function, but it seems that each language gives it a different symbol (e.g., not, .NOT., !, −, ~, ¬, and /). Of the 16 binary functions, the *and* and *or* functions are typically provided (also with a variety of symbols). From these three functions (*not*, *and*, and *or*) all Boolean functions can be defined. Some useful Boolean conditional operators that control the evaluation of expressions are the *andif* and *orif* operators. Ada uses the terms and then for *andif* and or else for *orif*. Functionally, these operators are like the *and* and *or* operators, but the second operand is evaluated only if it is necessary to determine the result. If we use the axioms

true or X = true
false and X = false

note that the second operand does not need to be evaluated in certain situations. There are two benefits of such conditional operators. First, expressions can be evaluated faster and second, it is easier to express certain conditions in one expression, such as the following:

```
if J>LOWER_BOUND and J>UPPER_BOUND then
        if DATA_VECTOR(J)≠0 then
                RESULT := 1/DATA_VECTOR(J);
        else
                REPORT_ERROR();
        end if;
else
        REPORT_ERROR();
end if;
```

A single conditional expression cannot be used with and in the above situation since the array subscript would always be evaluated and a subscript out of range may occur. But the expression can be simplified using conditional operators to

```
if J>LOWER_BOUND and J>UPPER_BOUND
                and then DATA_VECTOR(J)≠0 then
        RESULT := 1/DATA_VECTOR(J);
else
        REPORT_ERROR();
end if;
```

2.2 Character Types

Characters and string types are often confused because in many languages there is no distinction. A character is an indivisible symbol. A string is a sequence of zero or more characters. It is sometimes useful to note the distinction between characters and strings, because in some sense it is as important as the distinction between integers and arrays of integers. A character is not just a string of length one, just as an integer is not just an integer array of length one. Unlike numbers, there is not much one can do with single characters, whereas there are many things that can be done with strings. For this reason, some languages provide only strings.

Like numbers, the character type is often machine dependent. That is, each machine defines its own character set and the code for each character. Almost all IBM machines use the Extended Binary Coded Decimal Interchange Code (EBCDIC) and almost all non-IBM machines use the American Standard Code for Information Interchange (ASCII). This difference is immediately apparent when sorting a list of numbers and names. The sort is based on the comparison operation. Each character has a unique character code. Character comparison is based on character codes. While in both ASCII and EBCDIC the ordering for letters is the same (i.e., A⟨B⟨C...) the ordering is different for other characters. And so the character 0 is larger than A on EBCDIC machines, and A is larger than 0 on ASCII machines. Sorting algorithms based on character codes will produce different results on machines with different character codes. Other machine-dependent operations are the conversion functions from character to integer and integer to character. These conversion functions simply convert characters to character code and vice versa. A common method for obtaining the next alphabetic character on ASCII machines is the expression

```
INT_TO_CHAR( 1 + CHAR_TO_INT(X) )
```

where `INT_TO_CHAR` and `CHAR_TO_INT` are the conversion functions. This will not work on EBCDIC machines since the EBCDIC codes for the alphabet are not contiguous. In the table below, note that the characters "0" and "A" do not have the same order and that the letters "I" and "J" are not contiguous.

Some character codes:

Character	ASCII	EBCDIC
0	48	240
A	65	193
I	74	201
J	75	209

2.3 Enumerated Types

An elegant and simple generalization of the previously mentioned types is the *enumerated type*. An enumerated type is a finite set of values typically specified by listing every value or by giving the lower and upper bounds of some previously defined enumerated type. The second specification method is typically called a *subrange*. Enumerated types and subranges were first introduced in the Pascal language. Numeric, character, and Boolean types can all be considered as predefined enumerated types.

Programmers can use enumerated types for other than numeric, character, and Boolean types. Enumerated types can represent many kinds of data. As an example, consider the following types:

```
type DOOR is (OPEN, AJAR, CLOSED, LOCKED);
type BOROUGH is (BRONX, BROOKLYN, MANHATTAN, QUEENS,
                 STATEN_ISLAND);
```

The symbols OPEN through LOCKED are literals of the type DOOR. Enumerated types may seem like unusual types, but they would probably be one of the most commonly used types if they were available and used where appropriate. In many situations, a programmer with old habits will choose an integer representation when an enumerated representation is clearly better in terms of documentation and protection from mistakes.

Subranges are also enumerated types and are defined by specifying the lower and upper bounds of some previously defined range. In Pascal-like languages, a numeric type is typically specified as a subrange of some predefined numeric range. The bounds of a subrange are usually separated by the symbol ".." as in the following two examples:

```
type YEAR is 1900..1999;
type UNLOCKED_DOOR is OPEN..CLOSED;
```

Standard operators in Ada on enumerated types include the following:

FIRST returns the first element of the enumeration.
LAST returns the last element of the enumeration.
SUCC(X) returns the next element after X.
PRED(X) returns the element previous to X.

The enumeration also provides a natural ordering that can be used for defining comparison operators.

2.4 Numbers

Numbers are at once the simplest and most difficult of all data types. They are the simplest because everyone is familiar with numbers. They are the most difficult because computers represent numbers in many different ways, and it is often necessary to understand this complexity to implement even the simplest of programs. The concept of data type first appeared with the introduction of multiple representations of numbers. On the earliest computers, before the advent of high-level programming languages or even assembly languages, machines had many ways of representing numbers. Binary and decimal machines represent numbers differently. Some machines employ both representations by using binary encoded decimal. There is no finite representation that can be used to represent all the integers or the reals. Only a subset can be represented. The size of the subset depends on the number of bits used for the representation. The size is usually expressed as the number of digits of precision. Some machines allow representations that differ only by the number of digits of precision. Representations also vary depending on how the decimal or binary point is handled.

Two major methods that we examine in further detail are called the *fixed-point* and *floating-point* representations. These variations provided a rich and complex type system well before the introduction of programming languages. They provide an insight into the differences between compile-time and run-time type checking. The standard wisdom today is that compile-time type checking is superior to run-time type checking, but floating-point numbers provide a nice counterexample to the prevailing wisdom. To summarize, the exponent of a number is considered the type of a number. In the fixed-point method the exponents are calculated before the program is executed, while in the floating-point method, the exponents are calculated during execution of the program. To see the effect of this precursor to the data types of programming languages it will be instructive to look at some of the activities of a programmer during the 1950s.

Imagine a machine that represents numbers as eight decimal digits and a sign bit. No decimal point is explicitly represented. The decimal point is assumed to be at the extreme right. For example, "+00001984" represents the number 1984. Arithmetic operations for addition, subtraction, multiplication, and division assume integer numbers. The product of two numbers is represented as a pair of numbers, the first representing the amount of overflow. For example,

+12345678	first operand times
+00000100	second operand
+00000012	first number of resulting pair
+34567800	second number of resulting pair

Division returns a quotient and a remainder. For example,

+00000500	dividend
+00000003	divisor
+00000166	quotient
+00000002	remainder

The machine may seem limited by this representation and set of operations but it is a typical machine of the early 1950s. The range and usefulness of the representation can be extended significantly by simply imagining the decimal point somewhere other than the extreme right-hand side of a number. Such an imagination requires careful attention to avoid errors. Just as the operator of a slide rule had to keep track of a decimal point, the programmer of this machine had to keep track of the decimal point. Various methods were developed to aid the programmer in this task.

One simple method is to choose one place for the decimal point and to represent all numbers with the imagined decimal point in this fixed position. For example, one might choose the middle of the eight digit number. So, " +00025000" represents five halves. The use of the addition and subtraction operations remains meaningful for such a representation. However, changes must be made to the multiplication and division operations. The multiplication result must be shifted by four decimal digits. Multiplying five halves by three (represented as " +00030000") results in the pair " +00000007" and " +50000000". After shifting this pair by four digits, we obtain the desired result, " +00075000". A similar set of rules is necessary for division.

By using this representation throughout the program and shifting after each multiplication and division, the eight digit integer machine acts as if it were an eight digit machine with four digits of precision to the right of the decimal point. Typically the programmer must use the standard integers for addressing, input, output, and indexing. So the program typically contains both the imagined numbers and the standard numbers. The machine cannot tell the difference. To develop correct programs, the programmer must keep careful track of which numbers are standard and which ones have the unusual representation. This is type checking that must be done by hand. Sometimes it is necessary to convert a number from one representation to another. Conversion is just a left or right shift of four decimal digits. Such a conversion will occasionally encounter errors, since neither representation can represent all numbers of the other representation.

The above method does not provide a very wide range of numbers. To provide flexibility, a *scale factor method* can be used to keep track of the decimal point. In this method each number is tagged with a scale factor that indicates the location of the decimal point. The programmer determines the scale factors for every input, intermediate, and output number before programming the computer. The scale factor is defined as the power of ten by which the number must be multiplied to get the number actually represented. A scale factor of 0 means the decimal point is at the extreme right-hand side of the number. A scale factor of −4 means the decimal point is in the middle of the number. Five halves has seven different representations:

Representation	Scale Factor	Value
+00000025	−1	2.5
+00000250	−2	2.5
+00002500	−3	2.5
+00025000	−4	2.5
+00250000	−5	2.5
+02500000	−6	2.5
+25000000	−7	2.5

Conversion from one representation to another is achieved by shifting. Addition and subtraction can be performed only on numbers with the same scale factor. It is not possible to add the number "+00000025" with a scale factor of 1 (representing the number 250) to the number "+00000005" with a scale factor of 2 (representing 500) except by rescaling one of the operands.

Representation	Scale Factor	Value	
+00000025	1	250	
+00000005	2	500	
+00000030	?	?	Addition without rescaling
+00000007	2	700	Addition after rescaling first operand
+00000075	1	750	Addition after rescaling second operand

As the example indicates, it is important to rescale the correct operand to avoid loss of precision. Since overflow might also occur, it may be necessary to rescale in the opposite direction. The operands of multiplication do not need to be rescaled; the scale factor of the result is the sum of the scale factors of the operands.

The programmer who uses the scale factor method must take the following steps during programming:

1. Determine, from information about the physical quantities, the maximum sizes of all numbers . . . In the case of division, determine also the minimum sizes of divisors or the maximum sizes of quotients. Doing this will ordinarily require knowledge about input, intermediate results, and output; at the very least, the information must be available for the input.

2. Write the relationships between true numbers and scaled numbers by determining the necessary scale factors. These will ordinarily be the power of ten just larger than the maximum size of a quantity. Thus, if x in a certain problem can never be as large as 100, then the scale factor would be 2 . . .

3. Substitute the scaled quantities into the equations of the problem. Cancel exponents wherever possible.

4. Quantities to be added or subtracted must have the same scale factor. If this condition is not met in the scaled equation as it stands, some scale factors must be changed by shifting some of the numbers before addition or subtraction. The number of shifts required will be the same as the difference in scale factors in the scaled equation.

5. An "uncanceled" scale factor in division specifies a right shift necessary to avoid divide stop. An "uncanceled" scale factor in multiplication specifies a left shift of the product, which will cause no loss of significant digits at the left . . .*

These type-checking rules can be expressed concisely and formally. Let $x [n]$ represent the number x expressed with a scale factor n. Then the following formulas summarize the type-checking (where $\langle\langle$ and $\rangle\rangle$ denote left and right shifts).

$$x[n] + y[n] = (x + y)[n]$$
$$x[n] - y[n] = (x-y)[n]$$
$$x[n] * y[m] = (x * y)[n + m]$$
$$x[n] / y[m] = (x/y)[n - m]$$
$$x[n] \langle\langle m = x[n - m]$$
$$x[n] \rangle\rangle m = x[n + m]$$

Figure 2.1 shows an example with three inputs and one output. The numbers indicate the scale factors for the input, intermediate results, and final output.

Numbers with scale factors comprise a data type system. Each scale factor n represents a data type with its own set of values and operations. The above steps specify how to determine the types (i.e., the scale factors) and how to perform type checking for addition and subtraction and type conversion. All of these steps are performed by hand and should be part of the program documentation. Errors can be made in several ways. Clerical errors in type checking (such as improperly canceling exponents) could cause subsequent invalid additions or misscaled results. Misjudging the numerical range of inputs could cause overflow or underflow. For clerical errors, there is no automated error detection. In the second case, every multiplication, division, and conversion could check for overflow or underflow, in which case the system detects a run-time error. A third source of error is introduced because truncation results in approximations to the true result. *Numerical analysis* is a field of mathematics that can be used to determine error ranges with either fixed-point or floating-point methods.

---

* From D.D. McCracken, *Digital Computer Programming*, John Wiley and Sons, Inc., New York, 1957.

Let X, Y, and Z have initial scale factors of 3, 4, and 5 respectively.

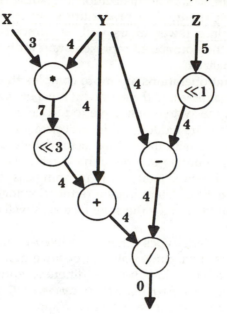

FIGURE 2.1 Flow diagram of "(X∗Y + Y) / (Y−Z)" with scale factors.

In many applications it is difficult to judge the range of numerical input or output. Often the range is too broad to permit accurate results for the entire range. Programmers often resort to the *floating-point* method in these situations. In the scale factor method, all scale factors are determined *before* coding. Such methods are often called *fixed-point* methods because the decimal point remains fixed. In the floating-point method, scale factors are determined during the computation. This approach requires that every number have a scale factor at run-time. A number is divided into two parts called the *exponent*, which specifies the location of the decimal point, and the *mantissa*,∗ which specifies the digits of the number. The exponent and mantissa are represented as a pair of numbers, most often combined in one word of memory. In our hypothetical machine, for example, the first two digits could be used for the exponent and the other six for the mantissa. However, there is only one sign bit, and two are required—one for the mantissa and one for the exponent. We solve this problem by arbitrarily adding 50 to the exponent. The decimal point is typically located at the extreme left-hand side of the mantissa. For example, five halves could be represented as "+55000025", where the exponent is 5 (obtained by

∗ The term *mantissa* is borrowed from mathematics, which means the decimal part of a common logarithm.

subtracting 50 from 55) and the mantissa is .000025. It is usual to *normalize* floating-point numbers. In normalization all leading zeros are discarded by adjusting the exponent. This procedure ensures maximal accuracy in computations, since fewer digits will be truncated on the right. So, "+51250000" is the normalized representation for five halves. Obviously, zero is not normalized.

Floating-point operations are more complex than fixed-point operations. Both the mantissa and the exponent must be computed. For addition and subtraction, the system may have to rescale one of the operands. All these complications are hidden within the operations, so that the programmer need not bother with the scaling factor details. The computer system provides either subroutines or special hardware. The use of these routines on other numeric representations is meaningless. So, the programmer must still perform type determination (either floating-point or fixed-point, and if fixed-point, determine the scale factor) as well as type checking and type conversions.

There are numeric types other than fixed-point and floating-point. Some representations include only the positive numbers. Even when the sign of the number is included, many different representations are possible, including *sign and magnitude, two's complement,* and *one's complement.* There is also a tradeoff between accuracy and cost. How many digits of precision should be used in a calculation? It is usually better to have more digits of precision, but each additional digit has a cost. More memory is required to store the extra digits and more time is required to perform the operations. In addition to decimal machines, there are binary machines. Wishing to satisfy all customers, some machines provide many representations.

FORTRAN Numbers

A team headed by John Backus at IBM developed and implemented the FORTRAN programming language in the middle 1950s. The goal of the FORTRAN project was to automate the programming job. The intent was to allow engineers and scientists to specify their program in the FORTRAN language, after which the FORTRAN compiler would do all the programming. A compiler is a program that translates a high-level programming language like FORTRAN into assembly language or machine language. As part of its job, the FORTRAN compiler automatically checks the numeric types, just as a human programmer would. Some people thought that languages such as FORTRAN would soon eliminate most programming jobs. Instead the job of programming evolved to a broader one. People conceived and implemented larger and more complicated programs, and became concerned with the larger issues of design, rather than merely coding. Languages such as FORTRAN increased productivity rates. But the increased demand for software exceeded the increased productivity, so the number of programming jobs has steadily increased rather than decreased.

The FORTRAN language, being the first programming language, is a landmark in the history of programming languages. The numeric types of FORTRAN reflect the numeric types traditionally used, except for the fixed-point methods. Unlike FORTRAN, machine and assembly languages do no type checking and so a number of any representation can usually be placed in any register or memory location. FORTRAN abstracted the concept of a memory location to a *variable*. Variables are denoted in the FORTRAN language by identifiers (up to six characters long). Each variable represents a location in memory and has an associated type that specifies the kind of numbers that can be stored in the location. No other kinds of numbers can be stored in that location. This restriction is enforced by the language. The programmer can specify the type of each variable. Variables can be specified explicitly by a declaration. If no explicit declaration of a variable is given, then the first letter of the identifier indicates the type. By default, any identifier beginning with a letter between *I* and *N* inclusive is an integer variable and all other identifiers are floating-point variables. The programmer can override this default.

The type information serves several purposes.

1. The compiler uses type information to determine which computer instruction should be used. This makes the job of programming much easier, since a FORTRAN programmer can use the symbol "+" to mean addition for any kind of number. One task of the FORTRAN compiler is to *translate* the plus sign to the appropriate computer addition instruction. This translation, called *operator identification*, can be determined only by knowing the types of the operands.

2. The compiler also uses type information to determine how much storage to allocate for each variable. Different number representations may have different storage requirements.

3. Type information also helps the compiler to detect errors. A *type error* is the improper use of a value of a data type. Making sure that all values are used properly according to their type is called *type checking*. If the programmer attempts to add an integer to a real, the compiler notes it as an error, because typically there is no computer addition instruction for mixed types.

Some people found these error checks to be annoying for certain cases. It is sometimes necessary to mix integers and reals. In machine or assembly language this requirement is met by calling a conversion routine that converts a number with an integer representation to a number with a real representation. The FORTRAN built-in conversion functions are FLOAT and IFIX. In the original version of FORTRAN, mixed type expressions were ruled out because it "was felt that if code for type conversion were to be generated, the user should be aware of that, and the best way to insure that he was aware was to ask him to specify them."* In some versions of FORTRAN automatic conversions were inserted for converting integers to reals, thus allowing mixed type expressions.

FORTRAN IV has four numeric types: INTEGER, REAL, DOUBLE PRECISION, and COMPLEX. Programmers use the DOUBLE PRECISION type when more digits of precision are required for real numbers. Some versions of FORTRAN use a "*n" following INTEGER, REAL, or COMPLEX to specify how many bytes of memory to use for a number (where *n* is the number of bytes).

The *range* of a numeric type is the set of numbers that it can represent. FORTRAN and most other languages do not specify the range of numeric types. An implementation of the language determines the range of each numeric type. To achieve efficiency for different machines every implementation may have different ranges. Ranges are *machine dependent,* which means that programs written on one machine may behave differently on other machines. For example, if one machine has a larger word size than another, then it is less likely to have overflow errors. The ability to run the same program on many machines with the same results is a highly valued and desirable property called *portability,* since the program can be ported to other machines. The difficulty and resulting inefficiency of attempting to make numeric representations the same on all machines means that numeric data types are not likely to become machine independent for a long time, but work on standards, such as the IEEE floating-point standard, may have a long-term impact.

PL/I Numbers

One of the most complex numeric type systems is found in PL/I. It is another programming language designed at IBM. PL/I was designed to be a general purpose language, one that could be used for any application. To achieve this generality, the designers wanted to allow maximal flexibility in the choice of number representations. PL/I data types are specified by one or more *attributes.* The attributes for PL/I numeric types are:

1. FIXED or FLOAT or COMPLEX.
2. BINARY or DECIMAL.
3. SIZE (determines number of digits of precision and location of decimal point).

Programmers can combine these attributes in many ways. Unlike FORTRAN, PL/I provides fixed-point methods (automated, of course, except for determining the ranges of input and output values). A "FIXED

* John Backus (1978a)

DECIMAL(6,2)" number has a fixed-point representation with six decimal digits of precision, and with two digits to the right of the decimal point. A "FLOAT BINARY(31)" number has a floating-point representation with 31 binary digits of precision. Assuming no upper limits on the precision, PL/I has an infinite number of numeric types. Every numeric literal in PL/I has exactly one numeric type that can be determined merely from the form of the literal. The literal "1234.56" is a FIXED DECIMAL(6,2) since it has six decimal digits, two to the right of the decimal point. The literal "0000101B" is a FIXED BINARY(7) and the literal "001234E−3" is a FLOAT DECIMAL(6). Numeric operations can be performed only on operands of the same type. PL/I has automatic conversions between every pair of numeric types. Tables for determining which conversions take place and the resulting type for each operation can be found in the PL/I language reference manual. Typically, the PL/I programmer is not aware of these automatic conversions, some of which take place at compile-time and others at run-time. In a few instances, the conversions produce surprising results (see Section 5.5).

The SIZE attribute specifies the number of digits of precision to be used in the representation. The SIZE attribute gives PL/I the possibility of machine independence. In practice, however, most PL/I compilers simply use the SIZE attribute to determine which of several machine-dependent sizes to use. Thus if the programmer has specified FIXED BINARY(10), the compiler may actually use a 16-bit field. Overflow beyond the ten bits would not be detected unless the SIZE condition was enabled. Programmers seldom enable the SIZE condition since it increases execution time.

Ada Numbers

New ways of organizing numeric types are still being created. In Ada there are just two numeric types, called *universal_integer* and *universal_real*. Unlike traditional numeric types, these two numeric types are truly the integers and reals. Neither of the types is really implemented in Ada. The programmer can only use *subtypes* of these universal types. An integer subtype is specified by lower and upper bounds of an integer range. The Pascal language was the first to specify integer types using subtypes. This specification provides more information about the numeric type, since it explicitly states the expected minimum and maximum bounds of the integer. Ada provides some predefined machine-dependent integer subtypes, called INTEGER, SHORT_INTEGER, and LONG_INTEGER, which have ranges symmetric about zero. The ranges of these predefined subtypes can be determined from the Ada *attributes* FIRST and LAST, which give the lower and upper bounds. The Ada language definition explicitly states that the actual implementation of all integer subtypes will be one of the predefined types, called a *parent* type. The range information is used to determine which of the predefined types will be used as the parent type.

The range information is also used as a constraint on integers of the subtype, and any violation of the constraint will raise the `CONSTRAINT_ERROR` exception. In Ada, there are no integer literals for each subtype; rather, all integer literals are of the type *universal_integer*. Ada provides implicit conversions from the universal numeric types to each subtype.

Ada numeric real numbers have an analogous set of properties, but there are additional complications. There are two kinds of real types: floating-point reals and fixed-point reals. A *floating-point real* is specified by giving the number of decimal digits of precision and an optional range constraint (consisting of lower and upper bounds). A *fixed-point real* is specified by giving a *delta*, and a range constraint. A delta specifies the maximum spacing between numbers of this type. Each numeric type defines a set of numbers called *model numbers*. An implementation of a type must be able to represent the type's model numbers exactly. To explain real types, the Ada language definition refers to yet another mysterious type called *universal_fixed* which is used solely for explanatory purposes.

One Numeric Type?

Why must a programmer worry about all these numeric types in order to do programming. After all, a number is just a number. And there are languages that do indeed treat numbers as just numbers. Both APL and SNOBOL have one numeric type and the programmer does not consider what kind of number representation to use. The programming language system takes care of those details. So why don't most languages have just one numeric type? The problem is efficiency. To implement numbers efficiently, the programming language system must have some help. Most machines have at least two different ways of representing numbers. Languages reflect this difference by using different numeric types.

Operations on Numbers

The classic four operations of addition, subtraction, multiplication, and division present a problem when applied to integer ranges. Addition and subtraction are complete functions on the integers but are partial functions on integer ranges. Since computer representations of numbers represent only a subset of the integers, all four operations may cause overflow or underflow. This problem is one that has frustrated language designers and programmers. Language designers can design languages with no limits on integers. Programmers can write elegant programs by assuming there is no limit on integers. But to be realistic, both language designers and programmers must face problems such as overflow.

Overflow occurs in a different way for floating-point numbers. First, the exponent may go beyond its range. A more serious problem is the approximation of the results of operations. If the result of an operation has more digits than the storage can hold, then the least significant excess digits are thrown away. Consequently, the floating-point operations are not always exact. Integer operations are always exact if they do not cause an overflow. The approximate nature of floating-point numbers causes some unusual results for those who are not familiar with computer arithmetic. For example, no competent programmer is surprised that 3*(1/3) is not 1. It is very close to 1, perhaps .9999999, but it is not 1. For this reason, it is a bad programming practice to compare for exact equality between floating-point numbers. It is acceptable to ask if one number is greater than another, but unacceptable to ask if they are equal. In the implementation of APL, this phenomenon was met with a novel approach. Falkoff and Iverson (1978) write,

> One difficulty we had not anticipated was the provision of sensible results for the comparison of quantities represented to a limited precision. For example, if X and Y were specified by Y←2÷3 and X←3×Y, then we wished to have the comparison 2=X yield 1 (representing *true*) even though the representation of the quantity X would differ slightly from 2.

> This was solved by introducing a comparison tolerance (christened *fuzz* by L.M.Breed, . . .) which was multiplied by the larger in magnitude of the arguments to give a tolerance to be applied in the comparison. This tolerance was at first fixed (at 1E-13) and was later made specifiable by the user. The matter has proven more difficult than we first expected, and discussion of it still continues . . .

Exercises

1. Work the following problem using the hypothetical machine of Section 2.4 and the scale factor method. There are three inputs: A is in the range 4000–500,000; B is in the range .0001 – 100 and C is in the range 1000–5000. The final output (in millions) is 100*A+C**2+B*C**3.

2. Explain the advantages and disadvantages of having run-time or compile-time exponent calculation of fixed-point and floating-point numeric types. Fixed-point numeric types must do compile-time type checking by taking into account the exponents, whereas floating-point numeric types do all this work (exponent calculation) at run-time.

3. Consider the following numeric representation. A rational number is the ratio of two integers. To represent such numbers, we just need two integers. Multiplication and division are simple, since only integer multiplication and division are needed. Addition and subtraction are more complicated, but they can also be implemented by using the four basic integer operations. For example $(a/b) + (c/d) = (ad + cb)/bd$. Rationals have some wonderful advantages over floating-point representations. Common rational numbers can be represented exactly, such as

one-third and one-seventh. When the expression (3∗(1/3)) is evaluated, the result is 1, not .99999999. There are no complicated floating-point operations to implement. The rational operations are easily constructed from the integer operations. What, then, are the disadvantages of the rational representations?

4. What problems do you think Falkoff and Iverson refer to in considering the fuzz factor (at the end of Section 2.4)?

*A*ggregate *T*ypes

3

An aggregate type is a data type whose values are collections of data. By contrast, the primitive types of the previous chapter are data types whose values are single indivisible data elements. An aggregate type does not *define* a new primitive data type, but rather *constructs* a new data type from previously existing data types. For this reason, aggregate types are sometimes referred to as constructor types. Each element of an aggregate value is typically accessed with some *index* value. The organization and implementation of the collection largely determine the accessing method. In this chapter three basic aggregate types are investigated: arrays, records, and sequences. Arrays are the most commonly used aggregate type. An array is characterized (in this book) as a fixed-size collection with each element dynamically accessible. A record can also be characterized as a fixed-size collection, but each element is accessed in a more restricted manner than the elements in an array. A sequence is a collection whose size may dynamically change at runtime.

3.1 Arrays

Arrays, like numbers, were among the earliest types. Before programming languages appeared, arrays were commonly used in assembly languages. Subscripted (or superscripted) variables are a common notational convenience used in mathematics and the sciences. Subscripted variables are used to denote a collection of data. A subscript identifies a particular element of the collection. The subscript might be used to indicate a time, a place, or a position in some arbitrary ordering of the data. Subscripted variables are represented in memory as a contiguous section of memory and indexed by the subscript.

Early language designers did not view arrays as a data type. The notion of *citizenship* is a useful metaphor for describing the extent to which data types are treated equally. *First class citizens* have full rights, which typically include assignment, literals, comparison operators, and parameter passing. Two types are considered to have the same citizenship if everything that can be done with one type can be done with the other type. In almost all languages, numeric types have the most rights. Other types may have a narrower range of features and are thus called *second class citizens*. Arrays are not first class citizens in most early languages, including FORTRAN and ALGOL 60. Neither language permits the assignment or comparison of array values. The individual elements of an array can be assigned or compared, but not the entire collection. In FORTRAN the array is an ordered set of data identified by a symbolic name; it is not a data type. Similarly, in ALGOL 60 an array is a collection of *fictitious variables*, rather than a variable whose value is a collection of values. Such viewpoints usually lead to complicated language definitions. For example, the description of parameter passing can be unduly complicated because data types and arrays must be described separately.

PL/I and APL were among the first languages to grant nearly full first class citizenship to arrays. PL/I allows array assignment and extends many arithmetic operators to arrays of numeric types. But PL/I still has some restrictions, such as not allowing procedures to return arrays. Neither PL/I nor APL allows arrays of arrays. Although APL arrays can be dynamically varying, they are considered in this section since APL is a major source of ideas about arrays. ALGOL 68 and Pascal granted even more rights to arrays, and notwithstanding some minor restrictions, arrays have become first class citizens. An array in both these languages is a data type; it has a set of values and a set of operations.

There are many difficult and subtle characteristics of arrays that we will discuss. In this section, we investigate arrays in terms of their characteristics rather than by language. The first two characteristics of an array are their index and element types. The index type is the type of the value used to select an element of an array, and the element type is the type of the elements stored in the array.

Index Types

A *subscript* selects an element of an array. The subscript has a type called the *index type*. Index types are almost always integers. So common and natural is the use of the integer type as the index type of an array, that many programming languages allow only integers as index types. An array must have *bounds* in order to store the array efficiently in memory. The bounds specify what values are valid subscripts. Typically the bounds are specified by giving a lower and an upper bound. The lower bound specifies the smallest value that can be used as a valid subscript and the upper bound specifies the largest value that can be used as a valid subscript. In most applications the lower bound is either zero or one. This occurs frequently enough that some languages only require a programmer to specify the upper bound. Some languages do not allow the programmer to specify the lower bound. FORTRAN has a lower bound of one, and some dialects of BASIC have a lower bound of zero, which cannot be changed by the programmer.

Beginning with Pascal, many languages allow enumerated types as an index type. This facility provides nice documentation and helps prevent errors. Consider the following two-dimensional array indexed by color and object:

```
type COLOR  is (RED, BLUE, YELLOW, WHITE);
type OBJECT is (BALL, CUBE, CYLINDER);
type MATRIX is array (COLOR, OBJECT) of INTEGER;
V: MATRIX;
begin
        V(BLUE, CUBE) := 5;
    ...
```

In addition to the readability of this program fragment, it is not possible to confuse the two indexes. If a programmer thought that the color was the second index and had written V(CUBE, BLUE), the compiler would flag the expression as an error. Enumerated types as index types are as easy to implement as integer types since most compilers represent enumerated types as integers. Other index types are often much more complicated to implement. For example, SNOBOL tables, whose index type is string, have a far more complicated implementation than SNOBOL arrays.

Ignoring the underlying implementation, we can say simply that an array associates a value of the element type with each value of the index type. This generalization of an array is called a *mapping*. Any type can be the index type of a mapping. Each dimension has its own index type. SNOBOL tables are mappings with string indexes. A mapping is a function from the index type values to element type values. Some high level languages (such as SETL) allow arbitrary mappings. Many of the topics discussed below can be applied to mappings as well as arrays, but most programming languages do not allow arbitrary mappings because it is not known how to implement them efficiently. Since the concept of arrays has been motivated by a particular kind of implementation and storage representation it would not be fair to consider mappings with complex index types as arrays.

Element Types

The element type is the type of the elements stored in the array. Typically the element type is a numeric type. But in the general case an element type may be of any type. PL/I allows arrays of any type except for another array. But PL/I permits arrays of structures of arrays! ALGOL 68 and Pascal have no restrictions on element types. To implement arrays efficiently the values of an element type must have a fixed amount of storage. Since each type in both Pascal and ALGOL 68 has a fixed amount of storage, all arrays in these languages can be implemented in an efficient manner.

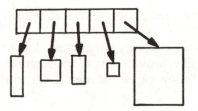

FIGURE 3.1 SNOBOL arrays using a level of indirection.

A *homogeneous* array is an array that has only one element type. In other words, all the elements of a homogeneous array are of the same type. A *heterogeneous* array is an array whose elements may be of different types. Most traditional programming languages do not permit heterogeneous arrays because they are incompatible with compile-time type checking and are harder to implement. SNOBOL, however, has heterogeneous arrays that are implemented as arrays of pointers to values. This device permits each element of a SNOBOL array to be of one fixed size, and so elements of a SNOBOL array are efficiently accessed despite the presence of varying-size elements. The real cost of SNOBOL arrays is storage management. Figure 3.1 shows a SNOBOL array that has values of many different sizes.

Dimensions and Nesting of Arrays

An array may have one or more dimensions. Each dimension has its own type and bounds. The size of a dimension is the number of valid subscripts in that dimension; for an integer index it is simply the upper bound minus the lower bound plus one. The total number of elements of an array is the product of the sizes of all the dimensions. To access an element of an array, a subscript must be provided for each dimension of the array. There may be a limit to the number of dimensions of an array, but in practice it is seldom reached since the vast majority of arrays have fewer than half a dozen dimensions. Even if a language did not permit arrays of more than one dimension it would be possible to have multidimensional arrays by using a function that converts any number of subscripts to one subscript. For example, a five-by-five matrix can be obtained by using a 25-element vector and a function as follows:

```
F: function (X, Y:INTEGER) return INTEGER is
        begin return (X-1)*5+Y end

V: array (1..25) of INTEGER;
begin
        V(F(3, 4)) := 5;
        ...
```

The function F maps two indexes (between 1 and 5) to a single index between 1 and 25.

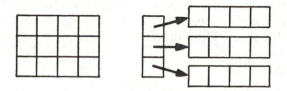

FIGURE 3.2 A two-dimensional array and a one-dimensional array of one-dimensional arrays.

Another way to achieve multidimensional arrays is by nesting arrays. A one-dimensional array of one-dimensional arrays can be used like a two-dimensional array, only the syntax is different:

```
V: array (1..5) of array (1..5) of INTEGER;
begin
        V(3)(4) := 5;
    ...
```

In the above example, V is an array of arrays and an element of one of the inner arrays is obtained by two subscripts separated by ")(" rather than a comma. Figure 3.2 shows the conceptual differences between a two-dimensional array and a one-dimensional array of one-dimensional arrays. One might wonder what are the actual differences between these variations. In one sense they are all the same, since they all have 25 elements and are accessed with two subscripts in the range 1 through 5. ALGOL 68 and Pascal demonstrate some of these differences. Pascal allows only one-dimensional arrays and considers a multidimensional array as an abbreviation for a nested array. The following two types have exactly the same meaning in Pascal:

```
type ONE is array (1..5, 1..5) of INTEGER;
type TWO is array (1..5) of array (1..5) of INTEGER;
```

These are different types in ALGOL 68. For example, ALGOL 68 permits different bounds on each of the one-dimensional arrays, which implies different amounts of storage for each one-dimensional array and a different storage mechanism than a two-dimensional array. ALGOL 68 also allows operations on any of the one-dimensional arrays as a unit. Pascal does not permit such operations or different bounds.

Array Values

If a data type is a set of values, then what is the set of values of an array type? In mathematics, array values might be things like vectors, matrices, and cartesian products, but all these mathematical objects do not incorporate the notion of the index. The bounds must be included somewhere, but exactly where is debatable. Again, ALGOL 68 and Pascal provide classic examples of this difference. In ALGOL 68, the bounds are part of the value of an array, not part of the type. In Pascal, the bounds are part of the type of an array, not the value. This difference has enormous implications for how arrays can be used.

The types

```
array (1..3) of INTEGER
```

and

```
array (5..7) of INTEGER
```

are two different types in Pascal. Coincidentally the values of both these types are the same, the set of all vectors of three integers. Since the type of an argument must match the type of a parameter in Pascal, it is impossible to write Pascal procedures that work on arrays of any bounds. This has changed in some recent Pascal standards, which permit a *conformant-array-schema** that allows array parameters with generic bounds.

The type

```
array () of INTEGER
```

is a type in ALGOL 68.[†] The values of this type consist of all one-dimensional integer arrays. Each ALGOL 68 array value consists of its bounds along with the elements of the array. This set includes the three-element arrays (3,4,5) with bounds 1..3 and (3,4,5) with bounds 5..7. Both array values, though different, both belong to this one type. Array assignment in ALGOL 68 is complicated. An array variable can only be assigned arrays with the same bounds. If the bounds of the source array are different from the array variable, then the lower bound can be *revised* with the @ token. Array parameters in ALGOL 68 need not specify bounds; instead, arrays are passed with their bounds. This device provides a natural method for writing procedures for arrays of any bounds.

APL has yet another interesting approach to arrays. The concept of shape specifies how the elements of a vector or matrix should be arranged. The APL expression

```
A ← 1 4 9 16 25 36
```

assigns a six-element vector to the variable A. The variable A can be *shaped* to a matrix of two columns and three rows with the expression

```
A δ 2 3
```

It thus appears that the underlying foundation of APL arrays is that of a one-dimensional array that can be viewed with any number of dimensions.

---

* Addyman (1980).

[†] To be technically correct, Row of Integral is a mode in ALGOL 68.

Array Sizes and Allocation Time

The bounds of an array determine its size and the amount of storage needed to represent the array. This storage must be allocated some time before its use. The time at which the allocation takes place has a major impact on the flexibility of the array bounds. In some languages, such as FORTRAN and Pascal, the allocation takes place at compile-time. Therefore, the compiler must know the actual bounds at compile-time. Other languages allocate arrays at run-time. The bounds and size of the array are fixed after allocation takes place. In many applications it is desirable to allocate arrays of just the right size at run-time. The advantages of run-time allocation over compile-time allocation are twofold. Since the programmer can allocate arrays that are exactly the right size, no storage is wasted. And the programmer does not need to determine in advance the largest array size that might be needed. Changing the bounds after allocation requires a radically different storage mechanism; we call such a type a sequence.

Array Operations

The most fundamental operation on arrays is subscripting. The operands are the array and the subscripts, and the value returned is an element of the array. The syntax of the operation typically looks like a function call, but some languages use square brackets rather than round brackets. In most languages the selected array element can also be assigned a new value. The subscripting operation is an error if any of the subscripts are out of bounds. Except for some specialized input/output operations, this is the only way to use arrays in languages such as FORTRAN and ALGOL 60. The restriction stems from the second class citizenship of arrays.

APL is best noted for its vector and matrix operations. APL has a wide variety of operations that create, transform, combine, and manipulate arrays. APL expressions are truly array expressions, not just numeric expressions. PL/I has a limited set of these array operations including array assignment, comparison, and component-wise numeric operations. PL/I allows selecting subarrays. Let A and B be two PL/I five-by-five arrays of integers; then the expression

```
A(*,3) + B(2,*)
```

will give as a value a one-dimensional array obtained by adding the third column of A to the second row of B componentwise. ALGOL 68 extended this capability by allowing bounds on selected subarrays. Let A and B be two ALGOL 68 five-by-five arrays of integers; then the expression

```
A(1:3, 3) + B(2, 3:5)
```

will give as a value a one-dimensional three-element array obtained by adding the first three elements of the third column of A to the last three elements of the second row of B. An ALGOL 68 *trimscript* is either a trimmer or a subscript. An ALGOL 68 *trimmer* is a pair of numbers that specify the lower and upper bounds, as in `1:3`. A trimmer, like a subscript, will select part of an array. But unlike a subscript, which selects a single element, a trimmer selects a range of elements, starting at the lower bound of the trimmer up to the upper bound of the trimmer. Note that whereas the type of `A(1, 3)` is integer, the type of `A(1:3, 3)` is an array of integers.

The APL unary operator `+/` sums the elements of any array. For example, if the array `A` is `(3,4,5)`, then `+/A` returns `12`. APL has a variety of operators of the form

    □/

where □ is some operator. Each operator of this form works in a similar way. The expression `*/A` returns the product of the elements of `A`. In APL this class of operators cannot be extended, but one can imagine a language that generalizes this notion. A *meta-operator* is an operator on operators. It is also sometimes called a *functional* since its operands are functions. The definition of `/` might be something like (where □ represents any binary operator):

    □ / (a1, a2, ..., an) = a1 □ a2 □ ... □ an

The Functional Programming (FP) language designed by John Backus (1978b) has many meta-operators including `/`. In some languages, programmers can define new meta-operators.

Another useful meta-operator for arrays is the "apply to all" operator, which takes a unary operation and applies it to all the elements of an array componentwise and returns an array of the same size and dimensions. It can be defined as:

    α □ (a1, a2, ..., an) = (□ a1, □ a2, ..., □ an)

This "apply to all" operator can be generalized to binary and other multiple-arity operations. Some languages may have special instances of these operators; in PL/I, for example, many of the numeric operators have been extended to work on arrays. But other languages, notably the FP language, have the general facility.

Miscellaneous Issues

An array is a collection of data elements. How small can this collection get? Certainly all languages would allow an array of two elements; but how about one or zero elements? Some may initially think that one-element or zero-element arrays are silly. Just for completeness' sake it might argued that they should be allowed. On more practical grounds, consider a program that allocates an array whose size depends on the number of input items. Unless code is written for special cases, such programs will not work properly for fewer than two input items. Languages such as

FORTRAN, PL/I, and Pascal allow one-element arrays but not zero-element arrays. Other languages, such as ALGOL 68, Ada, and APL, allow both one-element and zero-element arrays. There are no languages that allow zero-element but not one-element arrays; however, ALGOL 68, which has array constants for zero-element and two-element arrays, has none for one-element arrays!

The inability to express a constant of a data type is yet another example of the second class citizenship of arrays in many languages. DATA statements in FORTRAN and initialization attributes in PL/I are examples of limited ways of expressing a constant array. APL was one of the first languages to allow array constants. The elements of an APL array are separated by blanks (e.g., 3 4 5). In ALGOL 68 an array can be expressed as a parenthesized list of values separated by commas (e.g. (3,4,5)). In languages without this kind of expression, one must resort to temporary variables and *for* loops or sequences of assignment statements to express the same thing. The APL and ALGOL 68 array constants are more properly called array constructors since each element may be an arbitrary expression, rather than just a constant. The ALGOL 68 array expression (X, Y, Z+1) constructs a three-element array whose value may differ at each evaluation since the variables may have different values.

3.2 *Records*

COBOL was the first language to introduce the record type. Like an array type, a record type is a collection of values, each of which can be individually accessed. The elements of a record are called *fields*. Unlike the elements in an array, the different fields of a record may be of different types. The set of values represented by a record type is the cartesian product of its field types.

Selection is the operation that accesses a field of a record. Identifiers, called *selectors*, are used to name the fields of a record. Selection and selectors are the analogs of subscripting and subscripts. A major difference, however, is that a subscript may be an arbitrary expression that can evaluate to different subscripts at run-time. Records do not have index types, and selectors are not data types. So a selector cannot be replaced with a variable or an expression. This fact is important for languages with compile-time type checking; otherwise, a compiler could not always determine the type of value returned by a selection. Languages with run-time type checking would not need this restriction. But then, such languages could just use heterogeneous arrays for both traditional arrays and records.

The declaration, initialization, and selection of records occurs in different ways in different languages. Two examples will illustrate some popular methods. In the ALGOL and Pascal traditions, each field is given a unique name, such as:

```
type PERSON is
        record
                NAME:           STRING;
                AGE:            INTEGER;
                WEIGHT:         REAL;
        end record

    X,Y: PERSON;
```

The variables X and Y are records consisting of three fields named NAME, AGE, and WEIGHT. A record value in ALGOL 68 is expressed (like arrays) as a parenthesized list of values, one for each field of the record. If the type cannot be derived from context then it must be cast. An assignment to the variable X can be made thusly:

```
X := ("John", 4, 40.2);
Y.AGE := X.AGE;
```

The second statement shows selection. To select a field of a record, most languages use the syntax

```
X.AGE
```

This statement could be considered an operator in which the first operand must be a selector name and the second operand is a record. ALGOL 68 uses the notation

```
AGE of X
```

A second approach described here is the SNOBOL equivalent to records. The following excerpt is the SNOBOL version of the previous example:

```
DATA('PERSON(NAME, AGE, WEIGHT)')
X = PERSON('JOHN', 4, 40.2)
Y = PERSON()
AGE(Y) = AGE(X)
```

In SNOBOL creation and selection are functions. The function DATA creates functions for each identifier in the parameter, one for constructing the record and one for each field. Since SNOBOL does not type variables, no types are given for X, Y, NAME, AGE, and WEIGHT.

Depending on the language, the bounds of an array may or may not be part of the type. Likewise, the selectors of a record may or may not be part of the type. In ALGOL 68, the bounds of an array are not part of the type, but the selectors of an ALGOL 68 record are part of the type. Other languages (such as PL/I) do not consider the selector names as part of the type. For this reason, the last statement of the following program segment (properly translated) would be valid in PL/I but not in ALGOL 68.

```
type COMPLEX is
        record
                  RE, IM: REAL;
        end record;

type COORDINATES is
        record
                  X, Y: REAL;
        end record;

VAL: COMPLEX;
LOC: COORDINATES;

begin
        VAL := LOC;
        ...
```

The above assignment is also illegal in Ada but for a different reason. Ada uses name equivalence (see Section 5.6), and the names of the types of VAL and LOC differ.

3.3 Sequences and Strings

A *sequence* is an array whose size may vary during run-time. Sequences require a different kind of implementation strategy than arrays. Once storage is allocated for an array, it will not require any further storage. A sequence, on the other hand, may grow or shrink in size and it is not always known before allocation time how much storage will be required. Since arrays and sequences are so similar, some languages make no distinction. ALGOL 68 comes close to making no distinctions. ALGOL 68 requires the keyword flex before any array that may dynamically change in size. Some languages do not have any kind of sequence. Other languages make a special case for the most useful of all sequences, the character string.

A character string is a sequence of characters. Unlike fixed-sized numeric arrays, which are very useful, fixed-length strings are awkward to use. Character strings are used for names, addresses, labels, titles, and all manner of things that do not come in one fixed-size (except zip codes and four-letter words). It is interesting to observe the change in the treatment of strings from the earliest languages to more modern languages. FORTRAN did not permit strings, but later versions allowed character data to be stored in numeric variables. FORTRAN also allowed strings in output formats. ALGOL 60 is not much of an improvement. It permits strings to be passed as parameters to other functions. PL/I allows both fixed-length and variable-length strings, but insists on knowing the maximum length of variable-length strings. PL/I storage management of variable-length strings is simple; it simply allocates storage for the maximum length of the string plus storage for the length field. But a true string does not have such a length restriction; it can be of any length. The implementation of true strings requires dynamic storage management. SNOBOL was and perhaps still is the best available string manipulation programming language. It not only permits true strings, it provides a wide range of string functions, including a very sophisticated pattern matching facility. Because true strings require a smart storage management system, many languages (even recent ones) do not have a string facility. Pascal has only fixed-length strings, because one goal in the design of Pascal was an efficient, simple implementation.

One of the fundamental operations on strings and sequences is *concatenation*. Concatenation is a binary operation on sequences. It returns a sequence whose first part is the first operand and whose second part is the second operand. Search operations, pattern matching, and verification are common operations in many languages. Taking subsequences or replacement of a subsequence with another sequence are also commonly found in sufficiently rich programming languages. String comparison is usually based on lexicographical (or dictionary) order. This means that the string "CRAIG" is less than "TINA" even though "TINA" is shorter than "CRAIG".

Strings are not the only useful sequence data structures. LISP lists are sequences of atoms and lists. Three famous operations on LISP lists are

```
cons              car               cdr
```

The LISP names derive from the machine language instructions that were used by the first implementation of LISP. Other languages or systems give these operations different names, such as

```
makelist          first             rest
```

or perhaps the names

```
appendleft        value             next
```

The first operation constructs a longer list by concatenating an element to the beginning of the list. The second operation returns the first element of the list, and the third operation returns the list beginning with the second element.

Many types can be viewed as restricted versions of sequences. A *stack* of X is a sequence of X with restricted access. The allowed operations correspond to the LISP operations *cons*, *car*, and *cdr*, renamed to

```
push              top               pop
```

A *queue* differs from a stack only in that the pop operation takes an element from the opposite end of the sequence. The operations on a queue are usually named *insert* and *delete*. Stacks are sometimes called *lifos* (last-in first-out) and queues are sometimes called *fifos* (first-in first-out).

Another practical restricted version of sequences is found in input and output files. An input file could be considered a queue with no insert operation, and an output file could be considered a queue with no delete operation. Pascal formally defines files as sequences with restricted operations. One of the great strengths of the UNIX* operating system is the abstraction of a file as a simple sequence of characters with well-defined but restricted operations. For example, the new line character is just that, a character. So a UNIX file is just a sequence of characters, not a sequence of records. This approach simplifies most input/output operations, since only characters are read or written, not records.

Exercises

1. Consider those programming languages that allow zero element arrays. How many array types have zero elements, and for each such type how many different values are there?

2. Consider the +/ and */ operations, which return the sum and product of a vector. What values should be returned when these operations are applied to an empty array? How can this class of operators be generalized and also be applicable to zero-element arrays?

3. Consider the problems of processing arbitrary sequences of characters in which special character values are needed to denote such things as end of line, end of record, end of file. Suppose all characters are reserved for other meanings. Design a data type called STRINGPLUS that allows these special values without sacrificing any characters. Use the variant record or union type of Pascal, Ada, or ALGOL 68 and define concatenation and comparison for STRINGPLUS.

4. A complex number could be represented as an array or a record.

   ```
   type COMPLEX_ONE is array (1..2) of REAL;

   type COMPLEX_TWO is
               record
                          RE, IM: REAL;
               end record;
   ```

   Compare and contrast the above representations. What are the advantages and disadvantages?

---

* UNIX is a trademark of AT&T Bell Laboratories.

More Types   4

In this chapter we introduce types that are neither primitive nor aggregate types. These miscellaneous types may not be familiar to many programmers but nevertheless play an important role and influence many data type issues.

4.1 Pointer Types

Traditionally variables, as distinct from values, are not part of the data type system. Variables are part of the storage scheme and are not considered as values. This distinction is usually awkward when pointers are part of the type system, since a pointer's value is a variable. ALGOL 68 is an exception to this tradition. The ALGOL 68 term *reference* means a value that refers to a memory location containing another value. An ALGOL 68 data type without references is a constant (since no memory location is involved). An ALGOL 68 identifier with type int cannot change value and thus cannot appear on the left-hand side of an assignment statement. An ALGOL 68 data type with a reference is a variable. So an ALGOL 68 integer variable has type ref int. An ALGOL 68 data type with two or more references is a pointer value. An integer pointer has type ref ref int. Consider the ALGOL 68 declarations

```
int         CONSTANT1 = 5;
ref int     VARIABLE1 = loc int := READINT;
ref ref int POINTER1  = loc ref int;
int         CONSTANT2 = VARIABLE1*CONSTANT1;
```

The identifier CONSTANT1 is a name of a constant. It cannot be assigned a new value. Unlike Pascal constants, whose value must be known at compile-time, an ALGOL 68 constant may have a value that is computed at run-time. In the fourth line of the above example, the constant CONSTANT2 is given a value that depends on VARIABLE1, which has been initialized to a value read from some external file.

By including the concept of reference in the type structure, ALGOL 68 has simplified the concepts of constants, variables, and pointers. Without a clear model of values, variables, and pointers some confusing situations may arise. Other language definitions must cope with this additional complexity. Consider a subscripted integer array variable. In one context the array may represent a value, but in another context, such as the left-hand side of an assignment statement or an argument that is passed by reference, the subscripted array represents what is called an integer *l-value*. In a language that has not made the concept of reference a part of the type system, the type of all subscripted integer arrays is integer. There is no distinction between those subscripted arrays that will be used as values and those that will be used as variables. The type structure of ALGOL 68 clearly shows that subscripting a reference to an integer array returns a reference to an integer, not an integer. This convention would clearly allow such an expression to be on the left-hand side of an assignment statement. Likewise, selecting a field of a reference to a record returns a reference to the field, not the field's value. Some languages allow both call by value and call by reference. Parameter passing is formally call by value in ALGOL 68, but passing a reference value is equivalent to call by reference. So the ALGOL 68 calling mechanism is simple, but has great flexibility.

Pointers were introduced in PL/I in the early 1960s so that list processing could be done in a high-level language. At the time, type checking was not well understood, and no type checking was done for PL/I pointers (either at compile-time or at run-time). A PL/I pointer can point to anything and for this reason is called *untyped*. The concept of typed pointers was introduced in ALGOL 68 to overcome this lack of type checking ability. A typed pointer is a pointer that can point to variables of only one type. An integer pointer can point only to integer variables.

Pointers introduced another problem. A *dangling pointer* is a pointer that points to what used to be a variable but is no longer. This anomaly can occur if the variable is explicitly freed, or if a global pointer variable points to a local variable upon exit from a block. ALGOL 68 cannot detect dangling pointers at compile-time. Instead, a run-time check must be inserted at the right places to prevent assignments that might lead to dangling pointers. This check is sometimes called the *lifetime scope* check. An example of a dangling pointer is the assignment of VARIABLE2 to POINTER2 in the following program. The keyword pointer means "points to," which we use instead of ALGOL 68's ref, Ada's access, and Pascal's up arrow, ↑.

```
POINTER2: pointer INTEGER;
P: procedure is
        VARIABLE2: INTEGER;
begin
        VARIABLE2 := 5;
        POINTER2 := ADDRESS(VARIABLE2);
end P;
```

```
MAIN: procedure is
begin
        P;
        PRINT(POINTER2);
end MAIN;
```

In the above example, 5 is assigned to VARIABLE2 and the address of VARIABLE2 is assigned to POINTER2. But upon return from the procedure P, the storage for the variable VARIABLE2 is freed and the pointer POINTER2 is left dangling. Subsequent use of this dangling pointer is unpredictable. For example, the reclaimed storage may have been allocated to another variable. Pascal introduced a new solution to the dangling reference problem. To verify at compile-time that dangling references would not occur, Pascal pointers are allowed to point only to explicitly created anonymous variables on the heap. Pascal does not provide the ADDRESS function and so Pascal pointers cannot point to any other variables. In keeping with the spirit of Pascal, the ADDRESS function is also not provided in Ada.

As with any other type, one might ask what are the constants, values, and operators of a pointer type. The value of a pointer type is essentially an address of some location in memory where a value of some type is stored. One exception is the null pointer, which is used by nearly all languages to mean a pointer value that does not point to any storage location. It can be used for uninitialized pointer variables and for empty lists and trees. Null is usually the only literal of the pointer type.

The most important pointer function is the allocation function, which finds a fresh memory location. Another useful function is the previously mentioned address function. Programming languages allow comparison of pointers. Two pointers are considered equal if they point to the same object. Most languages do not offer any other operators on pointers. One exception is the C language, which allows pointer arithmetic. C arrays and C pointers are conceptually the same. Indexing into a C array is considered the same as adding a number to the C pointer. Thus a[j] means the value at location a+j.

4.2 *Union Types and Variant Records*

A union type is not an aggregate type, since it is not a collection of data. It is a constructor type, because union types are constructed from other types. It serves a variety of purposes and so different people will view union types in slightly different ways. Essentially, a union type combines the values of several other types, called the *alternative* types. Sometimes the word *variant* is used instead of alternative. A union type with two alternative types, integer and character, would have as values both integers and characters. Let x be a variable of such a union type. Either characters or integers may be assigned to x; but x has only one value at any one time which may be either a character or an integer. For languages with compile-time type checking, integer and character operators would not (in general) be valid if applied to X since it may have a value of the wrong type at run-time.

Union types are sometimes used for conserving storage space or giving different names to the same object (i.e., aliasing). Union types permit a number of logical variables to share the space of one physical variable. FORTRAN provides equivalencing for this purpose. COBOL has the REDEFINES capability for the same purpose.

A more important conceptual purpose of union types is the expression of a type that may consist of different categories of values not easily expressed as a single type. Consider a type, which we will call SCORE, whose values may be either an integer value or one of three noninteger values: UNKNOWN, UNDEFINED, or OTHER. If one were to try to just use the integer type to represent the SCORE type, one must somehow represent the three noninteger values. The following example uses such a representation and defines two functions: ADD1 and SUB1.

```
type SCORE is INTEGER;
constant UNDEFINED = -100;
constant UNKNOWN   = -101;
constant OTHER     = -102;

ADD1: function (X: SCORE) return SCORE is
begin
        if X=UNDEFINED or X=UNKNOWN or X=OTHER then
                return X;
        else
                return X+1;
        end if;
end ADD1;

SUB1: function (X: SCORE) return SCORE is
begin
        return X-1;
end SUB1;
```

There are several obvious flaws with this solution.

1. The first problem is that the above solution assumes that numbers -100, -101, and -102 can never be valid score values. That is, these numbers are reserved for special meanings.

2. The second problem is that the SUB1 routine does not consider the special values. For example, SUB1(UNKNOWN) returns a score of -99. The significant point is that no type errors can be detected by a compiler.

A second, alternative method is to use a collection of variables to store the information required for a SCORE value. One variable could be used exclusively for valid integer scores, a second variable for noninteger values, and a third variable to specify whether an integer or noninteger score is stored. This solution distributes the logical variable over three physical variables, but we can place them into a single record, as follows:

```
type SCORE is
        record
                AMOUNT:  INTEGER;
                PROBLEM: (UNKNOWN, UNDEFINED, OTHER);
                WHICH:   (GOOD, BAD);
        end record;

ADD1: function (X: SCORE) return SCORE is
begin
        if X.WHICH = GOOD then
                X.AMOUNT = X.AMOUNT+1;
        end if;
        return X;
end ADD1;

SUB1: function (X: SCORE) return SCORE is
begin
        X.AMOUNT = X.AMOUNT-1;
        return X;
end SUB1;
```

This example is an improvement over the previous example because there are no special meanings attached to integer values. Note that the SUB1 function works correctly, even though it it not properly written. It works correctly because the PROBLEM and WHICH fields do not change. However, note also that the AMOUNT field is not used properly when the SCORE is BAD. Using a union type should detect these type errors, but using a simple record type will not allow a compiler to detect such errors.

The blind use of a value of a union type as any other type will result in type violations and improper use of operators. This type checking cannot always be performed at compile-time. In most situations there must be some kind of run-time check. Therefore, some information must be kept at run-time that specifies the current type of the value stored in a union. This piece of information is called a *discriminant*, since it discriminates between the different alternative types. In the previous example WHICH played the role of a discriminant. Assignment to a union variable must update the discriminant as well as the value. Each use of the value must be checked for consistency with the discriminant. One way to do this is with the discriminated case statement.

A *discriminated case statement* is a multibranch statement (a generalized conditional statement), with one branch for each alternative type. At run-time the branch is determined by the current value of the discriminant. Examples will be given shortly. Another method allowed by some programming languages is to use *projection* operators, which convert a value from a union type to one of the alternative types, and *injection* operators, which convert an alternative type to a union type.

A second major issue concerning union types is the exact nature of a union. Is it possible to have a union of two integer types? The ALGOL 68 union type does not allow unions with related types, which are called *incestuous unions*. Two types are related if one can be coerced to another. For example, in ALGOL 68 int and ref int are related and cannot be part of the same union. Since every type is coercible to itself, each alternative type of an ALGOL 68 union must be unique. This notion is in contrast to the *discriminated union*, which has no restriction on the mix of alternative types. If two alternative types of a discriminated union are the same, they can still be distinguished by the discriminant. So the discriminated union is like a disjoint union, rather than a plain set-oriented, vanilla-flavored union. Pascal and Ada have both adopted the discriminated union under the name *variant record*.

Variant records are discriminated unions with no protection of the discriminant. An example of a variant record is

```
type SCORE is
    record
        case WHICH: (GOOD, BAD) is
        when GOOD => AMOUNT: INTEGER;
        when BAD  => PROBLEM: (UNKNOWN,UNDEFINED,OTHER);
        end case;
    end record;

ADD1: function (X: SCORE) return SCORE is
begin
    if X.WHICH = GOOD then
        X.AMOUNT = X.AMOUNT+1;
    end if;
    return X;
end ADD1;

SUB1: function (X: SCORE) return SCORE is
begin
    X.AMOUNT = X.AMOUNT-1;
    return X;
end SUB1;
```

The type SCORE is a record containing either an integer value or some problem condition. The record consists of three components. The first component is the discriminant and can be selected with the selector WHICH as in the previous example. The discriminant is an enumerated type and may have one of two different values, either GOOD or BAD. The second component of the record is selected by the selector AMOUNT but can only be selected *when* the value of the discriminant is GOOD. Likewise the third component selected by PROBLEM can only be selected *when* the value of the discriminant is BAD. Since AMOUNT and PROBLEM cannot be used at the same time, they can share storage. A major property of union types in all languages is that alternatives share storage.

The SUB1 function will cause an error if it is ever called with a BAD score. This error may not be detected in some languages and implementations. A compiler can easily insert code to physically check for the appropriate discriminant value before using AMOUNT. The discriminated case statement is often used to combine this checking with a multiway branch. The SUB1 function rewritten with this statement follows:

```
SUB1: function (X: SCORE) return SCORE is
begin
        case X.WHICH is
        when GOOD =>
                X.AMOUNT = X.AMOUNT-1;
        when BAD =>
        end case;
        return X;
end SUB1;
```

The above example illustrates the discriminated case statement. Depending on the type of X, one of two branches is chosen. *When* the WHICH value of X is GOOD the first branch is taken.

The ALGOL 68 union is not a discriminated union, but it still has a discriminant, which is not visible to the programmer. The discriminant is under complete control of the system and proper type checking can be performed. Consider the following example:

```
type PROBLEM_TYPE is (UNKNOWN, UNDEFINED, OTHER);
type SCORE is union ( INTEGER, PROBLEM_TYPE );

ADD1: function (X: SCORE) return SCORE is
begin
        case X is
        when INTEGER =>
            X = X+1;
        end case;
        return X;
end ADD1;

SUB1: function (X: SCORE) return SCORE is
begin
        case X is
        when INTEGER =>
            X = X-1;
        end case;
        return X;
end SUB1;
```

The important concept here is the type security provided by the hidden discriminant. An assignment to a union variable implies a hidden assignment to the discriminant. The case statement uses the hidden discriminant to determine which branch to evaluate. Each branch allows the opportunity to access one alternative as a constant.

There are two important advantages that variant records have over ALGOL 68 unions. First, variant records are nicely integrated with records that provide a nice syntactic and clean expression of complex types. Second, a variant record is a discriminated union and thus any two types, or even the same type, can be used for each variant. Consider the following example, which is awkward to translate into ALGOL 68.

```
type FIGURE is
    record
        X_LOCATION:   REAL;
        Y_LOCATION:   REAL;
        case SHAPE: (SQUARE, BOX, CIRCLE, ELLIPSE) is
        when SQUARE =>  SIDE:                REAL;
        when BOX =>     WIDTH, HEIGHT:       REAL;
        when CIRCLE =>  DIAMETER:            REAL;
        when ELLIPSE => X_AXIS, Y_AXIS:      REAL;
        end case;
    end record;
```

Ada extends the Pascal variant record so that it will be type-secure. The discriminant in an Ada record with *variant parts* cannot be explicitly changed. It is changed only when the variant is changed. Also, each access to a variant part is checked (if necessary) at run-time. This type still varies from the ALGOL 68 union type since in Ada it is possible to have a run-time error that raises the DISCRIMINANT_ERROR condition. It is not possible to have such an error in ALGOL 68.

In some programs a union variable might have only one alternative during its lifetime. This occurs when recursive data structures are constructed but not modified. In the unions discussed above, it was not assumed that a union variable would always have the same alternative. With such an assumption, the system could allocate exactly the amount of storage needed for that one alternative, rather than the amount of storage needed for the largest alternative. This approach can easily be adapted to PL/I, which does not have a union type or typed pointers. First let us consider a PL/I data structure without regard for storage efficiency:

```
1 FIGURE,
   2 X_LOCATION FLOAT BIN,
   2 Y_LOCATION FLOAT BIN,
   2 SHAPE FIXED BIN,
   2 SQUARE,
     3 SIDE FLOAT BIN,
   2 BOX,
```

```
   3 WIDTH FLOAT BIN,
   3 HEIGHT FLOAT BIN,
 2 CIRCLE,
   3 DIAMETER FLOAT BIN,
 2 ELLIPSE,
   3 X_AXIS FLOAT BIN,
   3 Y_AXIS FLOAT BIN;
```

This implementation reserves space for each alternative rather than sharing the space for each alternative. To overcome this waste of space the data structure could be written as

```
1 SQUARE_FIGURE,
 2 X_LOCATION FLOAT BIN,
 2 Y_LOCATION FLOAT BIN,
 2 SHAPE FIXED BIN,
   3 SIDE FLOAT BIN;

1 BOX_FIGURE,
 2 X_LOCATION FLOAT BIN,
 2 Y_LOCATION FLOAT BIN,
 2 SHAPE FIXED BIN,
   3 WIDTH FLOAT BIN,
   3 HEIGHT FLOAT BIN;

1 CIRCLE_FIGURE,
 2 X_LOCATION FLOAT BIN,
 2 Y_LOCATION FLOAT BIN,
 2 SHAPE FIXED BIN,
   3 DIAMETER FLOAT BIN;

1 ELLIPSE_FIGURE,
 2 X_LOCATION FLOAT BIN,
 2 Y_LOCATION FLOAT BIN,
 2 SHAPE FIXED BIN,
   3 X_AXIS FLOAT BIN,
   3 Y_AXIS FLOAT BIN;

1 FIGURE,
 2 X_LOCATION FLOAT BIN,
 2 Y_LOCATION FLOAT BIN,
 2 SHAPE FIXED BIN;
```

In this example, a reference to an arbitrary record would use the fifth record. But references to a specific kind of record would use the first four records. When using this technique the programmer must carefully prepare the records so that the initial fields are identical. This method works only because PL/I has untyped pointers, which can be used to point to any of the above five records. When a record is allocated one can allocate the exact amount of storage by referring to one of the first four records. If a record will be changing SHAPE then one must allocate the largest of the four records so that any shape will fit into the storage allocated.

Ada allows this approach but with type security. In Ada it is possible to declare variables with or without the discriminant. When an Ada variant record is allocated with a specified discriminant, the system will allocate only the amount of storage for that particular discriminant. This is called a *constrained* type in Ada, since values of this record may only have values for that one particular value of the discriminant. Consider the following Ada type declaration:

```
type SHAPE is (SQUARE, BOX, CIRCLE, ELLIPSE);

type FIGURE (TYPE:SHAPE := SQUARE) is
        record
                X_LOCATION: REAL;
                Y_LOCATION: REAL;
                case SHAPE is
                when SQUARE  => SIDE:            REAL;
                when BOX     => WIDTH, HEIGHT:   REAL;
                when CIRCLE  => DIAMETER:        REAL;
                when ELLIPSE => X_AXIS, Y_AXIS: REAL;
                end case;
        end record;

SQUARE1, SQUARE2: FIGURE(SQUARE);
OBJ1, OBJ2: FIGURE;
```

This Ada data type has the advantage of allocating exactly the amount of storage needed plus all the type security required to ensure that the values are used properly. The declarations of SQUARE1 and SQUARE2 allocate enough storage for square values. Only values with a square shape can be assigned to these variables. The declarations of OBJ1 and OBJ2 allocate enough storage to store any value of the FIGURE type.

Generic Types

A number of programming languages have a facility sometimes called a *generic* procedure. A generic procedure is more generally useful because it accepts a wider range of data types as its parameters. We may want a squaring function for both integers and reals. They could be provided as a pair of functions called INTSQUARE and REALSQUARE. Alternatively, one may wish to write one procedure that will do both by accepting either integer or real parameters. One might try

```
SQUARE: function (X:REAL) return REAL;
```

If the language does not have automatic conversion from integer to real, then this function will not square integers. If the language does provide automatic conversion from integer to real, it is still not acceptable, since only real numbers are returned. The ALGOL 68 union type works and can be written something like

```
SQUARE: function (X: union (REAL, INTEGER))
                 return union (REAL, INTEGER) is
begin
        case X
        when REAL    => ...
        when INTEGER => ...
        end case;
end SQUARE;
```

One problem with this solution is that the returned value is a union rather than either a real or an integer. Other languages provide different solutions. The PL/I generic facility provides different entry points depending on the types of the parameter. EL1 provides a construct called *oneof* which allows a parameter to be one of a number of different parameters, but unlike ALGOL 68 and PL/I, it may return values of different types. Most of these methods can be replaced with a more general approach using overloaded operators. Ada allows overloading of function names, so that the programmer may have two different SQUARE functions:

```
SQUARE: function(X:REAL) return REAL is
begin ... end

SQUARE: function(X:INTEGER) return INTEGER is
begin ... end
```

4.3 Recursive Types

A recursive definition of a data type is one that refers to itself. Recursive definitions are sometimes a very natural way of expressing certain things. The recursive definition of binary trees is more understandable than a nonrecursive definition. A binary tree of X is either empty or a record consisting of three things: an X and two binary trees called left and right. Other naturally occurring recursive types include lists, sequences, and all kinds of graph structures. The LISP s-expression was one of the first widely used recursive types in programming languages. An *s-expression* is either an atom or a parenthesized list of s-expressions separated by a blank. Although the integer numbers can be defined recursively, they are a primitive type in most programming languages. A positive nonzero integer is either one or the successor of a positive nonzero integer. The successor of a number is obtained by adding one to it. Similarly, lists, strings, sequences, stacks, and queues are easily defined as recursive types. However, some languages provide special features for these types.

Some types cannot be expressed without recursion. Using only the constructor types record, array, function, union, and pointer, it is not possible to express a linked list or a binary tree. All integer binary trees of depth 3 can be expressed as

```
type TREE0 is VOID;              -- empty tree
type TREE1 is
    record
        LEFT, RIGHT: TREE0;   -- leaf node
        INFO: INTEGER;
    end record;

type TREE2 is
    record
        LEFT, RIGHT: union (TREE0, TREE1);
        INFO: INTEGER;
    end record;

type TREE3 is
    record
        LEFT, RIGHT: union (TREE0, TREE1, TREE2);
        INFO: INTEGER;
    end record;
```

This is a particularly awkward way to work with trees. Lists and trees cannot be expressed without recursion because they are arbitrarily large data structures that cannot be represented by finite data type constructors. The power of recursive types implies a considerably more complex storage management than nonrecursive types. A variable of type TREE3 above must allocate sufficient storage to be able to store any tree of depth 3. Using this technique for an arbitrary tree (defined recursively) would require an infinite amount of storage for a tree variable:

```
type TREE is
        record
                LEFT, RIGHT: TREE;
                INFO: INTEGER;
        end record;

    ROOT: TREE;
```

The variable ROOT according to this definition should be allocated space for two trees and an integer. But the space required for each tree is another two trees and an integer. The pointer or access types can be used to get around the storage problem by inserting a level of indirection. A pointer always takes the same amount of space independent of what value it is pointing to; so recursive types with pointers will not take an infinite amount of space. The above tree definition can be rewritten as

```
type TREE is
        record
                LEFT, RIGHT: pointer TREE;
                INFO: INTEGER;
        end record;

    ROOT: TREE;
```

In this example the storage necessary for the variable ROOT is the storage needed for two pointers and an integer. Of course, in order to construct a tree one must dynamically allocate nodes as they are needed. One minor problem with this definition of a tree is that the empty tree cannot be represented. A simple change to the definition can remove this problem:

```
type TREE is
    pointer
        record
                LEFT, RIGHT: TREE;
                INFO: INTEGER;
        end record;

    ROOT: TREE;
```

Now the variable ROOT requires storage for a single pointer only, and the empty tree is naturally represented by the null pointer.

To make sure a recursive type can be stored properly, most programming languages have restrictions on recursive types. Pascal and Ada require all recursive types to have a pointer so that each recursive type requires a finite amount of storage. ALGOL 68 is a little more lax and requires either a pointer or an indirection through a procedure. Thus the following are legal recursive ALGOL 68 data types.

```
type C is function (F:C) return C;

type FUNC is function (A:INTEGER; F:FUNC)
                return INTEGER;
FACT: FUNC is
begin
        if A<2 then
                return 1
        else
                return A*F(A-1)
        end if;
end FACT;

begin
        FACT(5, FACT)
        . . .
```

Interestingly, with the recursive data type FUNC a recursive factorial function, FACT, can be defined that does not use explicit recursion.

4.4 Functions and Procedures as Types

A procedure or subroutine is a program called by another program. A procedure typically has the same structure as the main program. A procedure call may also pass parameters. There is usually a distinction between routines that return a value and those that do not. Some use the word *procedure* to refer to routines that do not return values and the word *function* to refer to routines that do return values. Procedure calls are statements and function calls are expressions.

Functions and arrays have some similar properties. Arrays and functions may be used in the same manner and their behavior may be identical. Many languages even use the same syntax for function calls and array subscripting. Other languages, like Pascal and ALGOL 68, use square brackets for array subscripting and parentheses for function calls. Arrays may have multiple subscripts of various types to access a particular element of an array. Functions may have multiple parameters of various types to compute a particular value of the function. In one respect the only difference seems to be the implementation, not the use of the type. Perhaps as an abstract data type, arrays and functions are the same. The choice of which to use is a performance issue involving the classic tradeoff between time and space. In what other respects do they differ? Unlike an array, a function may have a parameter whose type is not finite. The type of an array subscript is finite. Also unlike an array, functions may have side-effects and may depend on global variables. Even without side-effects and global variables, a function may have local static variables, and thus may remember a *history* of previous calls, which may in turn affect the value returned by the function.

Is it reasonable to consider procedures and functions as data types? One of the first languages to consider procedures and functions as first class citizens was ALGOL 68. ALGOL 68 does not distinguish between procedures and functions. In ALGOL 68 procedures return the nil value. In ALGOL 68 it is possible to have procedure variables, arrays of procedures, procedure passing, and even procedure constants. There are two operations that can be performed on procedures: assignment and application. The type of an ALGOL 68 procedure is a type constructor based on the types of all its parameters and the type of the return value. When the procedure is applied to parameters, the types of the parameters must be consistent with the type of the procedure. When procedures are assigned or passed as parameters the type must be compatible. This requirement ensures that the application of every procedure at run-time will be passed values with the expected types. Some languages (such as the original Pascal) do not have a well-developed notion of the procedure type. Consequently, type-checking holes may appear. If the procedure type is based only on the value returned and does not take into account the types of the parameters, then through procedure assignment and procedure passing a situation may occur where a procedure is applied to data of the wrong type with no compile-time (and probably no run-time) checks.

ALGOL 68 provides procedure constants. These are sometimes called *anonymous* procedures since they do not have a name associated with the procedure. The LAMBDA construct of LISP is an example of an anonymous procedure. Since Ada does not have anonymous procedures we will extend the language to include them and present all of the following examples using the Ada syntax. Without anonymous procedures, every procedure must be given a name. In the example below, imagine a procedure (named MAPALL) that applies another procedure to every item of a list. To print out every item in the list one might execute the expression

```
MAPALL(A_LIST, PRINT_ITEM)
```

and define the print procedure as

```
PRINT_ITEM: procedure (ITEM: ELEMENT_TYPE) is
begin
        PRINT_LINE ( ITEM.NAME, ITEM.VALUE )
end PRINT_ITEM;
```

If the PRINT_ITEM procedure is used nowhere else, then it makes sense to restrict the scope of PRINT_ITEM to just the statement in which it appears. Furthermore, there is no need to give it an explicit name. The example might thus be expressed as

```
MAPALL(LISTA,
        procedure (ITEM: ELEMENT_TYPE) is
        begin PRINT_LINE(ITEM.NAME, ITEM.VALUE) end
);
```

The expression beginning with procedure up to end is a procedure constant. Although it has no name, it is a well-defined procedure value. It is passed to another function; it could also be part of an assignment statement or explicitly called. The concept of anonymous procedures and functions might be new to many people but has been used in the lambda calculus and in mathematics for many years. The use of anonymous procedures does not affect data types other than the citizenship of procedure types. If a language offers a way of expressing constants for numeric types, character strings, arrays, records, and every type in the language except procedures, than procedure types are second class citizens.

Most languages provide only application and perhaps assignment operations on procedures. There are other operations on procedures that can be useful. A basic operation (at least in mathematics) is composition. The composition of functions results in a new function. Consider two integer unary functions F and G with one integer parameter. The composition of F and G is a third function that has the same effect as calling G and then calling F with the result obtained from G (i.e. F(G(x))). Most programming languages do not provide function composition and in most cases composition cannot be expressed in the language. One might try to express the operation as

```
type UNARYFUN is function (INTEGER) return INTEGER;

COMPOSE: function (F,G: UNARYFUN) return UNARYFUN is

        COMPOSITE: function (X:INTEGER) return INTEGER
        begin return F(G(X));
        end COMPOSITE;

begin
        return COMPOSITE;
end COMPOSE;
```

The difficulty that this function presents to normal programming languages is that the parameters to the function COMPOSE must be retained after return from the function. In a normal situation parameters as well as local variables are discarded because they are no longer needed upon return. In the above example both F and G should be remembered because the value that is returned will access these two values in the future. This problem is the procedure analog of the dangling reference problem (see Section 4.1). The *retention* model of storage management has been one proposal to solve both the dangling reference and dangling procedure problems. The retention scheme will retain any local variables or parameters that may be needed in the future, rather than disposing of them upon function exit.

One last note on syntax should be mentioned. Both Ada and Pascal provide a special syntax for declaring functions and procedures. When functions and procedures become first class citizens they can be defined like any other constant or variable. For example, the COMPOSITE function could have been declared like

```
COMPOSITE: UNARY := begin return F(G(X)); end;
```

Also note that we don't really need to name the COMPOSITE function, and so could have defined the COMPOSE function as follows:

```
COMPOSE: function (F,G: UNARY) return UNARY is
begin
        return  function (X: INTEGER) return INTEGER is
                begin return F(G(X)); end;
end COMPOSE;
```

Procedural Data Structures

In previous sections we have not amply demonstrated how to use the various data types for building data structures. Because the procedure data type is seldom used as a data structure, it is instructive to see some details of procedural data structures. Procedure data types are used frequently as parts of data structures, such as arrays of procedures, but this is not what we mean. Instead we show an example of how procedures could be used as a data-structuring device.

Consider the data type "set of integers." Assuming that our programming language does not have a predefined set type, we must consider how to represent a set of integers. In many applications, bit maps are used to represent sets. A bit map allocates one bit for each possible member of a set. If the bit is turned on, then the corresponding element is in the set. A bit map is not an appropriate representation for a set of integers because the number of possible elements that could be in a set is too large. Even restricting the range of integers that might be in the set to the range one to a million would require a bit map that is one million bits long. Another common representation is a linked list of the elements that appear in the set. To represent the set {3,5,7} a linked list of three elements would be constructed. It would not matter in what order the elements appear. This representation is appropriate as long as the sets do not become too large. To represent the set of all even numbers between one and a million would require even more space than the bit map representation. For more information on set representations see Section 9.1.

A procedural representation for sets does not have the disadvantages of the previous two representations. A procedural representation of a set is a Boolean function with one integer parameter. This Boolean function when passed a number will return true if the number is in the set and false otherwise. The empty set is represented by a function that always returns false:

```
type SET is function (X: INTEGER) return BOOLEAN;

EMPTY: SET := begin return FALSE; end;
```

Other sets, such as {4,7} and the set of even numbers, are easily represented.

```
FOUR_AND_SEVEN: SET := begin return (X=4) or (X=7);
end; EVEN: SET := begin return (X mod 2) = 0; end;
```

The above examples show that it seems easy enough to represent constant sets. Set operations must also be definable. Assuming a retention storage management scheme, operations are easily specified. The member, insert, and union operations are given below. Note that insert is written with a named function while intersection is written with an anonymous function:

```
MEMBER: function (X:INTEGER;  S:SET) return BOOLEAN is
begin
        return S(X);
end MEMBER;

INSERT: function (Y:INTEGER; S:SET) return SET is
        RESULT: SET :=
        begin return (X=Y) or else S(Y); end RESULT;
begin
        return RESULT;
end INSERT;
```

```
INTERSECTION: function (S1, S2: SET) return SET is
begin
        return   function (X:INTEGER) return BOOLEAN is
                 begin return S1(X) and then S2(X); end;
end INTERSECTION;
```

Procedural data types have some disadvantages. They are either awkward or difficult to implement in most programming languages. They may be inefficient, especially if many operations are used to construct large data items. In some cases, certain operations cannot be implemented. For example, in the set data type with a procedural representation it is not possible to provide a MAPALL procedure or any similar function. This is because it is either not possible or very expensive to enumerate all the elements of a set. It may be cheap to determine whether any specific element is or is not a member of a set, but only an exhaustive search will find all the members of an arbitrary set.

4.5 Other Types

There are many other data types that have been invented but do not neatly fall into one of the previous categories. These types may fulfill needs in specific data-processing environments. A few of these unusual types will be briefly mentioned in this section.

SNOBOL Patterns

SNOBOL is a programming language that has been specially designed for string processing. A concept, called a *pattern*, evolved into a data type in SNOBOL 4. ICON, a more recent programming language, continues the SNOBOL tradition and has generalized some of the concepts of pattern matching to what is called *goal-directed evaluation*.

A pattern specifies a class of strings. When compared to a specific string, a pattern either succeeds or fails. The pattern is like a grammar. Both grammar and pattern specify a formal language, which merely means a set of strings. The major operation on both grammars and patterns is testing for membership. In SNOBOL, testing for membership is called *pattern-matching*, while with grammars it is called *parsing*. A successful pattern match (or parse) occurs if the string is a member of the language, otherwise the operation fails.

The following list shows some of the basic pattern-matching facilities of SNOBOL:

'ABC'	matches only the string "ABC"
LEN(4)	matches any string of length 4
x | y	matches either string "x" or string "y"
x y	matches any string whose first part matches "x" and second part matches "y"
'A' ('B'|'C')	matches either "AB" or "AC"

The first two examples show pattern constants. Each expresses a fixed set of strings. In the first case, only one string is in the set. In the second case, all four-character strings are in the set. The next two examples show some pattern operators. The first operator, called alternation, may have arbitrary pattern operands. Likewise the second, called concatenation, may have arbitrary pattern operands. The last example shows a pattern expression involving both of these operators. Concatenation has a higher precedence, so parentheses are required for this example (otherwise it would match "AB" or "C"). Patterns may be assigned to variables, and more complex patterns may be formed from simpler patterns. For example,

```
VOWEL = 'A' | 'E' | 'I' | 'O' | 'U'
WORD = 'P' VOWEL ('T' | 'CK') | 'B' VOWEL 'G'
          | 'M' VOWEL ('TE' | 'SS')
SENT = WORD ' ' WORD ' ' WORD
```

assigns patterns to VOWEL, WORD, and SENT. The pattern SENT will match sentences such as "PAT BIG PET" and "PICK PACK BAG". Since these are dynamic assignments, the order of assignment is important. If the third assignment occurred before the first assignment, then SENT would match only two blanks (WORD, like all other SNOBOL variables, is initialized to the null or empty string).

SNOBOL patterns also provide many other facilities. For example, it would be nice to know the substrings that were matched, so SNOBOL allows (as part of a pattern expression) any match or partial match to be assigned to a variable. Recursive matches are more difficult but can also be accomplished with SNOBOL patterns. These additional complexities of SNOBOL patterns make them difficult to formalize.

Sets

A set is a fundamental mathematical abstraction. Few programming languages have set data types. Even Ada, a modern language based on Pascal, does not have sets. Pascal, the only widely used language with sets, allows sets only for enumerated types (or subranges). This is a very good restriction in Pascal and is compatible with Pascal's design goal of a simple and efficient implementation. Pascal sets can be easily and efficiently implemented as a bit map.

To generalize the notion of set to all types will complicate an implementation. For types with a very large number of values, the bit map may become unnecessarily long. For types with an infinite number of values, the bit map representation is not possible. Some dynamic data structure such as a list is a better representation in certain cases, but such structures imply dynamic storage management. These kinds of storage issues explain, in part, why the the set type is not included in most programming languages.

The programming language SETL is based on sets. The primitive types are the usual ones but the three basic type constructors are *tuple*, *set*, and *map*. The tuple is a heterogeneous varying-length array. This definition implies that SETL has run-time type checking and dynamic storage management. The map type is a set of pairs (a pair being a tuple of length 2). The first elements of all the pairs constitute the domain and the second elements constitute the range. A map may be used as a function. Updating a map is also allowed, and so a map is like an array with an arbitrary index type. Iteration for each of the constructor types is provided with a syntax familiar to mathematicians.

Types as a Type

The programming languages EL1 and Russell are just two of many languages that contain a data type that we shall call *type*. The values of type type are all types of the programming language. Such a type permits a flexible method for expressing generic routines. It also permits dynamic data types; that is, new data types can be constructed during the execution of the program.

The constants of a type type are the primitive types, and the operators of a type type are the constructor types. Thus INTEGER and CHARACTER are two constants and ARRAY would be a function of the type type. Ada is not particularly amenable to the type type construct, so let us invent our own data type system and type type. Let us have the primitive types INTEGER, CHARACTER, and TYPE. For constructor types let us use the cartesian product, discriminated union, function, and set—called, respectively, RECORD, UNION, FUNCTION, and SET. Each type constructor is permitted any nonzero number of arguments except SET, which is permitted only one. Type expressions are now just expressions made from these constants and constructors. A declaration would then consist of a name and a type expression. For example, some initialized declarations and code using type type could appear as

```
X: INTEGER := 5;
Z: RECORD(INTEGER, INTEGER) := (4,5);
T: TYPE := RECORD(INTEGER, CHARACTER);
type FUN is RECORD(TYPE, INTEGER);
ARRAY: function (INDEX, ELEMENT: TYPE) return TYPE;
STRING: TYPE := ARRAY(INTEGER, CHARACTER);
S: STRING;
```

This style of programming language suddenly introduces many new ideas that would previously not have been considered. Note in the above example that there might not be any distinction between a type declaration (such as FUN) and a type type declaration (such as T). New type constructors such as ARRAY and STRING can be defined. The exact nature and capabilities of a type type vary from language to language. One of the difficulties of such a style is that there is no clear distinction between compile-time and run-time actions.

Exercises

1. In the C language, pointers and arrays are essentially the same type. Consider the declarations

```
VAR1: array (1..10) of INTEGER;
VAR2: pointer INTEGER;
```

   Both VAR1 and VAR2 are equivalent with the following exceptions:

   a. VAR1 is a constant and cannot be assigned a new value. The array elements of VAR1 are variables, which can be assigned new values.

   b. The declaration for VAR2 allocates storage for the pointer. A separate statement is used to allocate a sequence of ten integer variables.

   Both VAR1 and VAR2 are considered memory addresses, and subscripts are considered pointer expressions that compute an address. What effect does this concept of an array have on programming? Are there any major conceptual differences between traditional arrays and C arrays that influence a programmer's view of types, values, and storage?

2. Comparison operators for procedures were not discussed. What are some possible interpretations for an equality operator on procedure values? Which of these interpretations can be implemented?

3. Why are sets not a fundamental data type of most programming languages?

4. Consider the type type and the following definition of a list type.

```
LIST: function (X: TYPE) return TYPE is
begin
        return RECORD(X, LIST(X));
end LIST;
```

   What problems might a programming language have with this type constructor? Can you rewrite this function to avoid these problems?

Further Reading

Wexelblat (1978) is a collection of papers on the history of early programming languages. Introductory books on programming language principles, such as Nicholls (1975) and Tennent (1981), provide auxiliary and related material. Tennent (1973) and Fleck (1978) discuss formalizing string patterns. The use of functions for accessing data structures is treated by Reynolds (1970) in a language called GEDANKEN. Procedural data types are described in more detail by Reynolds (1975). Further information on types as a type and dynamic data types can be found in Goodwin (1981), and Demers et al. (1978, 1980a). The roots of first class citizenship come from the orthogonality concept of ALGOL 68 (van Wijngaarden, 1975). More recently, Demers et al. (1980b) argue strongly for *Type-Completeness*. In extending APL, many questions on the meaning of type in regard to arrays are examined and evaluated by Gull and Jenkins (1979).

Data Type Issues

*T*ype *C*hecking

5

5.1 Type Errors

A *type error* occurs when an operation receives a value of the wrong type. For example, the integer addition operator expects integer values. If an integer addition operation receives a real value as an operand, a type error occurs. Without a type check, the integer addition operator would blindly add what it thinks are two integers. The real value would be misinterpreted as an integer value. This misinterpretation may make a big difference and is machine dependent. The real value 1.0 is misinterpreted as the integer value 16,512 on the VAX. Every operator expects operand(s) of specified type(s) and returns a value of some type. The occurrence of operands of the wrong type is a type error.

Another source of type errors is the invalid use of variables. A *typed variable* is a variable that will store values of one particular type. Invalid use of variables occurs only in a language with typed variables. Any attempt to store a value of the wrong type should produce a type error. If an integer variable is assigned a value other than an integer, a type error occurs.

Some errors that are traditionally not considered as type errors could become type errors by changing the set of types. A zero divide error occurs when the second operand to the division operator is zero. Since this is arithmetically undefined, an error occurs. If the numeric types are redefined to be the zero numbers and the nonzero numbers, then the second operand to division can be considered to be of type nonzero. With this view, division by zero is a type error. Other errors that fall into this category include dereferencing the null pointer, applying the first or rest operator to the empty list, and popping the empty stack.

Range and subrange errors are sometimes considered type errors. As you may recall, an integer subrange specifies a subset of the integers by giving the lower and upper bounds. The value assigned to a subrange variable must be checked against the lower and upper bounds. Range analysis is very difficult at compile-time, and most implementations defer the checks to run-time. Range analysis is equivalent to checking for subscript-out-of-bounds errors. In Pascal this equivalence is obvious since all index

67

types are ranges. Arithmetic overflow and underflow are special machine-dependent examples of range errors that are usually easier to detect because of special hardware.

5.2 Compile-Time and Run-Time Type Checking

Type checking verifies that operations receive data of the proper type, i.e., type checking detects type errors. It is most natural to think of type checking as occurring at run-time, when operations receive data. Run-time type checking occurs during the execution of the program. Before execution of the operation each data value of each operand is checked. But type checking at run-time has two drawbacks:

1. Run-time type checking increases execution time.
2. Typically it is not possible to determine the type of a value at run-time, particularly if data is not tagged with type fields.

Therefore, type checking usually occurs at compile-time. Compile-time type checking occurs during the compilation step before the program is executed. Compile-time type checking will check that each operator in every expression will always receive data values of the right type when evaluated at run-time. Compile-time type checking is typically a procedure that checks all operations, procedure and function calls, assignments, and other places in which values are used. Run-time type checks are typically inserted by the compiler into the run-time code for detecting type errors that may occur during the execution of the program. The following program declares two variables Y, an integer, and Z, a variable of any type. The keyword ANY is used to indicate a typeless variable, one that may be assigned a value of any type. The procedure P has one integer parameter. The program calls P three times.

```
Y: INTEGER;
Z: ANY;                    -- an untyped variable

P: procedure ( X: INTEGER ) is
begin
      ...
end P;

begin
        P(3);
        P(Y);
        P(Z);
        ...
end
```

For each call, the type of the argument must match the type of the parameter. In the first call the argument 3 is an integer constant and the compiler does not need to insert any run-time type check. In the second call the argument is the variable Y. The compiler notes that Y is declared as an integer and makes the assumption that the value of Y will always be an integer value. The assumption made by the compiler is a safe assumption because the compiler will also check every assignment to the variable Y to make sure that only integer values are assigned to Y. In the last call the argument is the variable Z. Because Z is not a typed variable the compiler does not know the type of the value stored in Z. To perform type checking the compiler must insert a run-time type check. This means that before executing the procedure call, the type of the argument must be checked. Most languages do not allow declarations such as Z, thus making it possible to do nearly all type checking at compile-time.

Beyond compile-time and run-time type checking there are two other alternatives. The four possible type checking schemes are:

1. Compile-time type checking.
2. Link-time type checking.
3. Run-time type checking.
4. No type checking.

Link-time type checking occurs during the link-edit phase when separately compiled program segments are brought together to form a single executable object. For example, assume that procedure P above is separately compiled with the segment

```
P: procedure ( X: REAL ) is
begin
      ...
end P;
```

The procedure types do not match, but when can this be checked? Not at compile-time because they are compiled separately. The compiler could insert a run-time check, but this is unpleasing because the run-time check slows down the execution speed. Many compilers simply do not ever check. The last alternative is to type check when the separately compiled programs are combined at link-time.

Most languages and compilers have a combination of these four alternatives: compile-time, link-time, run-time, and no checking. Seldom is type checking performed at link-time, so for the most part we will ignore this option until later in this chapter. When type checking is not performed at all for a particular situation, it will be referred to as a *type insecurity* or *hole* in the type checking scheme. A type insecurity means that type errors may go undetected. Some languages have been designed to have no type checking (BCPL and Bliss are examples). The desirability of such languages used to be at issue, but few people argue about the advantages of having no type checking today.

For most programming languages, type checking is performed at either compile-time or run-time. A compile-time check means that the compiler can verify that a value will be used correctly at all times during run-time. A run-time check means that the compiler will generate code to perform a check at run-time. If there is a type error, a compile-time type checker will issue an error or warning message at compile-time. A run-time type checker will issue an error message at run-time only if a type error actually occurs. This means that compile-time type checking has three advantages over run-time type checking, namely:

1. Compile-time checks issue error messages sooner than run-time checks.
2. Compile-time type checking insures that certain run-time errors never occur. Run-time type checking will detect errors but cannot prevent them.
3. Programs with run-time checks run slower.

The above observations imply that compile-time type checking is preferable. But sometimes it is easier to use run-time checks than to prove at compile-time that the value will be used properly at run-time. Zero division and Pascal subrange checks are good examples. More importantly, run-time checks provide a less restricted programming environment, which is sometimes desirable in highly interactive programming languages such as APL and LISP. These languages have *typeless variables* that can store values of any type. For example, a variable might be used to store a number at one time and a string at another time. These languages are sometimes called *weakly typed* or *typeless languages*, not because there is no type checking, but because the variables are typeless. All the values are typed, and if a value is used improperly at run-time then a type error occurs. This error checking can be provided by adding a type field to all values. The type field specifies the type of the value. When variables are typeless it is not possible to perform type checking at compile-time because one cannot in general determine the type of the value that will be stored in the variable.

The controversy between typeless languages and typed languages reveals a major division between the interactive interpretive-oriented programming languages (with run-time type checking) and the batch-oriented compiled languages (with compile-time type checking). There are of course LISP compilers and Pascal interpreters, but LISP is as naturally interpreter-oriented as Pascal is naturally compiler-oriented.

5.3 A Survey of Type Insecurities

A type error is a problem with a specific program. A type insecurity is a problem with a programming language. A programming language has

strong type checking if all type checking is done at compile-time and there are
no type insecurities. In such a language you are guaranteed that all type
errors will be detected at compile-time. Many type insecurities exist in
many languages. Some of the more infamous examples are described in
this section.

In PL/I, pointers are untyped. A use of a pointer in PL/I must be accompanied by information that specifies what the pointer is pointing to. This
information is given by the programmer. But it is not verified to be accurate
by the compiler or the run-time system. Therefore, a pointer could be pointing to a fixed binary number but used as if it were pointing to a floating
decimal number. Here is an example of adding two floating decimal
numbers as if they are fixed binary.

```
X, Y, Z:   REAL;
J:         INTEGER;
P1, P2:    POINTER;

begin
        X  := 3.45;
        Y  := 4.56;

        P1 := ADDRESS(X);
        P2 := ADDRESS(Y);

        Z  := P1->J + P2->J;
        ...
```

The PL/I notation P1->J means that the data pointed to by the pointer P1
is to be interpreted as if its type is the same as the variable J.

Pascal variant records have a type insecurity. The type discriminant is
not protected. The type discriminant can be assigned values that are quite
independent of the value assigned to the union. The discriminant might
never be used, as in the program below. Using Pascal variant records, it is
possible to add two floating-point numbers as if they were integers, as the
following program illustrates.

```
type U is record
                case TAG: (I, R) is
                when I => INT_PART:  INTEGER;
                when R => REAL_PART: REAL;
                end case;
            end record;

X, Y, Z: U;

begin
        X.REAL_PART := 3.45;
        Y.REAL_PART := 4.56;
        Z.INT_PART  := X.INT_PART + Y.INT_PART;
end
```

Independent compilation is the capability of dividing a program into parts; each part can be compiled independently of the other parts. The compiled parts are then linked into one object module. Most compilers allow independent compilation but seldom extend type checking to link-time or run-time to check for type consistency across separate compilations. Consider the following two program segments that are compiled independently:

```
/* first segment */
F: function (A, B: INTEGER) return INTEGER is
begin
        return A+B;
end F;

/* second segment, independently compiled */
F: function (A, B: REAL) return REAL is external;

X,Y,Z : REAL;

begin
        X := 3.45;
        Y := 4.56;
        Z := F(X, Y);
        ...
end
```

When a function is declared to be `external` (called *separate* in Ada), it means the function body appears in another separately compiled segment. Ada is carefully defined to avoid type insecurities, particularly among separately compiled units, so the above program would be issued type errors by the Ada compiler or linker. Most languages do not check and would add the two real numbers as if they were integers. This kind of error is a *link-time type insecurity.* Other link-time insecurities include external variables, which may be of one type in one program segment and some other type in another program segment.

Another classic type insecurity occurs in languages such as C and Pascal, in which procedures may be passed to other procedures. In some languages, the type of the procedure depends solely on the type returned, and does not include the type of the arguments. The following program adds two real numbers as if they were integers:

```
F: function (X,Y: INTEGER) return REAL is
begin
        return X+Y;
end F;

G: function (X,Y: REAL) return REAL is
begin
        return X+Y;
end G;
```

```
P: procedure (FUNC: function (...) return REAL) is
        X,Y,Z : REAL;
begin
        X := 3.45;
        Y := 4.56;
        Z := FUNC(X, Y);
end P;

begin                          -- main program
        P(G);
        P(F);
end
```

Note that this is a distinct problem from link-time insecurities because the above program segment is compiled all at once and yet will not produce any reported type errors. There is no type error in the first call to P. In the second call to P the function parameter F is indeed a real function and so there is no reported type error. But when the function F is called within P an undetected type error occurs. Many modern Pascal compilers have eliminated these type insecurities by suitable changes to the language. For example, the procedure heading can be changed to include the types of the operands as follows:

```
P: procedure (FUNC: function (REAL, REAL) return REAL;
```

A *subscript range* error occurs when an index into an array is out of bounds (i.e., is not between the upper and lower bounds of the array). This is not considered a type error in most languages. One of the many innovations of the Pascal language was the introduction of ranges and subranges. Pascal arrays are defined with these ranges or subranges. Assuming ranges and subranges are types, subscript range errors are type errors, and certain difficulties appear. First, determining whether a program has range errors at compile-time in the general case is an unsolvable problem. Therefore, in those cases where the compiler cannot verify the range of an expression, a run-time check should be inserted. This is equivalent to adding run-time checks for subscript range errors. Even so simple a statement as

```
X := X+1;
```

must have a run-time check, since if the range of X is i..j then the range of X+1 is i+1..j+1, which is not a subrange of i..j. Because run-time checks can become expensive, some compilers have an option that turns off the insertion of such run-time checks. This device is so common that the following implementation-dependent type insecurity can be found in many languages. If one knows how storage is allocated one could add two real numbers as if they were integers with a program similar to this:

```
A: array (1..4) of INTEGER;
X,Y,Z: REAL;

begin
        X := 3.45;
        Y := 4.56;
        Z := A(5)+A(6);
end;
```

If storage is allocated sequentially as declarations appear, then A(5) and X have the same address and A(6) and Y have the same address.* If so, then A(5)+A(6) will add X and Y as if they were integers rather than reals.

One classic problem with pointers is the misuse of the NULL pointer. The NULL pointer is used for a variety of purposes such as ending linked lists. It is good practice to check that a pointer is not NULL before using it. When this check is not made, unpredictable results may lead to difficult debugging sessions. One way around this problem is to eliminate NULL as a pointer value. Those situations that require a NULL pointer value can use a type such as

```
type U is union (VOID, pointer P);
```

The use of the U values must always check for the void value before using the pointer. This method converts a messy run-time error into a safely checked data type. Unfortunately, not many programmers are willing to give up ease of expression for safety.

There are some advantages to having type insecurities in a language; they are occasionally useful. The C language has formalized the idea of type insecurity with the *cast* construct. The cast construct allows data of some type to be interpreted as another type. Except in a few cases where the cast operation will actually change the representation of a value (primarily between numeric types), the cast operator merely changes the type of the value without changing the underlying representation. This approach allows the flexibility of untyped pointers in an otherwise typed pointer world.

5.4 Operator Identification and Overloading

The most fundamental way, and some will say the only way, of building expressions is to use operators and operands. An operation defines some function on the operand values. The operator symbol is used to denote the operation. If every operator symbol defines a unique operation then type

---

* This is true if integers and reals take the same amount of space. In certain implementations, reals take up twice the space as an integer, in which case A(7) and Y have the same address.

checking is straightforward (with the exception of implicit conversions). Each operator symbol would fully specify the types of the operands. The operator would also specify the type of the result.

Usually an operator symbol is used for more than one operation. In ALGOL 68 the "+" operator represents real addition, integer addition, string concatenation, and any operations defined by the programmer. This process is called *overloading* . To disambiguate overloaded operators the compiler must determine which operation is meant by the operator symbol. This is called *operator identification*. If the language does not permit the user to define overloaded symbols, the compiler can be built with a specialized operator identification routine for those overloaded operators defined by the language. If, however, the language does permit some degree of user defined operator symbols, the operator identification routine must be written in a general way. ALGOL 68 and Ada allow programmers to overload operator symbols.

In ALGOL 68, any number of functions can be associated with a single operator symbol, as long as certain restrictions are met. These restrictions prevent any possible ambiguity in the choice of an operation. Let A and B be any two functions associated with the same operator symbol. The types of the corresponding parameters of A and B cannot be *firmly related*, which is an ALGOL 68 term meaning that the types cannot be implicitly converted to each other in what is called a *firm context*.

The operator identification routine for ALGOL 68 is a strictly bottom-up procedure. Given the types of the operands, there will be at most one possible match with the list of available operations. (If there is more than one match possible, the ALGOL 68 compiler should flag the new operator as an error.) The operator identification algorithm is thus a simple search, which must take into account type equivalencing and implicit conversions. If no such operation matches the types of the operands, then an error occurs, which could be labeled as either an operand type error or undefined operator.

Unlike ALGOL 68, Ada does not permit implicit conversions in operations or procedure calls. Also, Ada employs name equivalencing rather than structural equivalencing (Section 5.6). Both of these facts contribute to simplifying the overloading mechanism in Ada. But there are two other differences that make Ada overloading more complex than ALGOL 68. First, Ada provides overloading of procedure names and constants of enumerated types in addition to operator symbols. And second, Ada permits overloading in every situation that is not ambiguous. Whereas ALGOL 68 operator identification is a strictly bottom-up algorithm, Ada requires both bottom-up and top-down passes to identify operators. This difference is immediately apparent when considering overloaded constants of an enumerated type. A constant is a zero-ary operator and thus there are no operands that can be used to disambiguate an overloaded constant. Overloaded constants must be disambiguated from context and so a top-down analysis is necessary. A top-down analysis may also be necessary for operators with operands. Consider the following overloaded Ada functions:

```
F: function ( X: INTEGER) return INTEGER;
F: function ( X: INTEGER) return REAL;

X: INTEGER := F(5);
```

The function F is overloaded and cannot be disambiguated by knowing only the type of the parameter. For this reason alone, this pair of functions is not permitted in ALGOL 68. An Ada compiler must resolve the ambiguity from context. Knowing that the returned value is assigned to an integer variable, the compiler will use the first function. An Ada compiler must also determine when a certain overloaded expression is inherently ambiguous. The following example cannot be disambiguated and is thus not legal Ada.

```
type COLOR is (RED, ORANGE, YELLOW);
type FRUIT is (ORANGE, LEMON, LIME);
P: procedure ( X: COLOR);
P: procedure ( X: FRUIT);

P(ORANGE);
```

Ada does not allow overloading of all identifiers, but let us imagine a language in which overloading has been extended to all identifiers. For example, let variables be overloaded. Consider

```
X, Y: INTEGER;
X, Z: (RED, YELLOW, BLUE);
Y: BOOLEAN;
Z: (RED, WHITE, BLUE);
```

Each identifier names two variables. We must be able to determine in an unambiguous way the binding of each applied occurrence. In the statements below the identifier X can only be bound to the integer variable in order for the statement to be correctly type checked.

```
X := 5;
X := X+Y;
if X=Y then ...
if Y then ...
```

In the last example, Y must be bound to the Boolean variable. Not all possible cases are unambiguous. Consider the ambiguous statements:

```
X := SUCC(X);
PRINT(X);
if X=X then ...
Z := RED;
```

The third statement has the interesting property that it is syntactically ambiguous but semantically unambiguous. It is syntactically ambiguous because the identifier X could mean either the integer variable or the color variable. It is semantically unambiguous because whichever variable it is, the comparison operator will return true.

Clearly, unrestricted overloading is undesirable. In fact, one could argue that overloading of any kind is undesirable, even for constants of enumerated types. But overloading has been quite successfully applied to operator names and input/output routines. We can only wait to see to what extent overloading will be used in future languages.

5.5 *Implicit Conversions*

There are many reasons for converting data from one type to another type. Integer values are sometimes used as real values. Sometimes real values are converted to integer values. Sometimes it is convenient to know the numerical value of a character. These conversions can usually be performed by calling conversion routines. To explicitly convert the real C to an integer value in ALGOL 68, one would write either

```
entier(C)
round(C)
```

The first routine removes the fractional part, which is called *truncation*. The second will add a half, then remove the fractional part. The first function will convert the real number .75 to 0 and the second function will convert .75 to 1. In Ada, to explicitly convert from an integer to a real, one would write

```
REAL(C)
```

An *implicit conversion* or *coercion* is a conversion that the compiler inserts into the code automatically. The programmer does not specifically state that the conversion is to take place. Instead the compiler makes the assumption that the programmer wants a conversion to take place. A very common implicit conversion is one from integer to real. Most languages would allow the following assignment statement, and the compiler would supply a conversion routine that will convert the integer value to a real value.

```
X: REAL;
J: INTEGER;

X := J;
```

Different languages allow different kinds of coercions. The conversion from integer to real is considered safe because the value of the number is not changed. For this reason, if a language allows any kind of conversions, it will probably allow coercions from integer to real. Coercions from real to integer are not considered as safe for two reasons. First, the sense of the value may be radically altered. Converting .25 to an integer results in zero, which is very different from a quarter. This conversion not only alters the type, it also changes the value. Consider the difference if the number is the denominator in a division expression! A second problem is that there are different conversion routines that could be used to convert real to integer, as described previously. These difficulties suggest that conversions from real to integer should be explicit rather than implicit.

Coercions complicate the process of type checking. For example, if a coercion from integer to real is allowed, then in places where a real value is expected, an integer value should be acceptable. This situation becomes potentially ambiguous if operator overloading also occurs. Consider the following overloaded operator in the light of an integer-to-real coercion:

```
function "○" ( X: REAL; Y:INTEGER) is ...
function "○" ( X: INTEGER; Y:REAL) is ...
```

Which function should be used when both operands are integer? ALGOL 68 avoids such ambiguities by allowing coercions to take place only in a certain context. In the above example, integers cannot be coerced to reals. PL/I has adopted a different solution to this problem. PL/I has specific rules on the order of conversions, so that even though many interpretations are possible, only one specific interpretation will take place.

The more coercions a programming language has, the less valuable type checking becomes. Potential type errors turn into coercions and thus go unreported. Coercions can be viewed as one way for the compiler to detect and "fix" errors in the program. But typically conversions are not reported, so the value of type checking is lost. The best example of coercions carried to an extreme are the PL/I numeric conversions. In PL/I all numeric types are convertible to all other numeric types—including bits, bit strings, and character strings. Some strange things happen as a result. Each PL/I fragment in the following example generates no compiler errors. Good PL/I compilers issue warning messages.

```
IF 1<X<5 THEN CALL Q;

DO J=1, J=2;

DO J=1 TO 2 BY .1;

A = 20 + 2/3;
```

The first statement will always call Q, since 1<X<5 always returns true. The subexpression 1<X returns either true or false, which is converted to either 0 or 1; since 5 is greater than 0 or 1, the entire expression returns true. The second statement will execute the loop body twice, both times with the

value of J equal to 1. The first = is assignment but the second = is a comparison. The expression J=2 returns false, which is converted to 1. The third statement goes into an infinite loop, since the float decimal constant .1 is converted to the fixed binary constant 0. The last statement assigns 2/3 to A. The expression 2/3 returns a fixed decimal number with precision (6,6) and when added to a fixed decimal constant 20 with precision (2,0) the resulting number, according to the PL/I conversion rules, has precision (6,6), so the value is truncated on the left by two digits.

It is worth examining the ALGOL 68 coercions, in part because they were carefully chosen, but primarily to observe coercions that are not immediately obvious. There are six coercions in ALGOL 68. They are called widening, dereferencing, deproceduring, uniting, rowing, and voiding. Widening is the coercion that includes conversions from integers to reals and from reals to complex numbers. Dereferencing is the coercion that converts a *reference to T* type to a *T* type. This coercion is a very common one, and is present in most programming languages. In many languages, it is an implicit assumption, so much that the reference manual doesn't even mention that it exists. An expression such as X+Y involves two dereferencing coercions, which convert the variables X and Y to integer values. Bliss does not have this coercion; dereferencing is the dot unary operator. To add the contents of X and Y one must write

    . X + . Y

In Bliss, the expression X+Y adds the addresses of X and Y.

Deproceduring is the coercion that converts a value of type *procedure with no parameters returning T* to a value of type *T*. Deproceduring means calling the procedure. The value the procedure returns is the value returned by the coercion. Deproceduring simply permits calling a procedure without the use of parentheses. Normally to call a procedure P with parameters, one must provide the arguments. If P has no arguments, then the parentheses following the P are empty. Some languages require that the parentheses be there, i.e.

    P ( )

Other languages permit simply

    P

In this last case, a potential ambiguity exists. Should the result of the expression P be the procedure P or should it be the value returned by calling P? The answer can be determined from context. In ALGOL 68 the context will dictate whether the deproceduring coercion should take place.

Uniting will convert a value of type *T* to a value of type *union of T and X and Y*... This coercion is useful when calling generic routines or assignment to union variables. For example,

```
X: union (INTEGER, REAL);
X := 5;

P: procedure (A, B: union (INTEGER, REAL)) is
begin
       ...
end P;

P(3, 4.5);
```

In the assignment statement an integer value appears on the right, but a union variable is on the left. The integer value is *united* to the type of X. The uniting coercion does not make any change to the value. In the call to P in the last statement, both arguments are of the wrong type; both must be united to the type of the parameters.

Rowing is an ALGOL 68 coercion that converts a value of type *T* to a value of type *row of T*. An ALGOL 68 row is just an array. This coercion will make an array of one element. Rowing is useful for variable-length arrays (called flexible rows in ALGOL 68) but is not too useful for fixed-length arrays. There are many situations where one may wish to initialize a variable-length array to a single element. In ALGOL 68 there are easy ways to assign zero-element arrays and two-element arrays to variables, for example:

```
X: array () of INTEGER;
X := ();
X := (2,3);
```

where X is a variable-length array of integers. But there is no easy syntactic way of assigning a single-element array, since parentheses are also used for ordering the evaluation of expressions. To overcome this minor problem, the rowing coercion was introduced, thus permitting the following assignment:

```
X := 4;
```

The last ALGOL 68 coercion is *voiding*. Like dereferencing, voiding is implicitly assumed by many languages. It is needed in ALGOL 68 to distinguish between procedures and functions. All ALGOL 68 procedures must return a value of some type. The type void is used to mean that it doesn't matter what is returned, since it won't be used further. Consider the procedure P below:

```
P: procedure   return VOID is
begin
        Y:=3
end P;
```

The type of the value of the last expression of an ALGOL 68 procedure is the type returned by the procedure. But a minor problem occurs in the last example in that the type of the last expression is integer but it should be void. This minor problem is solved in ALGOL 68 by the voiding coercion, which given any type *T* will convert it to the value of type *VOID*.

5.6 Type Equivalencing

One thing that all type checking algorithms must do is to determine when two types are the same. At first this appears to be a relatively simple task; but as the following simple example will show, there are questions that can be answered in a variety of ways. Are the types BLACK and WHITE the same types in the following program segment?

```
type BLACK is INTEGER;
type WHITE is INTEGER;

B: BLACK;
W: WHITE;
I: INTEGER;

begin
        W := 5;
        B := W;
        I := B+3;
        ...
```

Is BLACK another name for integer? Are BLACK and INTEGER names for the same type, or are they names for different but similar types? If they are the same type, then all the assignment statements are legal. If they are different, then (assuming no coercions are allowed) which of the assignment statements are legal? If they are different types, then is 5 a value of both types? These are some of the questions posed by such a simple situation.

The question of when two types are to be considered the same is called the type-equivalencing problem. There are two basic approaches, called *name equivalence* and *structural equivalence*. The basic approach of name equivalence is to say that types are the same only when they have the same name. The basic approach of structural equivalence is to say that types are the same if they have the same underlying structure. There are also other type-equivalence schemes that lie between these two basic approaches; but we shall just examine the basics of name and structural equivalence.

Using structural equivalence raises some difficult issues. Consider the following types:

```
type A is record
              X: INTEGER;
              N: pointer A;
          end record;
```

```
type B is record
                X: INTEGER;
                N: pointer A;
        end record;

type C is record
                X: INTEGER;
                N: pointer record
                                X: INTEGER;
                                N: pointer C;
                        end record;
        end record;

type D is record
                Y: INTEGER;
                N: pointer D;
        end record;
```

Structurally all of the above types are the same. Each type consists of a record with two components, an integer and a pointer to the same kind of record. ALGOL 68 uses structural equivalence and would consider types A through C to be different ways of spelling the same type. ALGOL 68 considers type D to be different since the component names of a record are considered part of the type. Additional complexities in the ALGOL 68 type-equivalencing scheme include unions, in which the order of the types does not matter. This means that

```
union (INTEGER, REAL)
```

is equivalent to

```
union (REAL, INTEGER)
```

The type-equivalencing scheme used in Pascal is unclear from the original definition, but the consensus now seems to favor name equivalencing. Ada formally specifies name equivalencing. Under this scheme, two type names are considered to denote different types, even if they have the same structure. The problem of using constants and operators for types BLACK and WHITE is solved in Ada by the concept of derived types. A derived type is indicated by the keyword new, as in the declaration

```
type GREEN is new INTEGER;
```

The type GREEN is a derived type from INTEGER and derives its characteristics from INTEGER. These characteristics include all constants and functions defined on INTEGERS.

One minor problem with name equivalence arises when type expressions are used and not named. In the following declarations, the types are structurally the same, but it is unclear whether they are name equivalent.

```
A:    record
        X, Y: INTEGER;
      end record;
```

```
B,C: record
        X, Y: INTEGER;
     end record;
```

The types of A, B, and C are called *anonymous types* since they have no name. Here, name equivalence is not clearly applicable. Here are a few interpretations.

1. An anonymous type is not equivalent to any other type. This would mean that A, B, and C have three different types.
2. Type expressions are used as the type name of anonymous types. This would mean that A, B, and C all have the same type.
3. Each occurrence of an anonymous type creates a new type. This means that B and C have the same type, which differs from the type of A.
4. Anonymous types are not allowed, in which case the above situation does not occur.

Ada uses the third interpretation (except for subtypes).

5.7 *Independent Compilation Issues*

There are many good reasons for separate compilation, but separate compilation raises a number of type checking issues. The interface between two independently compiled modules will include procedures and data. If this interface is not type checked, there is a type insecurity. There are several alternatives to this type insecurity.

Type checking could be performed at run-time. All external names could be accompanied by a type field and run-time code can be inserted to verify that parameter and argument types are equivalent. External variables must be checked before each use. Unfortunately, this adds considerable run-time overhead to procedure calls.

Type checking could be performed at link-time. When the two modules are linked together, the interface types could be checked. This solution requires a high degree of cooperation between the compiler and the linker. The compiler must generate the types of each external name. The linker must verify that the types are the same. It is not sufficient to check just the names even when the language uses name equivalence. Two modules may use the same type name, but different representations. Therefore the compiler cannot simply report the type names, but must also specify the underlying structure of each type name. The linker must become more sophisticated, not only resolving names but also verifying types of each name. The advantage of link-time checking over run-time checking is that with link-time checking there is no additional run-time expense.

Exercises

1. Subranges are normally not considered a type. Assume that subranges are types, and list the potential type errors in the following example. Also, assume that implicit conversions are allowed from one subrange to another if the first is contained in the second.

```
R1_VAR: 3..9;
R2_VAR: 4..10;
begin
        R2_VAR := 3;
        R2_VAR := R1_VAR;
        R2_VAR := R2_VAR + 1;
        R2_VAR := R1_VAR + 1;
        if R1_VAR≠3 then
                R2_VAR := R1_VAR;
        ...
```

For a particular operation, different combinations of values of the operands may produce type errors. If all combinations produce type errors, then the expression should be flagged as a type error at compile-time. If no combination produces a type error, the expression should never be flagged as a type error at compile-time or run-time. But suppose only some but not all combinations produce a type error, such as the examples above. Should these be flagged as type errors at compile-time even though the program may be written such that an illegal combination never occurs at run-time? What implementation problems arise if such expressions are considered compile-time type errors?

2. Consider the following example of overloading. For each occurrence of " + ", identify the operation implied, or if it is ambiguous, give all possible interpretations. Assume that " + " is already defined with integer addition.

```
function "+" (X:INTEGER; Y:LIST) return LIST;
function "+" (X:LIST; Y:INTEGER) return LIST;
function "+" (X:LIST; Y:LIST)    return LIST;

J,K: INTEGER;
A,B: LIST;
begin
        K:=J+J;
        A:=A+J;
        B:=J+K+A;
        A:=J+A+K;
        B:=(3+A)+(B+5);
end
```

3. For your favorite programming language (e.g., Pascal) and its compiler, when is type checking performed? Does your favorite compiler check ranges? If so, when? What type insecurities exist?

Which types are equivalent? Pay particular attention to such details as parameter passing, assignment, ranges, and pointers. Test the independent compilation features of your favorite compiler. Are type checks secure for external variables, parameters? How and when are they checked? What does the NULL pointer point to in your favorite implementation? What are the type-checking rules?

4. At the end of Section 5.7 four interpretations are listed. If you were designing a language with name equivalence, which would you choose, and why?

Further Reading

Type insecurities in Pascal are well documented in Welsh et al. (1977) and a collection of papers given in Section 5 of Wasserman (1980). Tennent (1978) and Berry and Schwartz (1979) examine further issues of the type-equivalencing problem. Eggert (1981) presents a version of Pascal in which all errors are compile-time errors. A number of papers on operator identification in Ada have appeared in *SIGPLAN Notices* and conferences on the Ada language (see Baker, 1982). Gannon (1977) reports on an empirical study of typeless and typed languages.

Type determination at compile-time for programs without declarations has been extensively studied for several languages, including ML by Milner (1978), APL by Miller (1979), Smalltalk by Suzuki (1981), SETL by Tenenbaum (1974), B by Meertens (1983), and in general by Cousot and Cousot (1977) and Kaplan and Ullman (1980). Also see Chapter 10 for further discussion.

Examples of Type Checking

6

6.1 Inductive Definitions and Type Checking

Given all the information of the previous sections, a compiler designer must put together a type-checking algorithm that will implement all the language design decisions concerning type checking. Type-checking algorithms can vary in complexity depending on the interaction of operator identification, coercions, and type-equivalencing methods. The context may also play a major role in determining the complexity of the type-checking algorithm. *Context* means that the surrounding situation may determine whether a certain rule is to be applied. For example, to type check an expression, one may need to know the declarations of the variables used in the expression. Before designing algorithms it is necessary to understand the complexity of type checking. In this section we present inductive definitions for describing type-checking rules.

Expressions in programming languages are defined recursively, and properties or characteristics of expressions can similarly be defined recursively. Before applying inductive definitions to type checking, we first present a simple language and a simple inductive definition. Consider the following language M:

Syntax of the Language

E ::= (let L be E in E) | EE | L
L ::= a | b | c | d | e

We would like to define certain functions on this language. For example, we might like to define the length of strings in the language. Let *Length* be a function from M strings to the integers that returns a count of the number of nonblank characters in the expression. Instead of conventional parentheses to indicate a function application, we shall use square brackets to surround syntactic expressions. So, for example, we would like to say:

Length[(let a be cc in *aabaa*)] = 17

We may use the following inductive method to formally define *Length*.

Length[(let L be E_1 in E_2)] = 10 + *Length*[E_1] + *Length*[E_2]
Length[E_1 E_2] = *Length*[E_1] + *Length*[E_2]
Length[L] = 1

Note that we must subscript duplicate occurrences of nonterminals so that there is no ambiguity in applying this definition.* To apply the definition to the expression

(let *a* be *cc* in *aabaa*)

we must first determine which grammar rules are used to generate the expression. Since the first alternative of the grammar is used we can say that

Length [(let *a* be *cc* in *aabaa*)] = 10 + *Length*[cc] + *Length*[aabaa]

The *Length*s of *cc* and *aabaa* can be determined similarly (by using the second alternative):

Length[cc] = *Length*[c] + *Length*[c]

Finally, using the last alternative we can finish up the computation:

Length[cc] = *Length*[c] + *Length*[c] = 1 + 1 = 2
Length[(*let a* be *cc* in *aabaa*)] = 10 + *Length*[cc] + *Length*[aabaa] = 10 + 2 + 5

Inductive definitions such as the above can be used for many such purposes, including defining the semantics of a language. We will come back to this topic in Chapters 12 and 13.

In this chapter we use inductive definitions to define type checking. To illustrate the process we will define a subset of expressions and types that may be found in most languages. Next we define "Type" as a function from expressions to types.

Syntax of Expressions
E ::= N | I | E(E) | E+E
N ::= 0 | 1 | 2 | ... | 32767
I ::= a | b | c | ... | z

We assume that all variables are declared with a type from the following grammar:

Syntax of Types
T ::= int | array-of-T | function(T)-returns-T

---

* Ambiguous grammars may make inductive definitions ambiguous. Although we have used an ambiguous grammar for the M language, the definitions given here are not ambiguous.

The symbol table, SymTab, will be a function from identifiers (I) to types (T). So if "a" is declared as "array-of-int" then SymTab[a] = array-of-int. An example of an inductive definition of the type of an expression can now be expressed as follows:

Type[N] = int

Type[I] = SymTab[I]

$$\text{Type}[\ E_1\ (E_2)\ ] = \left\{ \begin{array}{ll} X & \text{if Type}[\ E_1\ ] = \text{array-of-X} \\ & \text{and Type}\ [\ E_2\ ] = \text{int} \\ Y & \text{if Type}[\ E_1\ ] = \text{function(X)-returns-Y} \\ & \text{and Type}[\ E_2] = X \\ \text{error} & \text{otherwise} \end{array} \right.$$

$$\text{Type}[\ E_1 + E_2] = \left\{ \begin{array}{ll} \text{int} & \text{if Type}[\ E_1\ ] = \text{Type}[\ E_2\ ] = \text{int} \\ \text{error} & \text{otherwise} \end{array} \right.$$

The first line says that the type of an integer constant is an integer. The exact meaning of the second line depends on SymTab, which we have not defined. Presumably it would take into account scope rules and binding issues. If the identifier is undeclared, then this statement should result in a type error or undeclared-variable error. Unlike the other definitions in this example, the second line is *context sensitive*; this means that it depends on the surrounding context, in this case the declarations. All other definitions above depend only on the parts that make up the expression. The third line of the definition shows that the type of a subscripted array or a procedure call depends on the type of the array or the type of the procedure. The type of the subscript or parameter must match the corresponding part of the array or procedure type. One method for showing how type checking is performed on expressions is by drawing the parse tree and labeling each node with its type. Figure 6.1 gives an example.

The basic definition above can be extended to include type checking of all expressions and types in most languages. The type-checking definition does not state how a compiler should implement type checking; the definition is used to understand type checking. The method of definition presented in this example is also useful for defining many other properties of expressions and languages.

6.2 *Examples of Type Checking*

Type checking can be extended to include other properties. One example is dimensional analysis, a technique for detecting errors in formulas. A second example is range checking. Dimensional analysis has an elegant

let SymTab [a] = array-of-int
let SymTab [b] = function (array-of-int) -returns-int

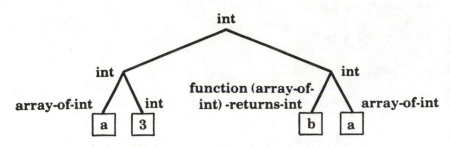

FIGURE 6.1   Parse tree and type checking of the expression "a(3)+b(a)".

compile-time type checking algorithm, but range checking becomes difficult if not impossible to perform completely at compile-time.

Dimensional Analysis

The distinction between dimension and unit is important. A *dimension* is some physical quantity that can be measured. A *unit* is a fixed quantity in some dimension. A dimension may have many units; for example, the dimension of length has feet, inches, and meters as units. Dimensional analysis can be performed at either the level of dimensions or the level of units. Most people use the term dimensional analysis for both these levels, but we shall make a distinction and use the term *unit analysis* for the latter case. The set of dimensions is a set of types including such elements as length, time, area, volume, speed, and energy. Dimensions have a very elegant organization called a *free Abelian group generated by a set of basis dimensions*. Instead of exploring this algebraic structure we shall adopt a simple representation of this group. A vector of integers can be used to represent our space of dimensions. Each component of the vector represents one of the basic dimensions. As an example, we shall use four basic dimensions: length, time, space, and money. Each four-element vector represents some dimension.

Vector	Dimension
(1,0,0,0)	length
(0,1,0,0)	time
(0,0,1,0)	mass
(0,0,0,1)	money
(3,0,0,0)	volume
(1,-2,1,0)	force
(-3,0,1,0)	density
(0,-1,0,1)	pay rate

There is one unique dimension, represented by (0,0,0,0), that is used for dimensionless quantities, such as angles and ratios. We will need the following vector operations.

(a,b,c,d) + (e,f,g,h) = (a+e, b+f, c+g, d+h)
(a,b,c,d) − (e,f,g,h) = (a−e, b−f, c−g, d−h)
n∗(a,b,c,d) = (n∗a, n∗b, n∗c, n∗d)

We can now describe dimensional analysis for some simple numeric expressions. We will use "Dim" as a function from expressions to dimensions (represented by vectors) and define D inductively as follows:

Dim[N] = (0,0,0,0)

$$\text{Dim}[X+Y] = \begin{cases} \text{Dim}[X] & \text{if Dim}[X]=\text{Dim}[Y] \\ \text{error} & \text{otherwise} \end{cases}$$

Dim[X∗Y] = Dim[X] + Dim[Y]

Dim[X/Y] = Dim[X] − Dim[Y]

Dim[X∗∗3] = 3∗Dim[X]

Dim[X∗∗Y] = value[Y] ∗ Dim[X]

Note that a problem exists for exponentiation. It is easy to provide compile-time type checking rules when the exponent is some integer constant. However, the function "value" should return the value of the enclosed expression and this may not be known until run-time. When the exponent is some arbitrary expression, one cannot calculate at compile-time the dimension of the result except in one special case, where the dimension of the first operand is (0,0,0,0).

Dimensional analysis as described above will check for dimension errors, but does not check for unit errors. Even though dollars and francs are in the same dimension, it would be an error to add them together without converting one to the other. Unit analysis is performed in the same manner as dimensional analysis. The only difference is that each component of the vector represents a unit rather than a dimension. The type-checking rules for unit analysis are exactly the same as for dimensional analysis.

To make unit analysis nice it would be useful to allow the programmer to specify the set of units. The compiler can then use this set and construct a vector to represent any combination of units. It would also be nice to allow a programmer to write constants with units. Using these two ideas, we can make explicit conversions from one unit to another as follows:

Units are {feet,inches,meters}
x,y : feet
a,b : inches

a := b + x ∗ (12 inches/feet)

Applying the type-checking rules to the expression reveals that all the units work out as expected. Without the explicit conversion factor, a type error would occur.

It might be desirable to express conversion factors between different units and let the compiler automatically insert conversion factors. An example of the input to such a compiler might be

Units are {miles,hours,minutes,mph}
Conversions are {
                         60 minutes = hours
                         1 miles/hours = mph
                         }

t1,t2 : minutes
distance : miles
rate : mph

rate := distance / (t1−t2)

The expression on the right-hand side of the assignment has type miles/minutes. But the variable "rate" has type mph. To perform the assignment the compiler must insert two conversions: (60 minutes/hour) and (mph hour/1 mile). The compiler must be aware of both the unit and dimension algebras. Two units are convertible if and only if they are in the same dimension. Each conversion defines a relationship between units, namely, that they are in the same dimension.

Subranges

A range is a totally ordered sequence of elements. A subrange of a range is denoted by giving a lower and an upper bound. Both bounds are members of the range, with the lower bound less than or equal to the upper bound. The values of a subrange consist of all elements between the lower and upper bounds, including the bounds. Subranges have proved quite useful in documenting programs by providing a formal way of specifying the expected range of values. Subranges have had less success at being accepted as a data type. Ada uses the notion *subtype*, which is not a new type but merely means a restriction on the set of permissible values that may be used. Subtype should not be confused with the Ada term *derived type*, which means a new type just like the old type (using name equivalence). Subranges have not been accepted as full-fledged data types because compile-time checking is too difficult or inconvenient to perform.

Even in languages without subranges, the issues presented in this section appear in disguised form. Arrays usually have a lower and an upper bound for each dimension. Each subscripting operation should validate the subscript by checking it against the bounds. This is usually a dynamic check and the error is usually called an "array subscript out of bounds'' error. In some cases, no check is made. An optimizing compiler could eliminate many of these checks by verifying that the subscript is in the proper range. For example, a compiler could tell whether a constant subscript is in range.

Without loss of generality we shall restrict our attention to integer ranges and subranges. A subrange can be represented as a pair consisting of the lower and upper bounds, which we represent as (l,u). We will use "Range" as a function from expressions to subranges.

> Given Range[E] = (X,Y)
> Let Lower[E] = X
>   Upper[E] = Y
>
> Range[N] = (N,N)
> Range[X + Y] = (Lower[X] + Lower[Y], Upper[X] + Upper[Y])
> Range[X − Y] = (Lower[X] − Upper[Y], Upper[X] − Lower[Y])

Type checking of the assignment statement is easy. The subrange of the right-hand side must be smaller than or equal to the subrange of the left-hand side.

> For X := Y
>   Upper[Y] ≤ Upper[X]
>   Lower[Y] ≥ Lower[X]

The difficulty with subrange checking is revealed with such simple assignment statements as (where X is a variable with some declared subrange):

> X := X+1

The upper bound of the left-hand side is smaller than the upper bound of the right-hand side, so an error may occur. To check for this error at compile-time requires either forbidding such statements or proving that, in the context in which the statement appears, the range of X+1 is a subrange of X. In general this analysis is far more complicated than any of the type checking algorithms in the rest of this chapter. It is comparable to the difficulties of proving programs correct. Alternatively the check could be made at run-time, but in a language that prides itself on strong type checking, subranges as a data type would be unacceptable.

Exercises

1. Consider the following language:

> E ::= (let L be E in E) | EE | L
> L ::= a | b | c | d | e

Give inductive definitions for the above language of the following functions:

Bcount: returns the number of *b*'s in the expression.
Depth: returns the maximum number of nested let expressions.
Meaning: returns the string represented by the expression.

2. Extend the example of type checking given in Section 6.1 to include the following:

Typed pointers.
Real values and constants.
Boolean values with " + " representing the Boolean or operation.
Assignment expressions.

3. Design and implement the algorithms for unit analysis or dimensional analysis.

4. Design and implement the algorithms for automatic conversion between units. Assume that the programmer must specify all units. Let the programmer further specify one or more conversions. Conversions may be redundant (that is, they may be derivable from previously specified conversions). For such a redundant conversion, verify that it is consistent with the set of previous equations. The type-checking algorithm should be extended to automatically insert conversions wherever appropriate.

5. Consider the problem involved in extending dimensional analysis with automatic conversions to integers. Design such a system to avoid the insertion of conversions that would require division. These conversions should not be used to avoid unexpected loss of precision.

6. Express the concepts of dimensional analysis using group theory. What is the algebraic relationship between units and dimensions? (Requires knowledge of abstract algebra.)

7. What are the type-checking rules for subranges for the multiplication operation?

8. Define a set of types for absolute and relative types. These types should be usable for absolute and relative measurements (such as temperature), and absolute and relative addresses in an assembler. What are the type-checking rules?

Further Reading

Inductive definitions on grammars are widely used for a variety of purposes and are sometimes known as attribute grammars. For examples, see Knuth (1968) or Stoy (1977) for applications to defining the semantics of programming languages. Cleaveland (1975) and Karr and Loveman (1978) discuss the incorporation of dimensional analysis techniques in programming languages.

Values, Variables and Storage

Traditionally, the concepts of reference (that is, variables and pointers) and of data type are separated in programming languages. ALGOL 68 is an exception since it combines both concepts into one data type system. Most programming languages separate the concept of data type from the concept of variables and values. That traditional view is compromised when a pointer type is introduced, mixing the concepts of data types and references. Storage mechanisms including sharing become part of the data type scheme. Excluding this anomaly, the concepts of data types and variables can be cleanly separated. This chapter illustrates the separation in several ways. Section 7.2 introduces applicative-style programming, which shows that variables are not a necessary part of programming. A data type specifies the amount of storage (Section 7.1) but does not specify a storage model (Section 7.3), scope, storage class (Section 7.4) or lifetime (Section 7.4). A data declaration usually brings all these seemingly disconnected parts together. The chapter ends with a brief discussion of garbage collection, which can make a big difference in how data types are perceived by the user.

7.1 Storage Requirements

How much storage does a value of a particular type require? A simple answer can be given. If type T has n different possible values, then it will require $\log_2 n$ bits of storage. For example, if T is a type of 32 values, then five bits are required to represent a value of T. In practice, this simple answer does not work well because of machine architectures, word sizes, and the time inefficiency of decoding compact representations. And some types, such as sequences and recursive types, have an infinite number of values. An enumerated type T with 32 elements is more likely to be stored in 8 or 16 bits rather than 5, because it is faster and simpler to store and retrieve a value in a byte or word of memory. The practice of minimizing the storage for some data type is called *packing*. There is usually a time-space tradeoff, and packing is exchanging time efficiency for space efficiency.

95

Numeric and character types have traditionally used a fixed number of bits of memory. A character in most systems today is 8 bits. There are some computer systems that use 7 bits, which is an advantage with a 36-bit or 60-bit word.* Short integers are typically 16 bits (which includes one sign bit) and long integers are usually 32 bits. Floating-point numbers are usually in the range of 16 to 36 bits. But what do all these machine sizes have to do with programming languages? Most programming languages like to claim to be portable and machine independent. In actual fact, a programming language is seldom independent of the word size of a machine. One cannot say in general that an integer in a particular programming language is X bits long. This usually depends on the machine, not the language. Given the length (in bits) of an integer, one can say something about the range of the integer. Some programming languages have formalized this dependence on machines by providing *environmental enquiries*. An environmental enquiry is a way of determining machine-dependent features such as the largest and smallest integers. ALGOL 68, for example, provides predefined constants such as `maxint`, which is the largest integer value. This value may vary from one machine implementation to another. Although it is to be expected that storage requirements of data types will vary from implementation to implementation, it should be surprising that the properties of such fundamental data types as integers also vary from implementation to implementation.

A value of an enumerated type is typically represented in the same way as integers. Most implementations do not pack enumerated types into the smallest possible space. One exception to this is the Boolean type. Some implementations will pack Boolean values, especially arrays of Boolean values.

Let n be the number of dimensions of an array and $D_1, D_2 \ldots D_n$ be the sizes of the dimensions. The total number of elements of the array is the product of $D_2, D_2 \ldots D_n$. Let E be the storage requirement for one element of the array. The total amount of storage needed for the array is $D_1* D_2*\ldots* D_n *E$. Sometimes the size of a dimension is not known at compile-time or sometimes the size information must be passed to a procedure along with the array. In these and other cases that arise, a *dope vector* must also be constructed and stored in memory. A dope vector includes such things as the number of dimensions (if the number of dimensions is variable at run-time), the lower and upper bounds of each dimension, and finally the size (in bytes) of each element. Sometimes the address of the first element is also included in the dope vector so that the dope vector and the array can be stored in different memory locations. Assuming each of the above quantities takes 4 bytes of storage, then the amount of storage needed for an array is $D_1 * D_2 *\ldots* D_n *E+8*n+12$ bytes.

---

* Five 7-bit characters can be packed into one 36-bit word.

If multidimensional arrays are implemented as nested one-dimensional arrays, then the storage requirements change. A dope vector is a little simpler in such a case; it consists of the lower bound, the upper bound, the size of the elements, and the address of the array. A one-dimensional array would then require $16 + D*E$ bytes (where D is the difference of the lower and upper bounds plus one). A nested array would require $16 + D_1 *(16 + D_2 *E)$ bytes, where D_1 is the number of elements in the outermost array and D_2 is the number of elements in each innermost array. Note that the dope vector is repeated for each element of the innermost arrays. This array requires considerably more space than multidimensional arrays, but there are some advantages. The array is segmented and does not require one contiguous chunk of memory. The bounds could vary from innermost array to innermost array. Figure 7.1 shows an array with both kinds of dope vectors.

Finally, let us consider heterogeneous arrays. The difficulty with heterogeneous arrays is the varying size of the elements. If the length of the largest element were known, then all elements could be placed in the same amount of space and the solutions of the previous two paragraphs could be applied. This length is not always known, however, and even if it were this solution may waste huge amounts of space if most elements are small relative to the largest element. Fast indexing into an array requires elements of a fixed length. This goal can still be accomplished by inserting a level of indirection. That is the array can be represented as a vector of pointers. The elements of the array can be stored anywhere in memory. The dope vector of such an array is the same as that of the homogeneous arrays (with the exception of the element size) but an extra pointer (usually four bytes) must be stored for each element of the array. That is the price for having heterogeneous arrays.

The representation of a record is typically a contiguous segment of memory, with the first field occurring first and subsequent fields following immediately. The minimum number of bits needed to represent a record is the sum of the number of bits needed to represent each field of a record. Since the various fields of the record may take different amounts of space, field selection is usually represented as an offset from the beginning of the record. Depending on the computer architecture, a field might not be able to begin at an arbitrary bit location. For example, characters must typically begin on a byte boundary. The process of lining up the fields of a record on the right boundary is called *alignment*. The need for alignment means that the number of bits necessary to represent a record is sometimes more than the sum of the bits necessary to represent each field of a record. Consider the record

```
record
        X: REAL;
        C: CHAR;
        Y: REAL;
end record;
```

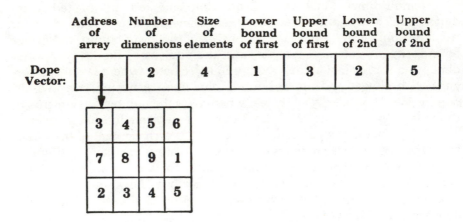

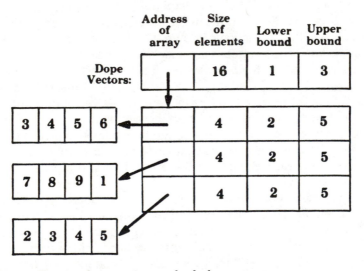

FIGURE 7.1   Two implementation methods for arrays.

Assuming that REAL values are represented with four bytes and that they must be aligned on a four byte boundary, then twelve bytes must be used to represent the above record, even though only nine bytes are needed to store the three fields. The extra three bytes must be used to align K on a four-byte boundary. See Figure 7.2. There is the occasional tricky code that accesses a field in an unusual way that assumes a certain alignment. These programs are usually not portable, since alignment is an implementation issue and is dependent on the machine architecture. Such programs usually involve some kind of type insecurity and should be avoided.

The storage requirement for a pointer value is independent of what it is pointing to. The value of a pointer is an address, which is one word on

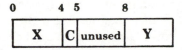

FIGURE 7.2 Record alignment (numbers indicate offset in bytes from beginning of the record).

most machines. The pointer type is what makes it possible to store recursive types. Consider the recursive type

```
type A is record
              X: REAL;
              N: A;
         end record;
```

The storage requirement for A is:

Storage(A) = Storage(X) + Storage(A)

The only solution to this recursive equation is to use an infinite amount of storage to represent A. Any finite amount of storage will not be able to store all possible values of type A. Changing the type of N from A to pointer A changes the storage requirement of A to:

Storage(A) = Storage(X) + Storage(pointer)

which is finite (typically eight bytes).

The storage requirement for union types is the maximum of the storage requirement for each alternative plus storage for the discriminant. The discriminant can usually be handled easily in a byte or word of memory.

The storage requirement for a procedure is usually just the space needed to point to the procedure entry. The storage requirement for a procedure is the same as for a pointer.

7.2 Doing without Variables

Is it possible to program without variables? Like the issue of Goto's in the late 1960s, the issue of programming with or without variables may be a major issue of the 1980s. Consider the implications of programming without variables. First, there would be no global or local variables of any kind. Without variables, there is no reason to have an assignment statement, since there would be no variables to assign to. Variables can appear in disguised forms. Input and output statements could not be used since they make implicit changes to input and output file variables. Call by reference would not make sense, since changes to the parameter imply that it is a variable. Loops would not make sense, since the only time you would want to reexecute a loop is when some variables have different values, thus giving different results. In fact, there is no purpose for statements. A programming language statement is one that changes the state of the machine and does not return a value. But if there is a machine state to change, there must be a disguised variable. So if there is no machine state for a statement to change and a statement does not return a value, then what good is a statement? When no variables exist then there are also no statements.

Is there anything left over to program with? Yes, there are expressions, including conditional expressions, and recursive procedures. This much is sufficient for programming; pure LISP is such a programming system. An expression, unlike a statement, returns a value. This value can be combined with other values, passed to procedures, and operated upon to obtain other values. There are claims that programming without variables is better than programming with them. Consider how much easier it is to understand such programs. There are no mysterious time-dependent changes to be wary of. There are no global variables, no side-effects, and no loops. These are some of the most difficult things for a beginning programmer to learn. Programming without variables is variously called *declarative programming, applicative programming*, and *functional programming*. Programming with variables is sometimes called *imperative programming*. A statement in a programming language is very much like a command. Assign 5 to X. Output "this string" to file Y. The previous two sentences are imperative sentences, and thus the name "imperative programming."

ALGOL 68 and Ada programs can be written in either an imperative or a declarative style. Such flexibility is possible in these two languages because of named constants whose value may be determined at run-time, recursive procedures, and expression-oriented syntax. The imperative program below computes the sum of the numbers in a linked list of numbers up to the first zero number or the end of the list.

```
type LIST is pointer
        record
                VALUE : INTEGER;
                NEXT  : LIST;
        end record;

SUM_UP_TO_ZERO: function ( A: LIST) return INTEGER is
        SUM : INTEGER;
        PTR : LIST;
begin
        SUM := 0;
        PTR := A;
        while PTR ≠ null and then PTR.VALUE ≠ 0 loop
                SUM := SUM+PTR.VALUE;
                PTR := PTR.NEXT;
        end loop;
        return SUM;
end SUM_UP_TO_ZERO;
```

To convert this program to a declarative-style program, the variables and loop must be transformed to a recursive procedure. The change can be achieved in a variety of ways, one of which is:

```
type LIST is pointer
        record
                VALUE : INTEGER;
                NEXT  : LIST;
        end record;

SUM_UP_TO_ZERO: function ( A: LIST) return INTEGER is
begin
        if A=null or else A.VALUE=0 then
                return 0;
        else
                return A.VALUE+SUM_UP_TO_ZERO(A.NEXT);
        end if;
end SUM_UP_TO_ZERO;
```

Named constants are considered valuable since they give additional information to the compiler for optimization. They also permit the detection of errors, since accidental assignments to named constants will be reported at compile-time. Named constants also make it easy for human readers to understand from the declaration that the value will not be changing. However, if one must specify the value of the constant at compile-time as Pascal demands, the value is reduced. C define statements are also not appropriate since they are compile-time substitutions. It is useful and sometimes necessary to determine the value of a named constant at run-time. For declarative programming it is essential that named constants be initialized dynamically.

7.3 Storage Models

Applicative programming does not require a storage model because there is no concept of a state or memory. It is purely value-oriented. Storage must be used for computation but this is transparent to the user. Imperative programming uses variables. To fully understand the behavior and meaning of variables, pointers, and operations such as assignment, we must construct a storage model. Three storage models will be examined in this section. They are called *value semantics*, *storage semantics*, and *pointer semantics*. Figure 7.3 is a pictorial summary of these three storage models.

Value Semantics

The value semantics model of storage is similar to that of applicative programming. The variable is considered an object, not the address of a storage location. Values may be stored in variables by assignment state-

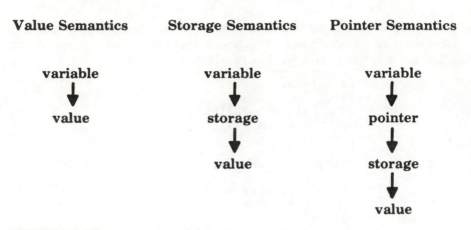

Value Semantics	Storage Semantics	Pointer Semantics

FIGURE 7.3 Three storage models.

ments. Because the concept of storage is bypassed, there is no concept of sharing values, pointers, or call by reference. Storage management is transparent to the programmer, as with applicative programming. If a language with value semantics includes arbitrary-size data types such as strings, the system must do storage allocation and garbage collection.

An assignment statement causes a transfer of a value to a variable. To distinguish this assignment statement from others it is called a *value assignment*. APL and SETL are examples of languages that use value semantics.

Storage Semantics

Storage semantics is the most common model of storage. Such languages as FORTRAN, COBOL, PL/I, C, and the ALGOL and Pascal families all use storage semantics. The major concept is that a variable is a storage location where a value is represented. A value has no time-dependent or place-dependent features. Storage does have both time and space properties. The value represented in storage may change over time. The allocation and freeing of storage is a critical issue. Different *storage classes* are sometimes provided by these languages to control the allocation and freeing of storage. This matter is further discussed in Section 7.4.

An *address* is the means of accessing a storage location. Addresses in a high-level language are represented as pointers. A storage location is *shared* if two or more different variables can access the location. Sharing is also called *aliasing* because the same storage location has more than one name. Sharing can occur when a global variable is passed by reference to a procedure. Within that procedure the parameter and global variable are aliases. When the same variable is passed as two different arguments to a procedure, then the two corresponding parameters share the same object. One common method of sharing is by the use of pointers. An object may have any number of pointers pointing to it. Aliasing troubles language designers, programmers, and verification experts. Proofs become much more difficult in the presence of aliasing. Programs are difficult to understand when multiple names refer to the same thing. When combined with call by reference (indicated here by the keyword var) aliasing can be subtle, as the following procedure shows:

```
MULT: procedure ( var A: array (1..10) of INTEGER;
                  var X: INTEGER) is
        J: 1..10;
begin
        for J in 1..10 loop
                A(J) := A(J)*X;
        end loop ;
end MULT;

B: array (1..10) of INTEGER;

begin
        MULT(B,B(3));
        ...
```

This is a classical aliasing problem that turns a seemingly innocent scalar multiplication routine into a difficult-to-find bug. After the procedure call, the first three elements of B are multiplied by B(3), but the remaining elements are multiplied by the square of B(3)! This particular aliasing problem can be eliminated by removing the var attribute on the second parameter.

The meaning of an assignment statement (using storage semantics) is to copy the value computed by the right-hand side to the storage referred to by the variable on the right-hand side. In most situations this assignment has the same behavior as the value assignment. The assignment of pointer values must be considered carefully. To assign a pointer value, only the address is copied, not the value pointed to by the address. This assignment is akin to the sharing assignment (described in the next subsection). As long as one thinks of a pointer value as being only an address, then the assignment used in storage semantics is the same as the value assignment. One example of the confusion that can occur is that in PL/I a string of characters is assigned by value, but in C a string of characters is assigned by sharing.

Pointer Semantics

The last storage model discussed here is *pointer semantics*. In this model, a variable is considered as a pointer to a storage location that contains the value. In an assignment such as A:=B;, the pointer to the storage location is copied rather than the value stored in the storage location. Since A and B share the storage the assignment is called a *sharing assignment*. In storage semantics it is analogous to the assignment of a pointer. The difference is

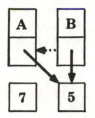

FIGURE 7.4 Value assignment in storage semantics (dotted arrow indicates copy).

FIGURE 7.5 Sharing assignment in pointer semantics: (dotted arrow indicates copy).

that in pointer semantics, the address is copied implicitly. See Figures 7.4 and 7.5.

Pointer semantics may lead to some unexpected behavior. For example, consider the following assignment statements, where both A and B are arrays of integers:

```
A := B;
B(5) := B(5) + 1;
```

In a language with value or storage semantics, the value of the array is copied. Incrementing the fifth element of B does not alter A. But in a language using pointer semantics, the value of the array is not copied by the first assignment; instead the storage is shared. Incrementing the fifth element of B will also increment the fifth element of A.

It may be difficult to distinguish the different storage models for simple types like numbers. How could one make a test to determine the storage model for integers? One might try something like:

```
B := 6;
A := B;
B := 4;
if A=4 then
        PRINT("POINTER SEMANTICS");
end if;
```

But this will not work because the third assignment simply changes B's pointer, not the value pointed to by B. To make the test work, an operation that will change the value pointed to by B must be used. But (typically) there are no numeric operations that will change the value. Thus, the primitive types in a language with pointer semantics may work just like their cousins in a language with storage or value semantics. To generalize this idea, call a data type *semantically transparent* if all primitive operations on the type create storage for new values, and do not alter any value currently represented in storage. This property might also be called write-once-only storage. If all data types in a language are semantically transparent, then value semantics and pointer semantics are equivalent! Ironically, SETL and other languages using value semantics are largely implemented using pointers and sharing assignment.

SNOBOL uses pointer semantics for all nonprimitive types. This includes arrays, tables, and data structures. Some languages use a combination of the storage models. The C language considers an array as a pointer. As a consequence, C arrays have pointer semantics. Other C data constructs, such as records, use storage semantics. In both SNOBOL and C, novice programmers may find that some array operations produce surprising results. One further difference between C and SNOBOL is the storage model used for character strings. In C, a string is considered an array of characters, consequently pointer semantics apply to C strings. In SNOBOL, a string is not an array. SNOBOL strings are semantically transparent and thus equivalent to value semantics.

7.4 Storage Classes, Lifetimes of Variables, and Garbage Collection

A value does not have a lifetime. It exists independent of time and space. The number 4 was not created or destroyed, neither does it have a home located in space. A programming language variable, however, does come and go and (with storage semantics) has a definite location in memory where values can be represented. The *lifetime* of a variable is the span of time from the allocation of space for the variable to the time that the space is freed. A *storage class* determines a variable's lifetime. Access to the variable during its lifetime is permitted, but access to it before or beyond its lifetime is an error. The lifetime of a variable is often related to its scope. In traditional block-structured languages, the lifetime of a variable begins upon entry to the block in which the variable is declared, and it ends upon exit from the block. This storage class is called *automatic* in C and PL/I, and *loc* in ALGOL 68. Upon each entry into the block, new storage is allocated for a new and fresh variable. Multiple entries into the block create multiple instances of the variable. This convention allows a natural way of expressing recursive procedures. But it does not make it easy to write functions that are history-sensitive. A function that is history sensitive may access values computed on previous calls to the function; therefore a history sensitive function must have some memory to save these values from call to call.

For example, pseudo random number generators often need to remember some information from the previous call. To accomplish this, one needs either a global variable accessible to others, or a local variable whose lifetime extends beyond the block. Sometimes such local variables are called *static*. In ALGOL 60 they were called *own* variables. Such a variable has a lifetime equal to that of the whole program. Its storage is allocated at the time the program begins and ends only when the program ends. In FORTRAN this is the only kind of storage provided. Storage for all variables in FORTRAN is allocated at program initiation time and kept until the end of the program. For this reason, recursive procedures are not allowed in FORTRAN.

The last common type of storage class is dynamic storage. This storage is called *based* storage in PL/I, and *heap* storage in ALGOL 68. Storage is allocated for a variable when an explicit command or procedure is called. The programmer has the responsibility of storage management for such variables and must allocate and free storage when necessary. Dynamic storage is useful for constructing list structures and arrays of varying sizes.

In a recent proposal, G.V.Cormack suggests that the programmer should be given better control over the lifetime and scope of variables. He suggests alternative lifetimes, such as a lifetime called *containing* that is the same lifetime as the block containing the block of the declaration. In fact, the programmer would be able to specify any lifetime for any variable including explicitly allocated variables.

7.5 Storage Management

We have discussed the amount of storage needed for representing values, when storage is allocated and freed, and storage models, but we have not yet described how storage is managed. This section gives a brief introduction to some standard storage management techniques used by programming languages. The easiest storage to manage is static storage, because it is allocated once at the very beginning and remains until the end. FORTRAN's storage management is that simple, because all storage in FORTRAN is static.

The next easiest is automatic storage. The stack model used for block structured languages is the standard technique for managing automatic storage. Automatic storage is allocated and freed using a run-time stack. Upon block entry, storage required for the block is pushed onto the run-time stack. At block exit, storage is popped off the stack. If we ignore dangling references, no access can be made to variables after they have been popped off the stack, so they can be freed at block exit time. Since the only block that can be freed is the active block most recently entered, a stack model will work nicely.

The most difficult storage to manage is dynamic storage. Since there is no predefined order of allocation and freeing of storage, no stack or other simple data structure can be used to manage storage. The problem is so difficult that a number of languages abandon the responsibility and let programmers worry about cleaning up their own storage. In Pascal, PL/I, and C dynamic storage is explicitly freed by commands that the programmer must put into the program. Care must be taken so that dangling references are not used. If everything that will be allocated remains in use until the end of the program, there will be no need for reclaiming storage. But in many programs, it is necessary to recycle storage. For these programs, the programmer must take care to free storage when it is no longer needed.

Other languages such as ALOGL 68, SNOBOL and Ada have taken the trouble to have automatic collection of unused dynamic storage. This process is usually called *garbage collection*. The major problem of garbage collection is the determination of which objects are no longer being used by the program. If no program variable can access the object (through any number of levels of indirection) then the object cannot ever be used and therefore can be recycled. One method of finding inaccessible objects is by a *marking* algorithm, which has the following steps.

1. Mark all objects in the system. One bit of storage is needed for each object in the system for this marking and unmarking.
2. For each program pointer variable, follow all paths (i.e., follow each pointer through all linked data structures). For each object along a path, unmark the object.
3. All marked objects are inaccessible from program variables, so they may be collected for reuse.

This method assumes several things about the language. It assumes that all created objects in the language can be found. It also assumes that the system knows where all pointers are in every object. These two assumptions are safe to make in a strongly typed language. In a type-insecure language, it is possible to hide pointers and thus invalidate the above method. The method has the advantage that the only overhead is the actual time for garbage collection and some additional memory for marking objects and locating pointers in data structures.

A second method, called the *reference count* method, adds a new field to each object to keep track of the number of pointers pointing to it. The reference count is maintained by adding and subtracting one for each pointer assignment or copy. In the pointer assignment

```
P := Q;
```

the reference count of the object pointed to by P before the assignment is decremented by one, and the reference count of the object pointed to by Q is incremented by one. The reference count method of garbage collection is much faster than marking algorithms since only one scan through memory will suffice to collect all unused storage. Any object with a reference count of zero can be reclaimed for use. One problem with this method is that cycles are not always deleted. In the program below, the object pointed to by Q is never deleted because its reference count is never nonzero even though the last assignment statement makes it inaccessible.

```
type LIST is pointer
        record
                    VALUE : INTEGER;
                    NEXT  : LIST;
        end record;

  Q: LIST;

  begin
            Q       := new LISTNODE;
            Q.NEXT := Q;
            Q       := null;
  end
```

Another major problem with the management of dynamic storage is fragmentation. *Fragmentation* occurs when all the free storage in the system is in small chunks, any of which by itself will not satisfy an allocation request. This situation can occur when many varying-length blocks of storage are allocated and freed. One method of garbage collection, called *compaction* , remedies fragmentation by combining all free chunks of storage. This sophisticated method requires moving blocks of memory. It then must, of course, update all pointers to those blocks being moved around in storage.

In traditional stack-based languages most allocation and freeing of storage occurs on a stack. This approach avoids the problems of dynamic storage management but introduces the problem of dangling pointers (or procedures, see Section 4.1). *Retention* is a storage management policy that alters the basic strategy of stack-based languages. Rather than freeing all local storage upon exit from a procedure, a storage management scheme using retention will retain storage that may be needed at a later time. This feature considerably alters the simple memory management scheme for stacks. Languages with retention require dynamic memory management.

Exercises

1. We have considered several different storage schemes for dope vectors and arrays. Compare their storage requirements, considering the following situations:

    Number of dimensions is fixed, sizes of dimensions may vary.
    Number and sizes of dimensions may vary, size of element is constant.

Number of dimensions is fixed, sizes of dimensions and elements
  may vary.

2. Rewrite the following programs without variables.

```
type LIST is access
    record
        VALUE: INTEGER;
        NEXT:  LIST;
    end record;

MINIMUM: function ( A: LIST ) return INTEGER is
    SMALLEST: INTEGER :=0;
    PTR: LIST;
begin
    if LIST ≠ null then
        SMALLEST := A.VALUE;
        PTR := A.NEXT;
        while PTR ≠ null loop
            if SMALLEST > PTR.VALUE then
                SMALLEST := PTR.VALUE
            end if;
            PTR := PTR.NEXT;
        end loop;
    end if;
    return SMALLEST;
end MINIMUM;

AVERAGE: function ( FROM,TO: INTEGER;
                    A: array () of REAL ) is
    SUM: REAL := 0.0;
    J: INTEGER;
begin
    for J in FROM..TO loop
        SUM := SUM + A(J);
    end loop;
    if FROM>TO then
        REPORT_ERROR("AVERAGE CALLED WITH NO RANGE");
        return 0;
    else
        return SUM/(1+TO-FROM);
    end if;
end AVERAGE;

GCD: function (X,Y: INTEGER) return INTEGER is
    R: INTEGER;
begin
    loop
        R := Y;
        while R>=X loop
            R:=R-X;
```

```
        end loop;
        if R=0 then
            return X;
        end if;
        Y := X;
        X := R;
    end loop;
end GCD;
```

3. Write a Pascal program to show that Pascal does not use pointer semantics. Is it possible to tell the difference between storage and value semantics in Pascal? If so, write a Pascal program to show the difference. [*Hint:* Use call-by-reference parameters.]

4. Write a SNOBOL program that will show that SNOBOL uses pointer semantics for nonprimitive types. Find some method to show that primitive types also use or don't use pointer semantics.

5. When would a `containing` storage class be useful?

6. Using only static storage, devise a technique to write recursive procedures and functions.

7. Let `set of X` be a type constructor for declaring sets for some type X. What are the storage requirements for this type?

8. Consider the type *type* for some language and determine a representation and its storage requirements. Contrast the differences between languages with a finite number of types and those with an infinite number of types.

Further Reading

MacLennan (1982) gives a clear description of the differences between values and objects. A good introduction to applicative programming is Henderson (1980). There are also annual conferences on LISP and applicative programming, including novel machine architectures. LISP and many other applicative languages have their roots in the lambda calculus developed by Church and his co-workers. Functional programming in the spirit of FP, the language of Backus (1978b), is based on the idea of combinators, a concept first introduced by Schönfinkel, and independently by Curry (see Curry and Feys, 1958). Functional programming and the combinatory logic of Curry are similar in that functions are defined by combining other functions, rather than being expressed by using parameters. Cormack (1983) proposes novel scope and lifetime rules. Garbage collection and compaction algorithms are described by Knuth (1973), Standish (1980), Cohen (1981), and Cohen and Nicolau (1983). Berry et al. (1978) discuss the issues of retention.

*D*ata
*A*bstractions

PART

III

Abstract Data Types

One of the most important programming concepts introduced in the 1970s was the abstract data type. Abstract data types provide a new way of organizing and designing programs that are both more reliable and easier to change. Although it is common to use the phrase *abstract data types* or *data abstractions*, we will just use the term *data type*, because for the most part there is no distinction. Similarly, the use of procedures is sometimes called procedural abstraction. Procedures were discovered quite early to be critical to good software design, and today procedural abstraction is the fundamental basis of quality software that is modular and reusable. Data abstractions extend this concept. Sometimes, people inaccurately think that a data abstraction is just a collection of related procedures. Others erroneously think a data abstraction is a programming language construct in an academic language. The next two chapters describe the motivation behind data abstractions and show how they are used in software. In Section 8.1, the concept as well as the programming language construct is examined. In Section 8.2, the early evolution of abstract data types is described. Section 8.3 and 8.4 show some ways of implementing abstract data types in languages with and without abstract data type facilities. Major examples of data abstractions are presented in the next chapter.

8.1   Concept and Construct

The essential idea behind abstract data types is:

> The separation of
>> the use of the data type
>> from its implementation.

The idea of separation is not new, but its application to data types, its formalization, and its inclusion in programming languages are new.

An abstract data type can be split into four major parts as shown in Figure 8.1. The first two parts, syntax and semantics, define how an application program uses the abstract data type. The last two parts, representa-

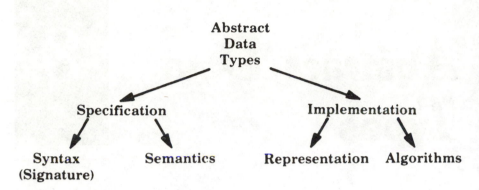

FIGURE 8.1 Abstract data types.

tion and algorithms, define a possible implementation of the abstract data type. To use the data type it is not necessary to know the implementation. In fact, it is important that knowledge about the implementation not be used. This point is the crux of data abstraction.

The syntax of the abstract data type specifies all the operator symbols or function names, the number and types of all the operands, and the type of the value returned. The syntax does not specify what value would be returned for a given input. The syntax is given in the declaration of a procedure. Consider the *bag of integers* data type with three operations, INSERT, REMOVE, and IN. The syntax specification of this data type can be easily provided by giving the procedure heading for each operation.

```
INSERT: function (X: INTEGER; B: BAG) return BAG;
REMOVE: function (X: INTEGER; B: BAG) return BAG;
IN:     function (X: INTEGER; B: BAG) return BOOLEAN;
```

The syntactic specification of a data type does not give the behavior of the type; as of yet, the semantics of the INSERT, REMOVE, and IN operations of the bag have not been given (but the operation names might suggest certain behavior). The semantics of a data type specify what value would be returned for each possible input value for every operation of the data type. The semantics for the bag type could be described in a natural language or in a formal language and in one of two styles.

The first style specifies a high-level representation and then specifies operational definitions on the representation. This style of definition should not be confused with the implementation. The definition of the semantics of the bag type in English using the first style could be:

Think of a bag as a container in which a number objects can be inserted or deleted. This bag can be considered as a sequence of numbers.

1. A bag is initially empty and is represented by the empty sequence.

2. An INSERT operation puts a new number on the end of the sequence.

3. The bag has a maximum number of allowable objects. Numbers inserted into a full bag are ignored.

4. A REMOVE operation scans the sequence for some occurrence of that number. If one is found, it is removed from the sequence. If there is more than one occurrence, only one is removed, the other occurrences are retained. If there are no occurrences, no change to the bag is made.

5. The IN operation returns true if the number occurs somewhere in the sequence; otherwise it returns false.

The second style is to describe the relationship between the different operations. This is usually accomplished by giving axioms or statements about the behavior of the operations. The second style of definition in English might go something like:

Consider a bag in which a number of INSERT and REMOVE operations have taken place. In many cases the order of the operations does not matter.

1. Two INSERT operations or two REMOVE operations can be interchanged.

2. An INSERT and REMOVE operation can be interchanged if they act on different numbers.

3. An INSERT operation followed by a REMOVE operation cancel each other if they insert and remove the same number.

4. A REMOVE operation on an empty bag can be canceled.

5. If only INSERT operations remain after the above cancellations, and there remain more INSERT operations than the maximum size of the bag, then the excess INSERT operations may be canceled.

6. The IN operation is easily defined for bags in which no more operations can be canceled. The IN operation will return true if there remains an INSERT operation for that number; otherwise it will return false.

There are a great variety of formal descriptive methods for specifying both the syntax and semantics of abstract data types. Some of these methods are discussed in Chapter 10.

The implementation of an abstract data type consists of the representation and the algorithms. The representation specifies how values of the abstract type are to be represented in memory. For example, the bag type could be represented as an array of integers or as a linked list of integers. The algorithms specify how the operations are implemented. They specify exactly how the representation is used and manipulated. Both the representation and algorithms must be coded in some programming language in order to have a working implementation. It is not necessary that the syntax and semantics be formalized in order to have an implementation.

The separation between the use of a data type (specified by the syntax and semantics) and the implementation is important for a number of reasons, one of which is motivated by a concern for correctness. Sometimes it is critically important to implement some part of a program correctly. Sometimes the correctness issues concern the implementation and manipulation of some data or data type. Abstract data types simplify these correctness issues by placing the code that physically touches the data in one place and then making this data inaccessible to the rest of the application program. The rest of the application program is permitted to use the data by using only the well-defined operations on the data. This restriction is sometimes termed *protection* or *encapsulation* . The data that is hidden by the abstraction is sometimes called *private* or *protected* data. Enforcement of such constraints is a major feature of the abstract data type facilities of some programming languages. Without such facilities, the enforcement may not be automated and thus is more likely to be breached.

What would such a breach of security be like? Consider the bag type represented as an array. Suppose someone wished to know the first element of this array for some reason, and the array was not protected. The programmer could simply subscript the array with the constant one and obtain the value and print it. What information is printed? It could be the first number inserted into the bag. It might be something else, depending on the implementation. If the implementation changes, so might this number. In this example, the programmer simply does not have any valid information. This breach may seem harmless, but changes to the implementation could affect what seemed to be the smooth running of the program. An even worse situation will occur if the programmer alters the value of the first element of the array. In this case, the bag will be corrupted; it will no longer accurately represent the value of the bag. To show the correctness of such a program is much more complicated because the correctness of the data type is not isolated to just the operations. It will also involve any part of the application program that accesses the data using unauthorized operations.

An abstract data type may have multiple implementations. Figure 8.1 is thus not quite accurate since only one implementation is shown. An abstract data type may be implemented in any number of ways and any implementation may be used. What implementation should be used in a specific situation? Assuming all the implementations are correct, the only difference among different implementations is performance. Some implementations may be better than others in that they take less space or take less time. Performance of data types may vary from one application program to another. It may also vary with different kinds of input to a single program. The choice of an implementation will thus vary for each situation. There may not be an implementation that is the best for all situations. Another major motivation for using abstract data types is the interchangeability of implementations. If a more efficient implementation is found it can readily be substituted for the older implementation.

To demonstrate the difference between the old traditional approach to solving problems and the abstract data type approach, we will consider a program that solves Rubik's cube. A Rubik's cube is a cube consisting of $3 \times 3 \times 3$ smaller cubes. Each plane of nine smaller cubes can be rotated independently of the other two planes in the same dimension. This is true of all planes in all three dimensions. In the start state, each face of the large cube consists of nine squares of the same color. Each face of the larger cube has a different color. When the planes are rotated the faces begin to have a mixture of colors. After a few random rotations of a few planes, it is not obvious which planes to rotate to go back to the start state. This puzzle has delighted many people around the world. It is also a good educational tool for those who teach group theory.

Imagine, then, writing a program that, given a cube in some arbitrary state, will generate a sequence of moves that will bring the cube back to the start state. To solve this problem one must first find a way of representing the cube. There are a number of possible approaches, but the most straightforward approach is to represent the cube as a three-dimensional array indexed by the face, row, and column. Each element of the array represents one of the six colors and this element tells us the color of the square indicated by the indexes. The declaration of the cube might thus be:

```
RUBIK: array (1..6, 1..3, 1..3) of 1..6;
```

This is not a very descriptive declaration for a cube. It is unreadable because the numbers do not mean much to a casual reader. This defect can, however, be easily overcome by using enumerated types:

```
type COLOR is (RED, BLUE,  GREEN,YELLOW,BLACK, ORANGE);
type FACE  is (UP,  DOWN,  RIGHT,LEFT,  FRONT, BACK);
type ROW   is (TOP, MIDDLE,BOTTOM);
type COL   is (LEFT,CENTER,RIGHT);
type CUBE  is array(FACE, ROW, COL) of COLOR;
```

```
RUBIK: CUBE;
```

Such a declaration is descriptive and conveys the meaning of the types in a pleasing manner. This approach is the standard approach that might be taken for writing a program for solving the cube puzzle. From here, the programmer may then either define some operations or proceed to solve the puzzle.

The abstract data type approach is different. The order of the questions is changed. The first question that is asked in the standard approach involves the representation of the object, not how it is to be used. The first questions in the abstract data type approach are: What are the operations? What operations are needed to solve the cube puzzle? Some operations will give us information; others will change the cube. Here is one possible set of operations:

```
type COLOR is (RED, BLUE,   GREEN,YELLOW,BLACK, ORANGE);
type FACE  is (UP,  DOWN,   RIGHT,LEFT,  FRONT, BACK);
type ROW   is (TOP, MIDDLE,BOTTOM);
type COL   is (LEFT,CENTER,RIGHT);
type CUBE  is private ;
type DIR   is (CLOCKWISE, COUNTERCLOCKWISE);

COLOR_OF:   function  (F:FACE; R:ROW; C:COL; T:CUBE)
                            return COLOR;
ROTATE:     procedure (F:FACE; D:DIR; in out T:CUBE);
INITIALIZE: function  return CUBE;
```

The data types COLOR, FACE, ROW, and COL remain the same. The data type CUBE is private, meaning that it is not accessible outside the data abstraction. A new data type, DIR, is added to specify the direction of rotation. It is needed here because the operations on the cube are being formalized, and one of the parameters for manipulating the cube requires this information. Next, the syntax of the operators is specified. The second operation is a procedure call that changes the third argument. It could have been a function returning a new cube.

To complete the specification of this abstract data type, the semantics of the operations should also be given. The step after specification could be one of two things. It might be the rest of the application program that solves the cube in terms of the cube operations, or it might be the implementation of the abstract data type. Only when one begins the implementation of the abstract data type does one need to specify the representation, which may very well be the same three-dimensional array used previously. To summarize,

> The traditional approach
>   first determines the representation,
> whereas the abstract data type approach
>   first determines how the data is to be used.

How do we know that a program is implemented correctly? For example, how do we know that a cube-solving program really solves the cube and does not cheat? Consider a person solving the cube. There are several methods. The first is to find a sequence of rotations that bring the cube to the start state. The second is to disassemble the cube and reassemble the cube properly. A third method is to peel off the colored plastic squares and paste them back on the cube. Only the first method really solves the cube without cheating. We could watch to make sure the person used that method. But how can we check that a computer program truly solves the cube? We could, of course, have the program print out a sequence of rotations that we would personally check. But the checking might be difficult to do if there is a long sequence of moves; it would also not guarantee that the program will honestly solve the cube tomorrow or next year. An alternative is to examine the program structure. If the program was designed using the traditional approach and the representation was used here and there throughout the whole program, one would have to examine the entire program to be convinced that it was an honest program. If the program was designed using the above abstract data type, then only the three operations need to be examined. Actually, only the rotation operation needs to be examined closely, since it is the only operation that changes the cube. Such an examination would be a more convincing and simpler demonstration that the program is honest.

Another observation to make about the two approaches above is that the abstract data type approach naturally leads to a better-structured and more modular program. The well-defined interface specified by the operators leads to independent development of two parts of the program. This clarity of structure is not necessarily produced by the first approach.

One might reasonably ask at this point how data abstraction differs from procedural abstraction. The difference is that a data abstraction is a collection of routines that all access common data or a common representation. The routines are tightly coupled. One routine from this group in isolation could not be called an abstraction since it may critically depend on the correctness or even the existence of the other routines in the group.

In summary, the important aspects of data abstractions are the following:

1. Data abstractions separate the use of a data type from the implementation of a data type.

2. Data abstractions simplify issues of correctness.

3. Data abstractions permit the exchange of (correct) implementations. Performance is ideally the only criterion for choosing an implementation.

4. Data abstraction is a software design technique that promotes modularity and independent development of the data abstraction implementation and the application program.

8.2 From SIMULA Classes to CLU Clusters

A major inspiration for the early work in abstract data types was the class concept developed in a programming language called SIMULA. SIMULA was designed for writing programs that simulate systems. An example of a class in the SIMULA tradition for the bag type is

```
class BAG(MAXSIZE: INTEGER) is

        BAG_ELEMENT: array (1..MAXSIZE) of INTEGER;
        SIZE: INTEGER := 0;

        INSERT: procedure (X:INTEGER) is
                J: INTEGER;
        begin
                if SIZE ≠ MAXSIZE then
                        SIZE := SIZE + 1;
                        BAG_ELEMENT(SIZE) := X;
                end if;
        end INSERT;

        REMOVE: procedure (X:INTEGER) is
                ...

        IN: function (X:INTEGER) return BOOLEAN is
                ...

    end class BAG;
```

The REMOVE and IN subroutines have been abbreviated. Compare this example to the operation declarations given for BAG at the beginning of this chapter. The first interesting note to make is that the second parameter to each routine has been omitted. It also appears that there will be only one bag object represented by the variables BAG_ELEMENT and SIZE. MAXSIZE is a parameter of the class that specifies the maximum number of objects the bag can contain. Additional insertions beyond this size are ignored. A class declaration by itself does not create any objects. The class must be called to *generate* objects. Since the class may be called any number of times, any number of bag objects can be generated. An example of declaring, generating, and using bags follows:

```
BAG_A: pointer BAG;
FIVE_BAGS: array (1..5) of pointer BAG;

begin
        BAG_A := new BAG(500);
        for J in 1..5 loop
                FIVE_BAGS(J) := new BAG(100);
        end loop;

        for J in 31..39 loop        -- insert numbers
                BAG_A.INSERT(J);        -- into BAG_A
        end loop;
        ...
```

In SIMULA, one uses the keyword ref rather than pointer, but the two keywords are similar enough in concept to warrant this liberty. The keyword new precedes a call to a class. It can be thought of as an allocator since it allocates storage for a new class. All class identifiers must be qualified; every reference to a class identifier must be preceded by a reference to a particular class. SIMULA uses a dot to separate a reference to a class and an identifier of the class. The expression FIVE_BAGS(3).REMOVE refers to the REMOVE procedure associated with the third bag of the array FIVE_BAGS. Just as one can access any class routine, one can also access any class variable. SIMULA class variables are traditionally not protected. One could write such things as

```
BAG_A.SIZE := 1;
FIVE_BAGS(3).BAG_ELEMENT(4) := 9;
```

In fact, note that if we replace the keyword class with record, then (ignoring the class parameters and binding rules), it appears that a class is just a record with procedure and function components. Even the syntax, using new and the dot notation, is like that of Pascal or Ada records. Consider the two differences: class parameters and binding. Each class parameter is just another field in the record. The class arguments are initialization values for these fields of the record. The binding problem concerns the identifiers found in the class routines that refer to the class variables. For example, in the INSERT procedure, SIZE is incremented by one. If the class is just a record, then SIZE must be fully qualified to specify which bag. To summarize, the SIMULA class is very much like a record with two minor exceptions: class parameters and binding of class identifiers in class routines.*

The binding problem raises an issue. It is sometimes useful to refer to the entire class in a class routine. In some languages the class that refers to itself is given a special keyword. In Smalltalk, the keyword is self. In SIMULA the keyword is this. Such a feature could be used to avoid the binding problem. Using this, the INSERT procedure can be rewritten as

```
INSERT: procedure (X:INTEGER) is
        J: INTEGER;
begin
        if this.SIZE ≠  this.MAXSIZE then
                this.SIZE :=  this.SIZE + 1;
                this.BAG_ELEMENT( this.SIZE) := X;
        end if;
end INSERT;
```

Rewriting the procedure using the Pascal with statement will almost return the procedure to its previous state.

```
INSERT: procedure (X:INTEGER) is
        J: INTEGER;
begin
        with this do begin
                if SIZE ≠ MAXSIZE then
                        SIZE := SIZE + 1;
                        BAG_ELEMENT(SIZE) := X;
                end if;
        end;
end INSERT;
```

---

* Inheritance, usually considered part of the class concept, is considered separately in Section 8.5.

The class concept in SIMULA proved to be quite useful. But there was one other significant step that was made before it evolved to the modern notion of abstract data types. This step was first made in a language called CLU, and the name cluster was used for the construct. A cluster is a SIMULA class with private variables. Some other minor syntactic changes were made as well. To avoid the binding and this problems of SIMULA, CLU cluster routines explicitly pass all parameters. Protection is provided by distinguishing between the internal representation of the data and the external representation. The internal representation is known only within the cluster. Outside the cluster, only a name is given for the type and only the visible operations of the cluster can be used on the data of that type.

8.3 Programming with Abstract Data Types in Languages without Abstract Data Types

This section investigates a variety of methods for using the concept of abstract data types in languages without abstract data type facilities. It should thereby become clear that an abstract data type is as much a design technique as it is a language construct. Most software is coded in programming languages that do not have abstract data type facilities; using such languages is not a reason for not using data abstractions. Although the construction of data abstractions in these languages has drawbacks such as nonautomated checking, it does provide a higher-quality software product.

There are a number of important decisions that must be made about the style of implementation of abstract data types. These issues involve the amount of formality that will be used, the style of procedure call, representation issues and of course the amount of protection that can be squeezed out of a language.

1. Should the implementation allow one object or many objects of the desired data type?
2. Can the implementation be put together in one place, separate from the rest of the program?
3. Should the implementation be value-oriented or variable-oriented?
4. Should the implementation have a sharing or value assignment (or perhaps none at all)?
5. What kind of protection can be offered? What will be offered?
6. Will the implementation be compiled independently?
7. Will generic operations (such as comparison operations and assignment) be permitted, and if not, can they be replaced?
8. Will there be any kind of generic facilities?

One or Many Variables

There is a simple and straightforward approach to implementing abstract data types in languages without them, but with a loss of generality. The approach, called *single-variable*, is to assume that only one instance of the data type is used. The implementing programming language should be able to compile a set of routines (or one routine with multiple entry points) with static variables accessible by only those routines. Under these conditions implementing a single-variable abstract data type is very economical and presents few problems with regard to the other issues discussed here. However, multiple variables of an abstract data type are usually desired and providing for this capability introduces many of the problems discussed below. To illustrate some of these concepts we will continue to use the bag abstract type. The following program segment illustrates how one might implement a single-variable bag type.

```
MAXSIZE: constant := 100;
BAG_ELEMENT: array (1..MAXSIZE) of INTEGER;
SIZE: INTEGER := 0;

INSERT: procedure (X:INTEGER) is
        J: INTEGER;
begin
        if SIZE ≠ MAXSIZE then
                SIZE := SIZE + 1;
                BAG_ELEMENT(SIZE) := X;
        end if;
end INSERT;

REMOVE: procedure (X:INTEGER) is
        ...

IN: function (X:INTEGER) return BOOLEAN is
        ...
```

In this example, there is only one bag. Therefore, operations do not include a bag parameter. For the same reason, there is no need for assignment or equality operations on bags.

Putting the Abstract Data Type in One Place

The Ada package is used for putting things together in one place because they are logically related. In the previous example the variables and procedures are all logically related. It is important to group these things together to make the program better organized and easier to read. This grouping can usually be done in other languages. In fact, it is preferable if the abstract data type is put into one file by itself and compiled separately. In PL/I, it is possible to construct one routine with multiple entry points, one entry point per operation. Data can be declared static inside the PL/I routine. Pascal cannot be used to group related declarations. In Pascal, declarations must appear in a particular order. All labels must appear first, followed by constants, type declarations, variables, and routines. One cannot change the order of these declarations. In consequence, the collection of things making up an abstract data type must be interspersed among all other declarations and routines. They cannot be gathered into one place separate from other declarations. This fact makes it very difficult to organize abstract data types in Pascal. Some modern Pascal compilers permit separate compilation. For these compilers, abstract data types could be placed in separate files. In subsequent examples we will use the following grouping construct:

```
adt BAGS is
    ...
end adt BAGS;
```

Value-Oriented and Variable-Oriented Abstract Data Types

A *value-oriented* implementation of an abstract data type views the data type as strictly a set of values and a set of operations on those values. Variables and storage issues remain outside the abstract data type. A *variable-oriented* implementation of an abstract data type views the data type as a set of variables and values, with some of the operations acting on variables of the data type. A value-oriented implementation may be easier and aesthetically pleasing, but variable-oriented implementations are often more efficient. Compare the following two implementations of the bag abstract data type.

```
adt BAGS is  -- variable-oriented implementation
    MAXSIZE: constant := 100;
    type BAG is
        record
            BAG_ELEMENT: array (1..MAXSIZE) of INTEGER;
            SIZE: INTEGER := 0;
        end record;

    INSERT: procedure (X:INTEGER, B: in out BAG) is
    begin
        if B.SIZE ≠ MAXSIZE then
            B.SIZE := B.SIZE + 1;
            B.BAG_ELEMENT(B.SIZE) := X;
        end if;
    end INSERT;

    REMOVE: procedure (X:INTEGER, B: in out BAG) is
        ...

    IN: function (X:INTEGER, B:BAG) return BOOLEAN is
        ...

end adt BAGS;
```

```
adt BAGS is          -- value-oriented implementation
    MAXSIZE: constant := 100;
    type BAG is
        record
            BAG_ELEMENT: array (1..MAXSIZE) of INTEGER;
            SIZE: INTEGER := 0;
        end record;

    INSERT: function (X:INTEGER, B:BAG) return BAG is
        RESULT: BAG := B;
    begin
        if RESULT.SIZE ≠ MAXSIZE then
            RESULT.SIZE := RESULT.SIZE + 1;
            RESULT.BAG_ELEMENT(RESULT.SIZE) := X;
        end if;
        return RESULT;
    end INSERT;

    REMOVE: function (X:INTEGER, B:BAG) return BAG is
        ...

    IN: function (X:INTEGER, B:BAG) return BOOLEAN is
        ...

end adt BAGS;
```

In the variable-oriented implementation, bag variables are passed to procedures or functions and directly modified. In the value-oriented implementation, bag values are passed to functions that create new bags. Variable-oriented implementations are more efficient but involve side-effects. Using these different implementations will also appear different.

```
X, Y, Z: BAG;                -- variable-oriented bags
INSERT(5, X);
REMOVE(8, Y);

X, Y, Z: BAG;                -- value-oriented bags
X := INSERT(5, X);
Y := REMOVE(8, Y);
```

One problem with both of the above styles is initialization of a bag value. It is important to initialize the SIZE of a bag to zero. This is easily accomplished in the two examples above. But in many programming languages it is not possible to initialize a component of a record in a type definition. One way of overcoming the initialization problem is to provide an initialization function. In the variable-oriented implementation it might appear as

```
EMPTYBAG: procedure (B: in out BAG) is
begin
        B.SIZE:=0;
end EMPTYBAG;
```

The single-variable implementations easily allow complete control over the variable, storage, and initialization. Unfortunately, most programming languages do not have similar facilities for multiple-variable implementations.

Protection

The inability to check for the proper use of data abstractions is one of the most serious drawbacks to implementing abstract data types in languages without abstract data type facilities. In a language without such facilities, protection is ad hoc and is usually done by assuming everyone is competent and friendly. In a language with built-in abstract data types, the compiler will perform this checking. In Ada, the keyword `private` can be used to provide the needed protection; its use means that the representation is not available outside the data abstraction. In a single-variable implementation, the data can be adequately hidden if the language provides the right scope rules. For example, in PL/I, an abstract data type implemented as a routine with multiple entry points hides all its static variables. In a language with separate compilation, variables can often be hidden in a single file by not declaring them external. In the case of the C language, a variable can be declared static, which means that it is known in the file, but is not known outside the file.

In languages without data abstraction facilities some protection can be provided by untyped pointers. PL/I pointers are not typed and therefore in a program using an abstract data type it is not necessary to specify the representation. Although C pointers are typed, it is easy to not fully specify what the pointer is really pointing to. Thus, in these languages, pointers can be used without fully specifying the data they point to; this fact decreases the likelihood of misuse because the representation is not readily available. Unfortunately, in both these languages, if one does know the representation, then it can be used and, of course, there are no compiler warnings.

The next program is an example of using pointers to hide the representation.

```
adt BAGS is      -- variable-oriented, using pointers
    MAXSIZE: constant := 100;
    type BAG is pointer BAGREP;
    type BAGREP is
        record
            BAG_ELEMENT: array (1..MAXSIZE) of INTEGER;
            SIZE: INTEGER := 0;
        end record;
```

```
INSERT: procedure (X:INTEGER, B: in out BAG) is
    J: INTEGER;
begin
    if B.SIZE ≠ MAXSIZE then
        B.SIZE := B.SIZE + 1;
        B.BAG_ELEMENT(B.SIZE) := X;
    end if;
end INSERT;
REMOVE: procedure (X:INTEGER, B: in out BAG) is
    ...

IN: function (X:INTEGER, B:BAG) return BOOLEAN is
    ...

    end adt BAGS;
```

The above program is compiled independently. Only the declarations for BAG, INSERT, REMOVE, and IN are made known to users of the bag abstract data type. The declaration for BAGREP and procedure bodies are kept "secret." In both C and PL/I this is easily done. There are other advantages to using pointers to represent abstract data types. They can always be used to pass and return values to and from functions. Some languages do not permit passing and returning certain types to or from functions. It is also more efficient to copy pointers in assignments, parameter passing, and function returns. But there are problems. One must now worry about allocating storage and about garbage collection. Initialization may be more difficult. Assignment becomes a sharing assignment, which is something that may be unexpected to unwary users.

A slightly more secure method is to replace a pointer with an index into a hidden array. The array index can be used in the same way as a pointer. The difference between these methods is that, even if the representation is known, the whereabouts of the array is not. Such an implementation might appear something like:

```
adt BAGS is    -- variable-oriented, using indexes
    MAXSIZE: constant := 100;
    type BAG is 1..100;    -- allow up to 100 bags
    ALLBAGS: array (BAG) of
        record
            BAG_ELEMENT: array (1..MAXSIZE) of INTEGER;
            SIZE: INTEGER := 0;
        end record;

    INSERT: procedure (X:INTEGER, B: in out BAG) is
        J: INTEGER;
    begin
        if ALLBAGS(B).SIZE ≠ MAXSIZE then
            ALLBAGS(B).SIZE := ALLBAGS(B).SIZE + 1;
            J:= ALLBAGS(B).SIZE;
            ALLBAGS(B).BAG_ELEMENT J:=X;
        end if;
    end INSERT;
```

```
    REMOVE: procedure (X:INTEGER, B: in out BAG) is
      ...

    IN: function (X:INTEGER, B:BAG) return BOOLEAN is
      ...

end adt BAGS;
```

Predefined Operations

Some operations, for example, assignment and comparison, can commonly be performed on all data types. These operations must also be considered when building new data types. In most cases they will fit in naturally and do the expected thing, but in some situations they do the unexpected. In Ada there are a number of mechanisms that can be used to solve such problems, but in most languages they cannot be solved.

Let us consider assignment first. When using pointers or indexes, the assignment operation becomes a sharing assignment. Some unexpected behavior may result. Consider the following segment of code:

```
X, Y, Z: BAG;

begin
        X:=Y;
        INSERT(6, Y);
```

One would naturally think of the assignment as a copy operation and the insertion of 6 into Y as not affecting X. But when bags are represented as pointers or indexes, the assignment only copies the pointer or index, not the value. This problem alone may be enough to discourage the use of pointers. However, in languages such as C and PL/I, the price of not using pointers is high. This is a serious tradeoff that must be considered carefully. It could be stated policy that data abstractions use pointers and sharing assignments, and that users should beware. One way to lessen the problem is to write a COPY or ASSIGN routine that would aid or replace the use of the assignment statement. The assignment routine might appear as:

```
ASSIGN: procedure (LHS: in out BAG; RHS: BAG) is
begin
        LHS.SIZE        := RHS.SIZE;
        LHS.BAG_ELEMENT := RHS.BAG_ELEMENT;
end ASSIGN;
```

The other serious problem is comparison. In most languages values of any type can be compared. Consider the following code segment:

```
X, Y, Z: BAG;

begin
        INSERT(5, X);
        INSERT(6, X);
        INSERT(6, Y);
        INSERT(5, Y);
        if X=Y then ...
```

The comparison is the predefined operation in the last statement. In the variable-oriented implementations discussed previously, the first four procedure calls would set SIZE to 2, the first two elements of X.BAG_ELEMENT to 5 and 6, and the first two elements of Y.BAG_ELEMENT to 6 and 5. If the representation is a pointer or index, then pointers or indexes are compared. If the representation is a record, then the SIZE and BAG_ELEMENT fields are compared. In either case the comparison returns false. In reality, one would want the comparison to return true since both X and Y represent the same bag, a bag containing 5 and 6. It does not matter in what order they were put into the bag. In general, a value of a data type does not necessarily have a unique representation. Even numeric types may have multiple representations for a number. In one's complement representation there are two representations for zero. As with assignment, one could provide an EQUAL function as a replacement for the comparison operator.

8.4 *Ada Packages*

The Ada package is used to group a collection of declarations and procedures. It offers both private and public declarations and it offers the possibility of separate compilation. It can be used to implement abstract data types. The bag abstract data type can be implemented as an Ada package in a variety of ways, which include the methods of the previous section. An example of the use of the package for separate compilation follows:

```
package BAGS is    -- variable-oriented implementation
    MAXSIZE: constant := 100;
    type  BAG  is private;
    procedure INSERT(X:INTEGER, B: in out BAG);
    procedure REMOVE(X:INTEGER, B: in out BAG);
    function IN(X:INTEGER, B:BAG) return BOOLEAN;

private

    type BAG is
        record
            BAG_ELEMENT: array (1..MAXSIZE) of INTEGER;
            SIZE: INTEGER := 0;
        end record;

end BAGS;
```

```
package body BAGS is

    procedure INSERT(X:INTEGER, B: in out BAG) is
        J: INTEGER;
    begin
        if B.SIZE ≠ MAXSIZE then
            B.SIZE := B.SIZE + 1;
            B.BAG_ELEMENT(B.SIZE) := X;
        end if;
    end INSERT;

    procedure REMOVE(X:INTEGER, B: in out BAG) is
        ...

    function IN(X:INTEGER, B:BAG) return BOOLEAN is
        ...

end BAGS;
```

The abstract data type has been split into two parts. The visible part occurs first. Declarations up to the keyword private are visible outside the package. The second part is called the *package body* and it can be compiled separately. Note that the syntax and representation are in the package and the algorithms are in the package body. The semantics of the abstract data type are not given at all.

It may seem odd that the representation of the abstract data type should be put in the package rather than the package body. Ideally, the representation should be in the package body so that one package body can be easily substituted for another. The representation is part of the implementation, and is likely to change from implementation to implementation. When the representation is in the package rather than the package body, then changing the package body will (in most cases) necessitate a change in the package itself. Those programs using the package would therefore also need recompilation. This unfortunate property is due to some design goals of a higher priority in Ada. These design goals include:

1. compile-time determination of storage requirements
2. independent compilation of package and package body

To determine the amount of storage needed for objects of the abstract data type requires knowing the representation. For this reason, the representation is placed in the package rather than the package body. In order to keep the representation private the programmer must use the private keyword. The representation does not need to be "secret" since the compiler enforces proper use.

8.5 Subtypes and Type Hierarchies

A type hierarchy is most generally a partial order on data types. Subtypes and supertypes are terms used to indicate this ordering. Type A is a subtype of B (or B is a supertype of A) if A is lower or smaller than B. This ordering or hierarchy is based on different criteria and there is no commonly accepted standard definition. In this section we simply list different viewpoints. Generally a hierarchy establishes common features of data types, particularly operations and/or values. Also a subtype is considered as some kind of restriction or specialization of another type. Two broad possibilities are the following. A is considered a subtype of B if all the values of A are values of B. Alternatively, A is considered a subtype of B if all the operations of B are also available as operations on A. A is said to *inherit* the operations of B, since B is often called the *parent* type.

We start off with a couple of possible hierarchies that are not commonly considered. The first one is based on the union type. Types A and B are subtypes of the union of A and B. This scheme produces a partial order on types, but it is usually not what is meant by a hierarchy. That is the subtype does not contain any operations or values of the supertype, because union values are tagged and must undergo some kind of projection operation to obtain a value of the component types. Another possible hierarchy is provided by polymorphic types (see Chapter 11). Here, array of integers and array of characters are subtypes of the array type. However, this hierarchy assumes that polymorphic types like array are types in their own right. That is usually not the case, because polymorphic types are collections of types and not types. In some languages with dynamic typing, such as SNOBOL and SETL, one may consider such a hierarchy because the languages allow heterogeneous arrays; thus one could consider various subtypes—for example, arrays with just integers or characters, arrays with just characters, or arrays with just alphabetic characters. But these languages do not have a well-developed notion of compile-time types, and most such type checking is done at run-time. The major concern in such languages is not subtypes but optimization by inferring types at compile-time.

Pascal uses the word subtype to mean subranges. The values of a subrange type are a subset of the values of some other type. Consider the following subranges:

```
type COLOR is (BLUE,GREEN,YELLOW,ORANGE,RED,VIOLET);
type WARM is YELLOW..RED;
type HOT is ORANGE..RED;
```

HOT is a subtype of WARM, which is a subtype of COLOR. In Pascal, subranges are really not considered types. For example, there is no compile-time type checking (and sometimes not even run-time type checking) for subranges. This notion of subtype has been extended in Ada to the idea of constrained types. A constrained type simply limits the values that may be assumed by a variable. Subranges, arrays with specified bounds, and variant records limited to a particular variant are examples of constrained types in Ada.

Another viewpoint that is sometimes adopted defines a type hierarchy by the coercions of the language. For example, if integers are implicitly converted to reals, then integers are considered a subtype of reals. The conversions make it possible to say that the integers inherit the operations of reals. Thus a square root operation defined on reals is also available for integer parameters, but note that the result is a real value, not an integer value. Note, too, that with this viewpoint a language with the uniting coercion (converting a value of type T to a value of a union type containing T) subsumes the union hierarchy previously mentioned.

If data types are considered as sets of operations on a universal domain (as in Russell), then the notion of a subtype can be defined by simply considering the available operations. Type A is considered a subtype of type B if the set of operations of type A is a superset of the operations of type B. A LIST type with operations prepend, append, first, rest, and empty is a subtype of QUEUE with operations prepend, first, rest, and empty. The terminology may appear quite confusing, for intuitively it may seem that QUEUE is a subtype of LIST, since it has a more restricted set of operations. But in common usage of the term, *subtype* means the opposite.

The best-known notion of subtype has been developed in the Smalltalk language. A Smalltalk class is based on SIMULA classes and for our purposes we can assume classes are just data abstractions. A class can be extended to a subclass (which is similar to SIMULA prefixing). The subclass inherits all the operations of the class and in addition can add its own set of operations. Every class is an object of some other class, and all classes are objects of the universal class *Object*, which contains such generic operations as assignment, comparison, and print. A subclass may override any of the inherited operations. Consider the following bag class:

```
class BAG is

    BAG_ELEMENT: array (1..MAXSIZE) of INTEGER;
    SIZE: INTEGER := 0;

    INSERT: procedure (X: INTEGER) is ... end INSERT;

    REMOVE: procedure (X: INTEGER) is ... end REMOVE;

    IN: function (X: INTEGER) return BOOLEAN ... end IN;

    function "="    (B: BAG) return BOOLEAN ... end;

end class BAG;
```

In this example, the comparison operator overrides the default comparison operation of the superclass *Object*. This provision is needed since the bag type has different representations for the same value, and the generic comparison operation would not correspond to the expected meaning of equal bags.

Let us now consider a subclass called `BIGBAG` that extends `BAG` by adding an operation, called `INSERT_MANY`, that will add an inexhaustible number of integers to the bag. New data structures are required to store the inexhaustible integers, and the `IN` and comparison routines must be overridden to take into account the inexhaustible integers. The subclass `BIGBAG` will inherit the `INSERT` and `REMOVE` operations from the `BAG` class and the assignment and print operations from the *Object* class.

```
class BIGBAG is BAG plus

    CBAG: array (1..MAXSIZE) of INTEGER;
    CSIZE: INTEGER := 0;

    INSERT_MANY: procedure (X: INTEGER) is ... end;

    IN: function (X: INTEGER) return BOOLEAN ... end IN;

    function "=" (B: BAG) return BOOLEAN ... end;

end class BIGBAG;
```

The Smalltalk approach conveniently allows the extension of record-like data structures. For example, a `PERSON` object may have information about a person's name, date of birth, and address. Various extensions can be made to this object for certain subtypes. A `STUDENT` object could be a subclass of `PERSON` with additional fields for student identification number, year, major, etc. An `HONORS_STUDENT` object could be a subclass of `STUDENT` with fields for honors thesis topic and honors advisor.

Note that the values of a Smalltalk subclass are not necessarily a subset of the values of its parent class. Another notion of subtype that does have this property uses predicates. A unary Boolean function on some type divides the values of that type into two parts, and each part can be considered a subtype. For example, the function `ISLETTER` on characters defines the alphabetic (and nonalphabetic) subtypes of characters. The `LETTER` subtype is defined using syntax introduced by Burton and Lings (1981):

```
ISLETTER: function (C: CHARACTER) return BOOLEAN is ...

subtype LETTER is CHARACTER which is ISLETTER;
```

The above facility would extend the Ada notion of subtype to arbitrary sets of values.

Of course, there remains the problem of whether such subtypes are really types that can or should be type checked at compile-time. The operations on such subtypes are unclear. Consider the integers as a subtype of the reals and consider the inheritance of multiplication and division. Do the types of the inherited operations change? For example, should the multiplication operation continue to be a function of two reals, returning a real, with integers converted to reals before calling the function? If this view is adopted, then subtypes are merely ways of defining coercions. Alternatively, a new multiplication operation with integer operands might be created. If so, should the newly created multiplication operation return a real or an integer? If the operation is closed under the subtype (e.g., multiplication), then it may safely return a subtype value. But if it is not closed (e.g., division) then it must continue returning a real number.

Another subtype notion involves implementation issues. One might desire a hierarchy of set types. The most general category of sets might have an inefficient implementation to take into account infinite sets. Subtypes such as finite sets, regular sets, limited-size sets (less than N elements), and character sets may have alternative implementations that are much more efficient than the most general category. However, one may not wish to view all these different kinds of sets as different types but rather as subtypes of one supertype. The Smalltalk subclass is not appropriate for this application because it assumes a common representation of the data.

Exercises

1. Design and implement bags with the following representation:

   ```
   array (CHAR) of INTEGER;
   ```

   Each element of the array indicates the number of characters in the bag. All elements are zero when the bag is empty. Discuss the performance differences between this implementation and those described in this chapter.

2. Consider the following function abstract data type:

   ```
   adt FUN_PACK is
           type  FUN   is private;

           DEFINE: function (F: function (X:INTEGER)
                                       return INTEGER)
               return FUN;

           APPLY: function (FN: FUN; X:INTEGER)
               return INTEGER;

   end adt FUN_PACK;
   ```

The function `DEFINE` initializes a function and `APPLY` applies that function to an argument. That is, for any integer X and any unary integer function F, the following always holds:

```
APPLY(DEFINE(F),X) = F(X)
```

Implement this data type so that computed values of the function F are saved. The first time that F is called with some integer argument, the computed value is saved on some list. Subsequent calls to F with the same integer argument will return the saved value rather than calling F a second time. Such an implementation requires that F be like a mathematical function: it has no side-effects, no history, and no dependence on global variables. In those cases where the computation time of a single call to F is large, and F is called many times with the same integer arguments, this implementation improves performance time.

3. Consider implementing the set abstract data type in some language (pick something like PL/I, FORTRAN, Pascal, C, or BASIC). Discuss the advantages and disadvantages of your implementation. Review the list of issues given at the beginning of Section 8.3.

Further Reading

Dahl and Hoare (1972) explore the use of SIMULA classes for data abstractions and coroutines. A variety of programming languages with data abstraction facilities have been proposed; some of the more well-known languages include

CLU	Liskov et al. (1977)
Alphard	Wulf et al. (1976)
Mesa	Geschke et al. (1977)
Euclid	Lampson et al. (1977)
Ada	Ichbiah et al. (1979)
Modula-2	Wirth (1980)
Smalltalk	Goldberg and Robson (1983)

Stroustrup (1986) has investigated a data abstraction extension of the C language. Research directions in data abstractions are discussed by Shaw (1976). A bibliography on data types and data abstractions can be found in Dungan (1979). Dewar et al. (1979) illustrate another approach to separating the implementation and use of a data type in SETL. Type hierarchies and subtypes are described in Burton and Lings (1981), Albano (1983), Sherman (1984), and Goldberg et al. (1983). Use of multiple implementations of a data abstraction is discussed by White (1983) and Sherman (1984).

*E*xamples of *A*bstract *D*ata *T*ypes

9

This chapter contains several larger examples of data abstractions. The previous chapter had smaller examples to show a variety of techniques and issues, but could not show the importance of larger data abstraction examples. In this chapter data abstractions built by using other data abstractions show how larger data abstractions might look in practice.

9.1 Character Sets

The character set is a good example to use for data abstractions because it occurs in a wide variety of implementations that are familiar to people. The domain of discourse (i.e., the set of all potential members) is the set of all characters, such as the ASCII or EBCDIC character sets. The operations of our character set will be:

emptyset( )   returns the empty set.
insert(c,s)   returns the union of s and {c}.
delete(c,s)   returns s − {c}.
union(s1,s2) returns the union of s1 and s2.
member(c,s)   returns TRUE if c is in s, otherwise FALSE.

We will assume a value-oriented implementation so that the character set data abstraction looks like the following:

```
adt CHAR_SET is
  type  CHARSET  is private;

  EMPTYSET: function                         return CHARSET;
  INSERT: function (C: CHAR; S: CHARSET) return CHARSET;
  DELETE: function (C: CHAR; S: CHARSET) return CHARSET;
  UNION:  function (SET1, SET2: CHARSET) return CHARSET;
  MEMBER: function (C: CHAR, S: CHARSET) return BOOLEAN;

end adt CHAR_SET;
```

137

For a set, there are two classical implementations: a linked list and a bit map. The linked list implementation places the members of the set into a linked list. Emptyset returns the empty list. Insert adds an element to the list, and delete takes one away. For a value-oriented implementation these changes require building a new list. The union operation combines two lists. The member operation is implemented as a linear search through the list.

The bit map implementation uses an array of Boolean values, one Boolean value for each element in the domain of discourse. Assuming characters are represented by eight bits, the character set could be represented by an array of 256 Boolean values. The empty set is represented by an array with all elements equal to false. The insert operation sets the appropriate element of the array to true, and delete sets the element to false. The union operation is the Boolean or operation on two Boolean arrays.

These two classic set implementations come in various flavors. One flavor is representation of the complement set. The linked list could be a list of those elements that are *not* in the set; the true value in a bit map could mean that that element is *not* in the set.

Another variation involving the linked list is whether to allow multiple occurrences of the same value in the linked list. For example, the expression

```
INSERT('X', INSERT('X', EMPTYSET))
```

returns a set with one element, but does the representation have a one-element or two-element linked list? If elements appear at most once in a linked list, then there is the additional option of unordered and ordered lists. An ordered list is sorted by some criteria.

Each representation has its limitations, advantages, and disadvantages. The bit map representations work only for small domains of discourse. The linked list representation will work over domains of any size except infinite sets (the complement representation will represent only cofinite sets in an infinite set domain). Space and time considerations vary considerably from implementation to implementation. Since the character domain is finite, any of the above representations will be adequate. In many languages, the string data type is a simple way to represent character sets. Strings are usually implemented more efficiently than a linked list of characters and so they may be a cost-effective representation. To show how strings might be used to represent character sets we shall assume that a string data abstraction exists with concatenation, substring operations, and a length operation. Note that our example shows how data abstractions can be used to build other data abstractions. Data abstractions can be built in a hierarchical manner just like procedural abstractions.

```
adt STRINGS is
    type  STRING  is private;

    EMPTYSTRING: function return STRING;

    function "+" (A,B: STRING) return STRING;
    -- returns the concatenation of A and B

    function "+" (A: STRING; B: CHAR) return STRING;
    -- returns the concatenation of A and B

    function "+" (A: CHAR; B: STRING) return STRING;
    -- returns the concatenation of A and B

    SUB: function (A: STRING; J: INTEGER) return CHAR;
    -- returns the Jth character of string A

    SUBSTR: function (A: STRING; J,K: INTEGER)
                        return STRING;
    -- returns the substring beginning at Jth character
    -- and ending at the Kth

    SUBSTR: function (A: STRING; J: INTEGER)
                        return STRING;
    -- returns the substring beginning at Jth character
    -- to the end of the string

    LEN: function (A: STRING) return INTEGER;
    -- returns the length of string A

end adt STRINGS;
```

A string representation is just a sequence of characters and so it is equivalent to the linked list representation. We must still choose from a variety of implementations, of which we shall show two: (1) unordered strings in which characters may be repeated and (2) unordered strings in which a character will appear at most once. The first one is easier to implement since we need not check for repeated elements:

```
adt CHAR_SETS is
    private type CHARSET is STRING;

    EMPTYSET: function return CHARSET is
    begin
        return EMPTYSTRING;
    end EMPTYSET;

    INSERT: function (C: CHAR; S: CHARSET)
                        return CHARSET is
    begin
        return S+C;
    end INSERT;
```

```
DELETE: function (C: CHAR; S: CHARSET)
                    return CHARSET is
    J: INTEGER;
    CH: CHAR;
    RESULT: STRING := EMPTYSTRING;
begin
    for J:=1 to LEN(S) loop
        CH := SUB(S, J);
        if CH≠C then
            RESULT := RESULT+C;
        end if;
    end loop;
    return RESULT;
end DELETE;

UNION: function (SET1, SET2: CHARSET) return
                    CHARSET is
begin
    return SET1+SET2;
end UNION;

MEMBER: function (C: CHAR; S: CHARSET) return
                    BOOLEAN is
    J: INTEGER;
begin
    for J:=1 to LEN(S) loop
        if SUB(S, J)=C then
            return TRUE;
        end if;
    end loop;
    return FALSE;
end MEMBER;

end adt CHAR_SETS;
```

Note that in the delete operation, all occurrences of the character must be deleted, not just the first one. The union and insert operations are simple.

In the next implementation (without repeated elements in the representation) the insert and union operations are more complicated and time consuming. In exchange, the delete operation is simpler and more efficient. The member operation remains unchanged but will be faster since the lists it searches will be the same length or shorter:

```
adt CHAR_SETS is
    private type CHARSET is STRING;

    EMPTYSET: function return CHARSET is
    begin
        return EMPTYSTRING;
    end EMPTYSET;
```

```
INSERT: function (C: CHAR; S: CHARSET)
                    return CHARSET is
begin
    if MEMBER(C, S) then
        return S;
    else
        return S+C;
    end if;
end INSERT;

DELETE: function (C: CHAR; S: CHARSET)
                    return CHARSET is
    J: INTEGER;
    CH: CHAR;
begin
    for J:=1 to LEN(S) loop
        if SUB(S, J)=C then
            return SUBSTR(S,1,J-1)+SUBSTR(S,J+1);
        end if;
    end loop;
    return S;
end DELETE;

UNION: function (SET1, SET2: CHARSET)
                    return CHARSET is
    J: INTEGER;
    RESULT: CHARSET := SET1;
begin
    for J:=1 to LEN(SET2) loop
        RESULT := INSERT(SUB(SET2, J), RESULT);
    end loop;
    return RESULT;
end UNION;

MEMBER: function (C: CHAR; S: CHARSET)
                    return BOOLEAN is
    J: INTEGER;
begin
    for J:=1 to LEN(S) loop
        if SUB(S, J)=C then
            return TRUE;
        end if;
    end loop;
    return FALSE;
end MEMBER;

end adt CHAR_SETS;
```

Ideally, the choice of implementation should be based solely on performance issues. The performance of these two implementations depends on the mix of operations used as well as the characteristics of the data. Thus the choice is difficult to determine analytically, and is perhaps best determined by benchmark tests.

The two implementations are interchangeable because of the deliberate decision to use data abstractions. Ada and other languages that have data abstraction facilities will guarantee this independence between use and implementation through type checking. In other languages, this enforcement must be accomplished in other ways. To illustrate what happens if this independence is not enforced, consider a programmer who is using the implementation with no repeated elements, and writes the following code:

```
S1, S2, S3, S4: CHARSET;
    ...

S3 := UNION(S1, S2);
S4 := DELETE('X', S3);
```

The programmer discovers that the two assignments are in a time-consuming loop. The programmer also thinks that in this particular situation, S1 and S2 do not share any common elements. The programmer thus rewrites the code as follows:

```
S1, S2, S3, S4: CHARSET;

    ...

S3 := S1+S2;          -- fast union
S4 := DELETE('X', S3);
```

It appears that the programmer has done everything correctly, but the situation is so precarious. There is the obvious problem that the programmer might be wrong and that S1 and S2 do share an element, in particular an X. In that particular case, X will not be deleted, and therefore will be a member of S4! Moreover, it may be that the two implementations written thus far are interchangeable, but there is no guarantee that any other implementation will be. Someone may decide that a complement set representation would be better. If this implementation is substituted, the "fast union" will compute the intersection! For these reasons, the above rewritten code, although more efficient, is discouraged because of the difficult long-term maintenance problems. Without automatic enforcement or the careful vigilance of all programmers, these circumventions of data abstractions can be costly.

There are many other representations of sets. Other data structures such as sorted binary trees would improve the sorting and searching efficiency of ordered lists. In Section 4.4 we briefly examined procedural data types. We will close this section with one other representation of sets that is similar to the procedural data types. It is a general method that can be used for any data type. This unusual implementation has several interesting properties. Operations that return a data value of the data type do nothing complicated. The operands are stored and evaluated at another time. Since only MEMBER does not return a CHARSET it is the only operation that must "figure out what the data is." This means that the first four operations are optimally efficient and MEMBER does all the work. When MEMBER is not called, this implementation is very fast, but when MEMBER is called often, it can be very slow.

This style of implementation is similar to lazy evaluation first discussed by Burge (1975) and Friedman and Wise (1976). *Lazy evaluation* is a method that evaluates expressions from the outermost function, rather than innermost expression. Arguments to functions are not evaluated until they are actually needed. The implementation below is like lazy evaluation in that CHARSET arguments are not evaluated until needed:

```
adt CHAR_SETS is
    type OPTYPE is (EMPTYSETOP, INSERTOP, DELETEOP,
                    UNIONOP);
    private type CHARSET is
      record
        case OP: OPTYPE is
        when EMPTYSETOP => ; -- no fields
        when INSERTOP =>   C: CHAR;
                           S: pointer CHARSET;
        when DELETEOP =>   C: CHAR;
                           S: pointer CHARSET;
        when UNIONOP =>    SET1, SET2: pointer CHARSET;
        end case;
      end record;

    EMPTYSET: function return CHARSET is
        S: CHARSET;
    begin
        S.OP := EMPTYSETOP;
        return S;
    end EMPTYSET;

    INSERT: function (C: CHAR; S: CHARSET)
                       return CHARSET is
        SET: CHARSET;
    begin
        SET.OP := INSERTOP;
        SET.C  := C;
        SET.S  := S;
        return SET;
    end INSERT;

    DELETE: function (C: CHAR; S: CHARSET)
                       return CHARSET is
        SET: CHARSET;
    begin
        SET.OP := DELETEOP;
        SET.C  := C;
        SET.S  := S;
        return SET;
    end DELETE;
```

```
UNION: function (SET1, SET2: CHARSET)
                    return CHARSET is
    SET: CHARSET;
begin
    SET.OP   := UNIONOP;
    SET.SET1 := SET1;
    SET.SET2 := SET2;
    return SET;
end UNION;

MEMBER: function (C: CHAR; S: CHARSET)
                    return BOOLEAN is
begin
    case S.OP of
    when EMPTYSETOP =>
        return FALSE;
    when INSERTOP =>
        return C=S.C or else MEMBER(C, S.S);
    when DELETEOP =>
        return C≠S.C and then MEMBER(C, S.S);
    when UNIONOP =>
        return MEMBER(C, S.SET1)
          or else MEMBER(C, S.SET2);
    end case;
end MEMBER;

end adt CHAR_SETS;
```

The data structures constructed by the above implementation are not modified by any of the other operations (i.e., the implementation is like a write-once memory). This fact makes assignment a value assignment even though pointers are used.

The implementation style described above is general and can be applied to practically all data types. First, determine the set of operations returning values of the desired data type. From this set, construct the representation that is a union with each alternative of the union representing one of the operations. Each alternative has a field for each operand of the operation. Next, code each operation by constructing a new value and assigning the operands to the appropriate fields. The hardest part of the method is designing and coding the rest of the operations.

9.2 Games

Sometimes it is useful to describe a class of abstract data types rather than one particular data type. In this section, for example, we wish to define a game abstract data type. The rules of the game will be the semantics of the abstract data type. But to describe some algorithms we need to know only the syntax of the abstract data type and just a little about the semantics. So we will design a class of data types that can be used for a large class of games. A particular game will determine the semantics of the data type.

Games have many common attributes, and a number of algorithms can be used on a large variety of games. To reveal this commonality and the generic game-playing algorithms we will organize games as abstract data types. The kind of games that will be considered will take into account any number of players, random events like the throw of a die, and hidden information. Further assumptions about games will be revealed as we design our data type. Variations on these assumptions can be obtained by adjusting the abstract data type design.

The game abstraction is composed of four types. The first type is called a SITUATION. A situation is a complete description of a game at an instant in time. It contains all information needed for further play. For Tic Tac Toe this information is the mark that has been made on each of the nine locations and the player whose move it is. The second and third types are called MOVE and PLAYER. A MOVE specifies an action made by a player. A PLAYER is an enumeration of the players. For each situation we will assume only one player can move. The result of making a move is a transition from one situation to another situation. Each situation determines a set of legal moves. A player plays by selecting one of these legal moves. The game must begin and end, so there are initial and final situations. The game begins with an initial situation and ends with a final situation. No moves can be made from a final situation. Games usually end with winners and losers. This concept will be represented with a type called OUTCOME. It may indicate winners and losers or perhaps some other kind of end result. In poker, for example, it may be a monetary result.

A game can be diagrammed as a graph with nodes representing situations and arcs representing moves. Nodes with no incoming arcs are initial situations, and nodes with no outgoing arcs are final situations. Each node could be labeled with a player to indicate whose move it is. The end nodes (representing final situations) could be labeled with the outcome of the game rather than a player. Figure 9.1 shows a small part of the graph for Tic Tac Toe. Random events can be represented in a variety of ways. A pseudo player called *random* could be asked to make a move whenever a random event is required. Alternatively, a move can represent not just one transition from a situation but many transitions. One transition is randomly selected. This second alternative will be used in our design.

The syntax of the game abstract data type as a value-oriented implementation can now be fully described. Assume the existence of a LIST data type with operations FIRST, REST, and APPEND.

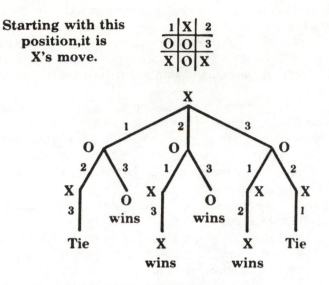

FIGURE 9.1 A small part of the Tic Tac Toe game tree.

```
adt GAME is
        type SITUATION is private;
        type MOVE      is private;
        type PLAYER    is private;
        type OUTCOME   is private;

        type MOVELIST is  LIST(MOVE);
        type SITLIST  is LIST( record
                                SIT: SITUATION;
                                PROBABILITY: REAL;
                             end record );

        INITSIT:   function
                                return SITUATION;
        WHOSEMOVE: function (SIT:SITUATION)
                                return PLAYER;
        GENMOVES:  function (SIT:SITUATION)
                                return MOVELIST;
        LEGALMOVE: function (SIT:SITUATION; M:MOVE)
                                return BOOLEAN;
        MAKEMOVE:  function (SIT:SITUATION; M:MOVE)
                                return SITLIST;
        KNOWNINFO: function (SIT:SITUATION)
                                return SITUATION;
        FINALSIT:  function (SIT:SITUATION)
                                return BOOLEAN;
        RESULT:    function (SIT:SITUATION)
                                return OUTCOME;

    end adt GAME;
```

A brief explanation of each function is in order.

1. INITSIT will generate an initial situation. For some games, like chess and backgammon, this function will always produce the same initial situation. In other games such as bridge and Boggle, INITSIT may have to generate a random initial situation. That process may involve a simulation of shuffling and dealing a deck of playing cards.

2. WHOSEMOVE returns the player that should make the next move given some situation. For many two-player games, moves may simply alternate. But this is not generally true. In the game of Boxes, a player gets another move if he or she completes a box. In Blackjack a player may make another move after each hit. Our procedure assumes that in any given situation only one player may move.

3. GENMOVES will generate a list of all possible moves that can be made in a particular situation. An empty list is returned if there are no moves. This result only can occur in a final situation. Our procedure assumes that there are only a finite number of possible moves that can be made from any situation. This assumption excludes games in which a player can make one of an infinite number of possible moves, such as games which allow unlimited bidding. If a player can bid any arbitrary amount, then this implies a choice from an infinite number of possibilities.

4. LEGALMOVE tests the legality of making a move. It will return true if move M is a legal move from situation SIT. This procedure contains the same information as GENMOVES. The two procedures must be consistent. In fact, LEGALMOVE can be written as

```
LEGALMOVE: function (SIT: SITUATION; M: MOVE)
                     return BOOLEAN is
    LIST_OF_MOVES: MOVELIST := GENMOVES(SIT);
begin
    while LIST_OF_MOVES ≠ null loop
        if M=FIRST(LIST_OF_MOVES) then
            return TRUE;
        end if;
        LIST_OF_MOVES := NEXT(LIST_OF_MOVES);
    end loop;
    return FALSE;
end LEGALMOVE;
```

5. MAKEMOVE will make an actual move. It will compute a new situation based on the old situation and the move. If there are no random events, then a list of one situation with a probability of 100% is returned. If there are random events, then a list of each possible situation with the probability of that situation occurring is returned. The roll of a die can be represented by generating six situations with equal probability. MAKEMOVE only makes the specified move; it does not decide which move to make, which is a strategic decision that players make.

6. KNOWNINFO returns the information that a player is entitled to have. In a complete-information game, like chess and backgammon, this procedure could simply return the situation unchanged. In other games, like bridge, it should blank out unavailable information such as the cards held by other players.

7. FINALSIT will return true if the situation is a final situation and false otherwise. Note that like LEGALMOVE this function could be expressed in terms of GENMOVES since GENMOVES will return an empty list if the situation is final.

8. RESULT returns the outcome of a game. Only final situations should be passed to this function, otherwise an error is raised. For many two-player games the outcome is usually one of three possibilities: (a) first player wins, (b) second player wins, or (c) tie.

The game abstract data type is a formal means for describing the rules of the game. It does not describe a strategy or specify how players might play. It describes the entire range of possible games.

To describe a strategy we need a procedure outside the abstract data type, which, given a situation, will choose a move. Each player will have a possibly different strategy, so let us have an array of procedures named PLAY:

```
PLAY: array (PLAYER) of function (S: SITUATION)
                              return MOVE;
```

Each player should have access to the public parts of the game abstract data type but should not have access to the internals of the abstract data type nor to other players' strategies.

We can now express some general algorithms about games. One algorithm is the impartial referee. The referee coordinates the game, asks players to make a move when it is their turn, and gives the appropriate information to each player:

```
REFEREE: function return OUTCOME is
    SIT: SITUATION;
    NEXTMOVE: MOVE;
begin
    SIT := INITSIT();

    while not FINALSIT(SIT) loop
        NEXTMOVE := PLAY(WHOSEMOVE(SIT))(KNOWNINFO(SIT));
        if LEGALMOVE(SIT, NEXTMOVE) then
            SIT :=  -- randomly select one
                    -- of MAKEMOVE(SIT, NEXTMOVE);
        else
            REPORT_ERROR("Illegal move -- try again");
        end if;
    end loop;
    return RESULT(SIT);
end REFEREE;
```

Another useful algorithm is the well-known minimax procedure. It is called *minimax* because one player attempts to maximize his or her own gains, while the other player attempts to minimize the first player's gains. It assumes there are (a) no random events, (b) two players, and (c) a complete-information game (i.e., a game with no hidden information). So MAKEMOVE returns one SITUATION and KNOWNINFO is the identity function. The minimax procedure can be used to determine the best strategy for each player (shown in the second procedure below). The procedure as implemented below will return the value of the outcome of the game if both players always play their best. The procedure

```
VALUE: function (R: OUTCOME) return INTEGER;
```

will return a number indicating the value of the outcome. Bigger numbers are more valuable for one player and smaller numbers are more valuable for the other player. The numbers chosen for a game with three outcomes might be something like:

1. 100 if player 1 wins
2. 50 if a tie
3. 0 if player 2 wins

The minimax procedure in its pure form (as shown below) is not used because it almost always takes too much time. Consider a game such that at each situation there are n possible moves and the game always takes m moves from initial situation to final situation. Then the minimax procedure is called more than m^n times!

```
MINIMAX: function (SIT: SITUATION) return INTEGER is
    LIST_OF_MOVES: MOVELIST;
    NEXT_MOVE: MOVE;
    V, W: INTEGER;
begin
    if FINALSIT(SIT) then
        return VALUE(RESULT(SIT));
    else
        LIST_OF_MOVES := GENMOVES(SIT);
        V := MINIMAX(MAKEMOVE(SIT, FIRST(LIST_OF_MOVES)));
        while REST(LIST_OF_MOVES) ≠ null loop
            LIST_OF_MOVES := REST(LIST_OF_MOVES);
            NEXT_MOVE := FIRST(LIST_OF_MOVES);
            W := MINIMAX(MAKEMOVE(SIT, NEXT_MOVE));
            if WHOSEMOVE(SIT)=PLAYER'FIRST then
                V := MAX(V, W);
            else
                V := MIN(V, W);
            end if;
        end loop;
        return V;
    end if;
end MINIMAX;
```

```
BESTMOVE: function (SIT: SITUATION) return MOVE is
    LIST_OF_MOVES: MOVELIST;
    V, W: INTEGER;
    BEST, NEXT_MOVE: MOVE;
begin
    LIST_OF_MOVES := GENMOVES(SIT);
    V := MINIMAX(MAKEMOVE(SIT, FIRST(LIST_OF_MOVES)));
    BEST := V;
    while REST(LIST_OF_MOVES) ≠ null loop
        LIST_OF_MOVES := REST(LIST_OF_MOVES);
        NEXT_MOVE := FIRST(LIST_OF_MOVES);
        W := MINIMAX(MAKEMOVE(SIT, NEXT_MOVE));
        if WHOSEMOVE(SIT)=PLAYER'FIRST and W>V
        or WHOSEMOVE(SIT)≠PLAYER'FIRST and W<V then
            V:=W;
            BEST:=NEXT_MOVE;
        end if;
    end loop;
    return BEST;
end BESTMOVE;
```

Because of the enormous amount of time the minimax procedure consumes, it is desirable to have a faster solution. The minimax procedure returns an exact result, a faster solution may be achieved by accepting an approximation. One method is the addition of a JUDGE function which, given a situation, will approximate the value of the situation—that is, it will guess at what the minimax function might have returned. The JUDGE function depends on the game; for chess, the function may take into account such things as the number of chess pieces on both sides and the position of both sides. In the minimax procedure the only numbers returned are the ones returned by the VALUE function. The JUDGE function may return any number between the two extremes. Designing and implementing a JUDGE procedure is difficult and ad hoc. The minimax procedure and the JUDGE function are combined by using the minimax procedure up to a certain depth of nesting and then using the JUDGE function. The MINIMAX function is replaced with the following function.

```
BESTGUESS: function (LEVEL: INTEGER; SIT:SITUATION)
                        return INTEGER is
    LIST_OF_MOVES: MOVELIST;
    NEXT_MOVE: MOVE;
    V, W: INTEGER;
begin
    if LEVEL=0 then
        return JUDGE(SIT);
    end if;
    LIST_OF_MOVES := GENMOVES(SIT);
    V := BESTGUESS(LEVEL-1, MAKEMOVE(SIT,
                    FIRST(LIST_OF_MOVES)));
```

```
    while REST(LIST_OF_MOVES) ≠ null loop
        LIST_OF_MOVES := REST(LIST_OF_MOVES);
        NEXT_MOVE := FIRST(LIST_OF_MOVES);
        W := BESTGUESS(LEVEL-1,
                        MAKEMOVE(SIT, NEXT_MOVE));
        if WHOSEMOVE(SIT)=PLAYER'FIRST then
            V := MAX(V, W);
        else
            V := MIN(V, W);
        end if;
    end loop;
    return V;
end BESTGUESS;
```

As the depth of nesting is increased the quality of play should improve, but the computation time will increase exponentially.

The above set of functions illustrate the usefulness of separating the details of a game from the abstract notion of a game. We have described a variety of general purpose functions that will work on a wide variety of games. Each game can be written to be independent of the general purpose functions. We shall conclude this section with one example of a game: Tic Tac Toe. A situation will be represented by a list of ten elements. The first element will specify whose move it is and the remaining nine elements will indicate the status of each of the nine squares of Tic Tac Toe.

```
adt GAME is

    type STATUS is (BLANK, X, O);
    type SITUATION is array (0..9) of STATUS;
    type MOVE is 1..9;
    type PLAYER is STATUS range X..O;
    type OUTCOME is (XWINS, OWINS, CATSGAME);

    INITSIT: function return SITUATION is
        R: SITUATION := (X, BLANK,BLANK,BLANK,
                            BLANK,BLANK,BLANK,
                            BLANK,BLANK,BLANK);
    begin
        return R;
    end INITSIT;

    WHOSEMOVE: function (SIT: SITUATION)
                            return PLAYER is
    begin
        return SIT(0);
    end WHOSEMOVE;

    GENMOVES: function (SIT: SITUATION)
                            return MOVELIST is
        LIST_OF_MOVES: MOVELIST := EMPTY_LIST;
        J: INTEGER;
```

```
    begin
        for J in 1..9 loop
            if SIT(J)=BLANK then
                LIST_OF_MOVES := APPEND(LIST_OF_MOVES,J);
            end if;
        end loop;
        return LIST_OF_MOVES;
    end GENMOVES;

    LEGALMOVE: function (SIT: SITUATION, M: MOVE)
        return BOOLEAN is
    begin
        return SIT(M)=BLANK;
    end LEGALMOVE;

    MAKEMOVE: function (SIT: SITUATION, M: MOVE)
        return SITLIST is
        NEWSIT: SITUATION;
    begin
        if LEGALMOVE(SIT, M) then
            NEWSIT := SIT;
            NEWSIT(M) := WHOSEMOVE(SIT);
            return MAKE_SIT_LIST(NEWSIT, 100);
        else
            ERROR();
        end if;
    end MAKEMOVE;

    KNOWNINFO: function (SIT: SITUATION)
                        return SITUATION is
    begin
        return SIT;
    end KNOWNINFO;

    FINALSIT: function (SIT: SITUATION)
                        return BOOLEAN is
    begin
        -- return true if there are no blanks
        -- or there are three in a row;
    end FINALSIT;

    RESULT: function (SIT: SITUATION) return OUTCOME is
    begin
        -- return one of TIE, X or O according
        -- to the Tic Tac Toe rules;
    end RESULT;

end adt GAME;
```

Exercises

1. Add the equality operator to the character set for all three implementations in Section 9.1.

2. In the function body of LEGALMOVE what assumption is made about predefined operations? What effect will this have if the assumption is false?

3. Write a procedure that will play any game in which the moves of every player are selected randomly. Do not use PLAY or REFEREE.

4. Consider the implementation of a game (such as Poker, Nim, Go, Blackjack, Checkers, etc.) using the game abstract data type. The algorithms are usually determined by the representation (i.e., the data structures). Give two different representations and discuss the performance tradeoffs.

Polymorphism

10

Polymorphism, meaning "existing in many forms," is a term applied to programming language constructs that may have many data types. For example, a polymorphic procedure will have a parameter of any type and each call to the procedure may pass values of different types. The type of the parameter is called polymorphic since it may assume values of many different types. There are many other words meaning the same thing as polymorphism. The languages CLU and Alphard use *type generators*, and Ada uses the adjective *generic*. *Parameterized types* and *schemes* are other words that have been proposed. In this chapter we shall use the terms "polymorphism" and "polymorphic types."

In previous chapters we have seen many predefined polymorphic types, called type constructors. For example,

```
array (N..M) of X
```

is a polymorphic type whose parameters are N, M, and X. Likewise, records, unions and procedure types are polymorphic types. Most languages also have polymorphic operations and procedures. A polymorphic procedure has one or more parameters, each of which can be one of many types. Three basic polymorphic operations are assignment, array subscripting, and function application. Overloaded operators are not examples of polymorphic functions. The difference is in the implementation. A polymorphic function usually has just one algorithm for implementing the function. An overloaded function usually has a different algorithm for each type. For example, the addition and equality operations must usually use a different algorithm for each type; there is no general algorithm for all equality or addition operations. But the assignment and application operations are generally implemented in one specific way for all types.

In previous chapters we introduced user-defined data types. We now extend this idea to user-defined parameterized types. The techniques introduced in previous chapters are not sufficient to create constructor types like arrays. Whereas in previous chapters we designed and implemented sets of characters, in this chapter we consider such ambitious goals as implementing sets for an arbitrary data type.

10.1 Polymorphic Parameters

A polymorphic type has one or more parameters. A polymorphic type with arguments is called an *instance* of the the polymorphic type, and such an instance is a type of the polymorphic type. Thus the polymorphic type represents a collection of types, and this collection is generated by the range of possible parameter values. A polymorphic procedure has one or more parameters with polymorphic types. A polymorphic procedure represents a collection of procedures, one for each type of the polymorphic types. For polymorphic types and procedures to be executable, one must specify the type parameters to generate a nonpolymorphic type or procedure. This task is called *instantiation* because it creates an instance of the polymorphic type or procedure. Instantiation is normally done at compile-time, so it is necessary to know at compile-time the parameter values to polymorphic types and procedures. In the following examples we shall use lower-case identifiers for those type parameter values that are normally known at compile-time. We shall also explicitly list all parameter values to polymorphic procedures. Later we shall discuss syntactic issues and implicit parameters. We will examine three kinds of parameters: values, types, and restricted types.

Values

The bounds of a Pascal array are part of the type. Since Pascal requires that all types be known at compile-time it is not possible to write a procedure that accepts a variable size array as a parameter. Let us imagine an extension to Pascal that would allow Pascal procedures to accept arrays of variable sizes. This extension requires that the bounds of the array must also be passed. The following procedure counts the number of occurrences of the value KEY in an arbitrary-size array:

```
NUM_OCC: function (n,m: INTEGER;
                   X: array (n..m) of INTEGER;
                   KEY: INTEGER)
                return INTEGER is
        COUNT: INTEGER := 0;
        J: INTEGER;
begin
        for J in n..m loop
                if KEY=X(J) then
                        COUNT:=COUNT+1;
                end if;
        end loop;
        return COUNT;
end NUM_OCC;
```

The parameters n and m are deliberately in lower-case to emphasize that they are compile-time constants. For each call of the procedure NUM_OCC, the values of the first two parameters are known since the bounds of all Pascal arrays are compile-time constants, and they must be known to do complete Pascal compile-time type checking.

NUM_OCC is a simple example of a polymorphic procedure. The third parameter, X, represents a collection of possible types. Each call to this procedure specifies (via the first two parameters) the type of the third parameter.

Polymorphic types may have numeric parameters or other value parameters that are used to specify such things as sizes. Consider the following data type BAG, represented as an array of some fixed size. The parameter specifies the maximum number of elements that may be stored in a bag.

```
type BAG (max: INTEGER) is
        record
                VALUES: array (1..max) of INTEGER;
                CURRENT: INTEGER;
        end record;

A_BAG: BAG(100);      -- an example declaration using BAG
```

Types

Another kind of parameter is a type parameter. A bag of integers and a bag of characters have many similarities. The concept of bag is independent of the type of object stored in the bag. Likewise, the procedure NUM_OCC can be generalized to arrays of an arbitrary type. To make these generalizations and also make all parameters explicit we must introduce a new type called *type*. A brief discussion of such types appears at the end of Chapter 4. In this chapter we need this type to make type parameters visible. As an example, consider the following polymorphic procedure:

```
NUM_OCC: function (t: TYPE;
                   X: array (1..100) of t;
                   KEY: t)
                return 0..100 is
          COUNT: 0..100 := 0;
          J: 1..100;
begin
          for J in 1..100 loop
                   if KEY=X(J) then
                             COUNT:=COUNT+1;
                   end if;
          end loop;
          return COUNT;
end NUM_OCC;
```

This procedure has three parameters. The first introduces the type, and the other two are polymorphic types based on the first parameter. Like the numeric parameters of the previous section, the type parameters must also be compile-time constants to do compile-time type checking. However, an examination of the above procedure should convince one that if the arguments are properly typed then the instantiation of NUM_OCC will be properly typed. This conclusion implies that it is not necessary to know the values of the type parameters at compile-time. Another issue that we defer to later is the comparison that we make on elements of type t. There may be some types that do not have a comparison operation.

To complete this section we give an example of a parameterized BAG type:

```
type BAG (t: TYPE) is
        record
                    VALUES: array (1..100) of t;
                    CURRENT: INTEGER;
        end record;

A_BAG: BAG(INTEGER); -- an example declaration using BAG
```

Types with Operator Restrictions

In the previous section we noted a difficulty with operations performed on an arbitrary type. Some polymorphic procedures require certain operations. We can formalize such requirements by adding more parameters. The comparison operator can be a parameter of the NUM_OCC procedure and thus no mystery operations appear in the procedure body.

```
NUM_OCC: function (t: TYPE;
                    X: array (1..100) of t;
                    KEY: t;
                    EQUAL: function  (A, B: t)
                                            return BOOLEAN)
            return 0..100 is
        COUNT: 0..100 := 0;
        J: 1..100;
begin
        for J in 1..100 loop
                    if EQUAL(KEY, X(J)) then
                            COUNT:=COUNT+1;
                    end if;
        end loop;
        return COUNT;
end NUM_OCC;
```

Now, this procedure clearly states all requirements for type t in its parameter list. Polymorphic types often require certain operations that must be performed on elements of the type parameter. It is important that these operations be included along with the type parameters, and most languages with polymorphism provide a special syntax for this purpose. Examples from several languages are as follows:

```
t: type where t has                          -- CLU
        EQUAL: proctype(t, t) returns (bool);

t:form<EQUAL>                                 -- Alphard

type t with ( function EQUAL(t, t) : boolean;); -- Russell

type t needs attributes                       -- Schemes
        ( function EQUAL(t, t) returns boolean )

generic type t is private;                    -- Ada
        with function EQUAL(A, B: t)
                return BOOLEAN is EQUAL;
```

Some of these constructs provide other facilities. For example, in Alphard and Russell, the constructs can be used in any declaration and are used to restrict the class of operations that may be used.

In the procedure NUM_OCC we specified the EQUAL function separately from the type. We could do the same thing for parameterized types, but most programming languages gather the operations of the type with the type, as the above examples show. This approach is appropriate since such operations are properly considered part of the type rather than a second parameter. However, most of these languages do not go far enough. Only the syntactic part of the operator is specified, but often certain properties of the operation are necessary as well. An equality operation has certain properties that are assumed by the polymorphic type. Ideally these properties should be fully specified. Alphard encourages the formal specification of all required properties of each operation passed with each type parameter.

10.2 Binding and Type-Checking Issues

In the previous section we looked briefly at different kinds of parameters to polymorphic types. In this section we will look at syntactic questions as well as semantic issues concerning the power of polymorphic types and the kind of type checking that can be provided at compile-time.

Static and Dynamic Parameters

We need to distinguish between compile-time parameters and run-time parameters. A compile-time parameter is one whose values are always known at compile-time. The compiler uses this information to compile the program. A run-time parameter is one whose value is not generally known until run-time and therefore the compiler must generate code to handle all potential values. In most languages types are static, meaning that in all constructs, every type is known at compile-time, and all type parameters are compile-time parameters. Static types require that parameters to polymorphic types be compile-time values. Dynamic types are types that are created at run-time and that the compiler cannot generally anticipate. Allowing run-time parameters for polymorphic types would allow dynamic types since the values of the parameters are determined at run-time. A language with dynamic types must defer to run-time many of the traditional tasks of a compiler such as determining storage sizes, type checking, and procedure instantiation. Because of these complexities most programming languages shy away from dynamic types. However, there are occasions when dynamic types are particularly useful. Determining the bounds of an array at run-time is particularly useful. If the bounds of an array are part of the type, then there is strong motivation to allow some dynamic types.

For the most part we shall assume that parameters to polymorphic types and procedures are compile-time constants. To distinguish between compile-time and run-time parameter values we adopt a notation used by Tennent (1981). Parameters are split into two lists. The first list is placed in square brackets and includes all compile-time parameters. The second list is placed in round brackets and includes all run-time parameters. Such a notation will help us understand what must be known at compile-time and what values are dynamic. The `NUM_OCC` procedure heading would look like:

```
NUM_OCC: function [t: TYPE; n,m: INTEGER]
                (X: array (n..m) of t; KEY:t)
            return t;
```

An instantiation of polymorphic procedures and types is now easier to explain. It simply means that compile-time parameters are known at compile-time. Two instances of the `NUM_OCC` procedure are

```
NUM_OCC[INTEGER,1,100]
```

and

```
NUM_OCC[CHARACTER,5,8] .
```

Sometimes instantiations may be given a new name. For example, `INT_NUM_OCC` may stand for `NUM_OCC[INTEGER,1,100]`. Polymorphic types will normally have only compile-time parameters. An alternative notation adopted by languages such as SIMULA and CLU uses

```
INTEGER$NUM_OCC
```

rather than

```
NUM_OCC[INTEGER]
```

Explicit and Implicit Parameters

In previous sections we have seen some different syntactic methods for expressing the parameters of a polymorphic type or procedure. In this section we examine yet another method. Consider the following type:

```
type BAG[t: TYPE] is
        record
                VALUES: array (1..100) of t;
                LAST: 0..100;
        end record;

INSERT: procedure [t: TYPE] (B: BAG(t); X:t);
```

From this polymorphic type we may create two instances of the bag type as follows:

```
type INT_BAG is BAG[INTEGER];
type CHAR_BAG is BAG[CHARACTER];

BAG1: INT_BAG;
BAG2: CHAR_BAG;
```

The INSERT procedure must be instantiated with a type. This can be done explicitly by passing the type of the first argument. We have already mentioned several different syntactic methods:

```
INSERT(INTEGER, BAG1, 5);
INSERT[INTEGER] (BAG1, 5);
INTEGER$INSERT(BAG1, 5);
```

But consider an implicit approach. One natural way of using the INSERT procedure is

```
INSERT(BAG1, 5);
INSERT(BAG2, 'A');
```

There is enough information in each procedure call to determine which INSERT procedure is intended. The compiler can usually determine the missing parameters. The compiler can consider the name INSERT as an overloaded operator and use an operator identification algorithm to resolve the binding.

The Semantics of Polymorphism

Polymorphism is often viewed as a syntactic issue. Polymorphic procedures and types are considered as parameterized macros that are expanded at compile-time. After expansion of all polymorphic procedures and types, the compiler does normal parsing and type analysis. In this light, polymorphism does not have any semantic meaning, but let us consider the semantic implications of this syntactic-oriented view. For each polymorphic type one must determine which instantiations are required by the program. If it is not the programmer's responsibility to specify these instances, as Ada requires, the compiler must perform this initial task. After the compiler determines a list of instances, the compiler replicates and instantiates each polymorphic routine or type with the appropriate static parameter values. This task may be difficult if implicit parameters are used. After this phase, each polymorphic type and procedure has been replaced with a collection of nonpolymorphic (i.e., normal) types and procedures. Every such derived type and procedure is compiled as if it were a separate entity. Some difficulties that occur with macro preprocessors will also occur during the process described above. Recursive polymorphic types and procedures cannot be expanded, just as recursive macros cannot be expanded. Some instances of a polymorphic type may be legal and others might not be legal. For example, a type error may be detected only when certain type parameters are used. Another disadvantage of a syntactic view is that since all derived types and procedures are treated independently, much duplication occurs during compilation and run-time. Nearly identical procedures are compiled and nearly identical code must be duplicated for each instance of a polymorphic type or procedure. Clever optimization techniques may undo some of this work, but the duplication is inherent in the syntactic viewpoint.

A semantic view of polymorphism overcomes many of the above disadvantages. With a semantic view of polymorphism, polymorphic types and procedures could be type checked before they are instantiated. Efficient implementations are possible with a semantic view, since polymorphic types do not need to be replicated. Recursive polymorphism also becomes possible.

With a semantic viewpoint, polymorphic types and procedures are parsed as part of the language (rather than treated as syntactic sugar on a nonpolymorphic language). Compilation of polymorphic procedures usually includes type checking of the procedure body before any instantiation takes place. Each use of a polymorphic procedure must also be type checked, but unlike the syntactic viewpoint, the polymorphic procedure call does not require that we type check the body of the instantiated procedure. Thus it may considerably reduce the amount of type checking needed.

Implementation of polymorphic procedures with a semantic foundation is more flexible and can achieve considerable optimizations. One option is to mimic the syntactic viewpoint and replicate the code for each possible instantiation. Another option is to make the static parameter a run-time parameter. In the polymorphic procedure body, this additional parameter can be used to select the appropriate code that varies between instantiations. A combination of these two extremes may provide the optimal implementation.

To illustrate some of these semantic considerations, consider the following polymorphic procedure:

```
NUM_OCC: function [t: TYPE]
                  (X: array (1..100) of t; KEY: t)
                  return 0..100 is
        COUNT: 0..100 := 0;
        J: 1..100;
begin
        for J in 1..100 loop
                if KEY=X(J) then
                        COUNT:=COUNT+1;
                end if;
        end loop;
        return COUNT;
end NUM_OCC;
```

Before even considering how `NUM_OCC` is used, the compiler can type check the procedure body. From the procedure body, the compiler can determine that the only requirement on type `t` is that it have an operator = that accepts two operands of type `t` and returns a value of type `BOOLEAN`. Consider the following two function calls to `NUM_OCC`:

```
AGES:  array (1..100) of INTEGER;
NAMES: array (1..100) of STRING;

begin
        ...
        NUM_OCC(AGES,  5);
        NUM_OCC(NAMES, "Alpha");
```

From the declarations of `AGES` and `NAMES` (as well as the literals) the compiler can determine that the polymorphic procedure `NUM_OCC` has type parameters `INTEGER` and `STRING`. Both types meet the requirements for parameter type `t`, so everything is correctly typed.

We can now consider the code that might be generated by a compiler that will implement this particular example. Replication of code could be used by duplicating the procedure, one for each type used. This is also what a syntactic view of polymorphism would do. For the above example, two copies of `NUM_OCC` would be generated, with the only difference in code being the address of the equality routine. In one copy, the `STRING` equality routine would be used, and in the other the `INTEGER` equality routine would be used. Each copy of the routine would be given a unique name (or address), and calls to `NUM_OCC` would generate code to call one of the two copies. This implementation can be represented as follows:

```
NUM_OCC1: function (X: array (1..100) of INTEGER;
                    KEY: INTEGER)
          ...

NUM_OCC2: function (X: array (1..100) of STRING;
                    KEY: STRING)
```

```
        . . .
    NUM_OCC1(AGES,   5);
    NUM_OCC2(NAMES, "Alpha");
```

Alternatively, the compiler can generate code that will in effect make the type parameter an extra run-time parameter. We will call this the *shared code approach*. This implementation consolidates the code and thus will require less memory but cost more time for processing the extra parameter to NUM_OCC. The end result of a shared code approach is equivalent to a procedure with an extra run-time parameter inserted by the compiler that specifies the type. The following code illustrates this approach.

```
NUM_OCC: function (THE_TYPE: INTEGER;
                   X: array (1..100) of ANY;
                   KEY: ANY)
                 return 0..100 is
        COUNT: 0..100 := 0;
        J: 1..100;
        EQUAL: procedure (X,Y:ANY) return BOOLEAN is
        begin
                if THE_TYPE=1 then
                        INT_EQUALITY(X,Y)
                else
                        STRING_EQUALITY(X,Y)
                end if;
        end EQUAL;

begin                     -- body of function NUM_OCC
        for J in 1..100 loop
                if EQUAL(KEY, X(J)) then
                        COUNT:=COUNT+1;
                end if;
        end loop;
        return COUNT;
end NUM_OCC;

        . . .
        NUM_OCC(1, AGES,  5);
        NUM_OCC(2, NAMES, "Alpha");
```

The choice of implementation depends on the programming language, the compiler, the programmer, and/or the specifics of a program. A compiler might always opt for the shared code approach, but an optimizing compiler can do better. If a polymorphic routine is used with only one type parameter value, then obviously the type should be instantiated. Recursive polymorphic routines have no choice (unless maximum depth is known); they must be implemented using a shared code approach. If a polymorphic routine is used with many different type parameters, and each one is called only a few times during execution, then the shared code implementation is best. If one of the above uses is executed very frequently, it might be best to instantiate that one occurrence and use a shared code approach for all other cases. In general it is not clear how to determine automatically what the best implementation strategy should be for an arbitrary program.

Working out the details of a semantic framework for polymorphism is not always easy. If one is willing to accept certain restrictions on polymorphism, one can comfortably define the semantics of polymorphism in a fairly simple way. To allow generalized polymorphism that includes self-application requires many mathematical details. These details are sometimes considered in a simpler framework such as the lambda calculus.

Type Inference

A popular polymorphism style developed by Robin Milner (1978) and adopted in such languages as ML and HOPE can be characterized as polymorphism and strong type checking without declarations. Rather than declaring variables with a type, the programmer simply uses variables and the compiler infers their types. Given an arbitrary expression with variables of unknown types, a *type assignment* assigns some type to each variable. A valid type assignment is one that results in correctly typed expressions. *Type inference* is the problem of determining all possible valid type assignments. For example, in the expression X=5, one can infer that the type of X must be an integer since only integers can be compared with integers. But the variables in the expression X=Y may have many valid type assignments. If we assume that the operands of the comparison operator must have the same type, we may infer that the types of X and Y must be the same. Type schemes can express this constraint. A *type variable* represents a type, and expressions with type variables represent a set of types. We use Greek letters for type variables. A *type scheme* assigns a type expression to each variable. An *instance* of a type scheme is the uniform replacement of each type-variable with some type. If every instance of a type scheme gives a valid type assignment, then the type scheme is valid. The most general valid type scheme, called the *principal typing*, or *principal type scheme*, is one in which every valid type assignment is an instance of the type scheme. The principal type scheme for the above simple example is

```
X: α
Y: α
```

where α is a type-variable. This scheme expresses the constraint that the type of X must be the same as the type of Y. Now consider the more complex expression

```
F(A,G(C)) = G(A)
```

The principal typing is

```
A:  α
C:  α
F:  α × β → β
G:  α → β
```

where $\alpha \times \beta \to \gamma$ means a function with two parameters of types α and β which returns a value of type γ. As long as the type-variables α and β are replaced uniformly with some type, the expression is correctly typed. Any other type assignment produces incorrectly typed expressions.

Hindley (1969) used the unification algorithm to deduce automatically the principal type scheme. This device can be used as a basis for introducing polymorphism into a programming language. When type-variables are used to express the type of an expression, this shows that the expression is polymorphic. Type-variables are not variables in the programming language, nor does the language include a type *type* with type values; type-variables are used merely to introduce polymorphism by representing classes of types. Such an expression cannot be evaluated until all type-variables are resolved; this occurs naturally as the program is compiled or executed. Expressions can be polymorphic, but not values.

A polymorphic procedure in ML may optionally declare parameters with or without type variables. Consider the example NUM_OCC where functions have been substituted for arrays. This function can be written in an ML-style either as

```
NUM_OCC: function (X: function (Y: INTEGER) return α;
                   KEY: α
                   return INTEGER is
        ...
     end NUM_OCC;
```

or as

```
NUM_OCC: function (X; KEY) is
begin
        COUNT := 0;
        for J in 1..100 loop
                if KEY=X(J) then
                        COUNT:=COUNT+1;
                end if;
        end loop;
        return COUNT;
end NUM_OCC;
```

In both cases above, the compiler determines that NUM_OCC is a polymorphic function of type

```
( INTEGER → α ) × α → INTEGER
```

This is so in the second case because KEY must have the same type as X(J) and because the function returns COUNT. Often the type of a variable can be deduced from its use. ML has adopted the philosophy that declarations should be optional wherever their type can be deduced from context. This convention makes programs more concise. It also leads to a natural way of introducing polymorphism without introducing any new syntax other than type-variables.

ML has a semantic view of polymorphism instead of a syntactic view (based on only macro-like expansion). For example, ML type checks polymorphic procedures before instantiation, and ML allows recursive polymorphic types and procedures. But at run-time there are no polymorphic procedures or values. Before evaluation of an expression all type-variables are replaced with concrete types. This does not prevent the use of polymorphic procedures within other polymorphic procedures; it only requires that the evaluation of every expression have no unresolved type-variables.

A disadvantage of the Milner-style type checking is that polymorphism is based only on type parameters. Array bounds and sizes cannot be used as type parameters. In addition there can be no type parameters that carry along operations. In the examples of the next section, we shall see the consequences. Leivant (1983a) has further developed type inference to include such things as type coercions and overloading.

10.3 Polymorphic Sorted List Example

To illustrate how polymorphic types are used in a variety of languages we present a simple example. The sorted list data abstraction is an ordered set of values. Two important parameters are the type of values to be sorted and the ordering. For example, integers can be sorted in either an ascending or descending sequence, and strings can be ordered by length or dictionary order. We will consider three operations on sorted lists.

> *emptylist*()   Creates an empty sorted list.
> *add*(v, sl)   Adds a new value v to the sorted list sl.
> *traverse*(sl, p) Applies procedure p to each value of the sorted list sl.

The polymorphic sorted list type has two parameters: the type of the values to be sorted, which we will call VTYPE, and the ordering operation, which has two parameters of type VTYPE and returns a Boolean value. Let the symbol "$\leq$" represent the ordering operation. It must have the properties of a total ordering relation, namely, for all a, b, and c,

> $a \leq b$ and $b \leq c$ implies $a \leq c$
> $a \leq b$ and $b \leq a$ implies $a = b$
> $a \leq b$ or $b \leq a$

The ordering operation is a parameter of the sorted list data abstraction. To work properly, it must have these attributes, but there is no practical system today that can automatically enforce these requirements. Recent work on Clear (by Burstall and Goguen 1977), Larch Shared Language (by Guttag and Horning 1983), and OBJ2 (by Goguen 1984) explore promising systems that will automate such enforcements.

A major issue that we will encounter in our examples is how and where to specify the *ordering* parameter. If the language allows parameterized data abstractions this may be a straightforward issue. In those languages that do not have parameterized types, the ordering operation can be passed as a parameter to one of the three operations. Intuitively the *add* operation is the only operation that requires use of the ordering operation and so it may seem that we should pass the ordering operation as a third parameter to *add*. But this turns out to be the worst place to pass the ordering operation. This is because there is no way we could guarantee that the same ordering operation is passed every time that *add* is called. If different ordering operations are passed, a mixed list will be created. To make the sorted list more robust it is better to pass the ordering operation to either the *emptylist* or *traverse* procedures. Passing the ordering operation to *traverse* implies that we do not store the data in a sorted manner. Instead we sort the data every time we traverse the data. An advantage is that we can traverse the same list with different orderings. Passing the ordering operation to *emptylist* means that we cannot change the ordering until the next empty list. In exchange, we can implement more efficient sorting methods, and *traverse* does not need to sort the data every time it is called. In the implementations below we shall pass the ordering operation to the *emptylist* procedure whenever we cannot make it a parameter of the data abstraction.

PL/I or C Style of Sorted List

Our first implementation of the sorted list will be in a C-like or PL/I-like language with untyped pointers. These languages do not have polymorphic types, but a good resemblance to polymorphism can be achieved by using untyped pointers to represent arbitrary types and passing the ordering operation to the *emptylist* procedure. As in previous examples, we shall use the name ANY to represent untyped pointers. This implementation requires that all sorted list values be pointers to values. We shall also use a variable-oriented abstraction since this is compatible with the programming style of these languages.

```
adt SORTED_LISTS is

    type ORDERING is function (X,Y: ANY) return BOOLEAN;

    type SORTED_LIST is
        record
            ORDER: ORDERING;
            VALUES: ANY_LIST;
        end record;
```

```
type ANY_LIST is pointer
    record
        FIRST: ANY;
        REST: ANY_LIST;
    end record;

EMPTYLIST: procedure (SL: out SORTED_LIST;
                        ORDER_OPER: ORDERING) is
begin
  SL.ORDER := ORDER_OPER;
  SL.VALUES := null;
end EMPTYLIST;

ADD: procedure (V: ANY; SL: in out SORTED_LIST) is
  T: ANY_LIST;
begin
  if SL.VALUES= null then
    SL.VALUES = new ANY_LIST(V, null);
  else
    T:= SL.VALUES;
    while T ≠ null loop
      if SL.ORDER(V, T.FIRST) then
          T.REST := new ANY_LIST(T.FIRST, T.REST);
          T.FIRST := V;
          return;
      end if;
      PREV := T;
      T:= T.REST;
    end loop;
    PREV.REST := new ANY_LIST(V, null );
  end if;
end ADD;

TRAVERSE: procedure (SL: SORTED_LIST;
                        PROC: procedure (X:ANY)) is
  T: ANY_LIST;
begin
  T:= SL.VALUES;
  while T ≠ null loop
    PROC(T.FIRST);
    T := T.REST;
  end loop;
end TRAVERSE;
```

end adt SORTED_LISTS;

In this example, the ANY type is a pointer to an arbitrary value. The operation on ANY values include pointer comparison (really just comparison with NULL) and pointer assignment. Operations on the value pointed to by ANY is just ORDER.

Note that since this is not a macro implementation, only one copy of each procedure is compiled, not one for each kind of sorted list. Also, the compiler performs no type checking, nor is any type checking provided at run-time. For example, the following segment that uses the sorted list procedures has a type error that will not be caught by typical PL/I compilers:

```
type INT_NODE is ...      -- an element of an integer
                          -- sorted list
type STR_NODE is ...      -- an element of a string
                          -- sorted list

INT_ELEM: INT_NODE;       -- an integer node

INT_LIST: SORTED_LIST;    -- an integer sorted list
STR_LIST: SORTED_LIST;    -- a string sorted list

ADD(INT_ELEM, STR_LIST);  -- a type error that will not
                          -- be detected by PL/I
```

Ada Style

We next consider languages with polymorphic data abstractions and a syntactic view of polymorphism. Ada is a good example of such a language, which requires explicit instantiation of polymorphic types and procedures. Unlike PL/I, Ada has complete type checking and allows the ordering operation to be a parameter of the abstraction rather than an operation. Also unlike PL/I, Ada does not require that values be pointers. An Ada-style sorted list would look something like:

```
generic type VTYPE is private;
    with function "<" (X,Y: VTYPE)
                        return BOOLEAN is "<";
package SORTED_LISTS is

    type SORTED_LIST is pointer
        record
            FIRST: VTYPE;
            REST: SORTED_LIST;
        end record;

    EMPTYLIST: procedure (SL: out SORTED_LIST) is
    begin
        SL := null;
    end EMPTYLIST;

    ADD: procedure (V: VTYPE;
                    SL: in out SORTED_LIST) is
        TEMP: SORTED_LIST;
    begin
        ...
    end ADD;
```

```
TRAVERSE: procedure (SL: SORTED_LIST;
                        PROC: procedure (X:VTYPE)) is
        ...
    end TRAVERSE;

end package SORTED_LISTS;
```

To use the above polymorphic abstraction is a little awkward. First, each instantiation must be made explicit using the new construct as follows:

```
package S_SORTED_LISTS is new SORTED_LISTS(STRING,
                                          S_ORDERING);
package I_SORTED_LISTS is new SORTED_LISTS(INTEGER,
                                          I_ORDERING);
```

Each of the instantiated packages comes with three operations that are accessed by prepending the package name to the operation name. Thus the *add* operation of the S_SORTED_LISTS package is called S_SORTED_LISTS.ADD. This approach can be improved by renaming the operations and overloading them. The following two declarations rename the ADD operation of the two instantiated packages back to ADD:

```
ADD: procedure (V:INTEGER;
                SL: I_SORTED_LISTS.SORTED_LIST)
        renames I_SORTED_LISTS.ADD;

ADD: procedure (V:STRING;
                SL: S_SORTED_LISTS.SORTED_LIST)
        renames S_SORTED_LISTS.ADD;
```

Now the programmer can use the name ADD as a typical polymorphic procedure.

This cumbersome set of statements to instantiate and rename operators is not typical of most languages with polymorphic data abstractions. Usually, instantiation may be automated and operator names are automatically overloaded. Such automation is easier to accomplish if the language adopts a semantic view of polymorphism. Unfortunately, such automation makes the system less flexible. With Ada-style renaming, an existing data abstraction can be easily fitted into an existing application by simply renaming packages and operations.

ML style

We next consider the Milner style of polymorphism as exemplified by the ML language. In this language, declarations need not be used if they can be determined from context, although in our example we declare everything. Because the type checking algorithm is based on unification, polymorphic types can have only type parameters; it cannot handle nontype parameters such as bounds and operators. So, as in the PL/I style, we must pass the *ordering* operation to the *emptylist* procedure. To be compatible with the previous examples, we do not use the syntax of ML, nor the spirit of ML that would encourage a value-oriented implementation.

```
adt SORTED_LISTS is

    type ORDERING (vtype:TYPE) is
        function (X,Y: vtype) return BOOLEAN;

    type SORTED_LIST (vtype:TYPE) is
        record
            ORDER: ORDERING (vtype);
            VALUES: LIST (vtype);
        end record;

    type LIST (vtype:TYPE) is pointer
        record
            FIRST: vtype;
            REST: LIST (vtype);
        end record;

    EMPTYLIST: procedure (SL: out SORTED_LIST (vtype);
                          O: ORDERING (vtype)) is
    begin
        SL.ORDER := O;
        SL.VALUES :=  null;
    end EMPTYLIST;

    ADD: procedure (V: vtype;
                    SL: in out SORTED_LIST(vtype)) is
        ...
    end ADD;

    TRAVERSE: procedure (SL: SORTED_LIST (vtype);
                         PROC: procedure (X:vtype)) is
        ...
    end TRAVERSE;

end adt SORTED_LISTS;
```

The ML style has much in common with the PL/I style. They have similar data structures because both must incorporate the *ordering* operation as part of the value rather than part of the data type like the Ada style. Both have implicit instantiation. However, there is a major semantic difference. Whereas the PL/I style does no type checking, either at compile-time or at run-time, the ML style does complete compile-time type checking. This difference is best observed by noting the use of ANY and type in both examples. The ML style is based on a semantic view of polymorphism and so type checking is performed before any instantiations. This differs from the

Ada style, which is based on a syntactic view of polymorphism. It is possible to have a combination of the last two styles. For example, Russell has implicit instantiation, is based on a semantic view, and allows operators to be a parameter to polymorphic types.

Exercises

1. Extend the sorted lists examples by adding the *delete* operator.
2. Design and implement a polymorphic set type. Define the operations *emptyset, insert,* and *member.* What operation(s) are needed with the type parameter? How can these operation(s) be passed to the data abstraction in a PL/I-style or ML-style language?
3. What types can we infer about the variables in each of the following expressions?

```
F(A, F(5, true))

G: function (X, Y) is
begin
        if Y = null then
                return X;
        else
                return APP(FIR(X), G(TA(X), Y));
        end if;
end G;
```

4. Consider the type of the following expression:

```
X(X);
```

Does x have a type? What type properties can we infer about x?

Further Reading

Gehani and Gries (1977) discuss problems with polymorphic types. Various forms of polymorphism have been tried in a number languages, notably Ada, Alphard (Wulf et al. 1976), EL1 (Wegbreit, 1974), ML (Gordon et al., 1978, 1979), HOPE (Burstall et al., 1980), Russell (Demers et al., 1978), and POLY (Harland, 1984). Mitchell and Wegbreit (1978) introduced Schemes as type-parameterized definitions. Thatcher et al. (1979) and Ganzinger (1983) discuss parameterized types in the context of algebraic specifications.

Hindley (1969) used the unification algorithms developed by Robinson (1965) to determine the principal typing of expressions. Milner (1978) further developed this notion, which has been used in ML and HOPE;

further work on polymorphic type inference has been done by Damas and Milner (1982), Leivant (1983a), Mitchell (1984), McCracken (1984), and many others.

The semantics of polymorphism has been a recent area of interest and is discussed by MacQueen and Sethi (1982), Coppo (1983), Taghva (1983), Reynolds (1983), Leivant (1983b), and more recently at the 6th session of the POPL, 1984; see Wand (1984), MacQueen et al. (1984), and Mitchell (1984). Lambda calculus models are often used in such work since lambda calculus provides a simple but nontrivial notation for exploring different polymorphism semantics; see Barendregt (1981), Meyer (1982), Reynolds (1984), and Bruce and Meyer (1984). Burstall and Goguen (1977), Guttag and Horning (1983), Bert (1983), and Goguen (1984) discuss the issues involved in the formalization of properties of passed operations of type parameters.

Data Type Specifications

PART
IV

PART

IV

Data Type
Specifications

*S*pecifications

This chapter introduces methods for defining data types. Specifications are written for many purposes. First, a specification says exactly what and how a data type behaves. This information enables a programmer to implement the data type, and it enables users to use the data type. Second, a specification provides a means for checking the correctness of a data type implementation, through either testing or formal verification. Third, a specification may provide a means for the automatic implementation of data types.

The two most important qualities of specifications are precision and communication. Specifications must be precise and unambiguous so that they are difficult to misunderstand or misinterpret. Natural language is easily misunderstood and can be ambiguous, whereas a formal language can be made precise and unambiguous. However, it is equally important that specifications be easy to read. Specifications are used to communicate between people; both the user and the implementor must easily grasp their meaning. Natural language is easier to read but not precise, and most formal languages are precise but difficult to read. These two conflicting goals are not unique to data type specifications, and they present a challenge to the computer science community.

Related to the work in data type specifications is the work on program specifications and formalisms for defining the semantics of programming languages. Besides a natural language approach we shall briefly examine operational, axiomatic, denotational, and algebraic approaches to specification. *Operational semantics* is a general term used to refer to one technique for the definition of programming languages. The technique is based on a procedural description of the language. Usually an abstract machine or interpreter is defined and the programming language is defined in terms of actions on the abstract machine. This is a natural approach since the definition can closely model the actual implementation of the programming language. Examples include the Vienna Definition Language (Lucas et al., 1968; Wegner, 1972) and SEMANOL (Anderson et al., 1976). This general approach is also applicable to program specification.

A logical (or axiomatic) approach pioneered by Floyd and Hoare has given us an implementation-independent way of specifying the behavior of a program. This approach defines the semantics of a programming language by using axioms that specify the behavior of programming language constructs. Input and output assertions specify a program. These assertions can be proven consistent with a program by using the axiomatic definition of the programming language. The denotational approach developed by Scott gives a mathematical description of programming languages and is based on recursive domain equations. This approach constructs functions that map programs into a semantic domain. One can also use a denotational-like approach in defining programs and data abstractions. The algebraic approach is similar to axiomatic semantics in its use of axioms. In this chapter we give brief examples of all these approaches. We then fully develop the algebraic approach and give larger examples of its use for defining data types.

11.1   Example Specification of an Editor

As our example, we choose a text editor with a few simple commands. The editor *edits* a file, which is a linear sequence of records. Records are considered primitive data objects and are not defined in further detail. In fact, the editor example could be considered a polymorphic type in which *record* is a type parameter. Editor commands change the file by inserting, replacing, and deleting records. Commands operate on the *current record*, which is a particular record of the file. In the English and operational specifications, the file is an implicit parameter to each editor command. In the functional and algebraic specifications, the file is an explicit parameter.

11.2   English Specifications

The English specification of the editor is given by a list of commands with a brief, one-sentence description. The exceptions are given separately to simplify the description of each operation.

Operations

NewFile: Initialize; create an empty file with no current record.

Insert(NewRecord): Insert NewRecord after the current record and make the NewRecord the current record.

Replace(NewRecord): Replace the current record with NewRecord.

Delete: Delete the current record and the following record becomes the current record.

Advance: Make the next record the current record

Back: Make the previous record the current record

Copy(*m,n*): Copy by inserting *m* records (beginning with the current record) after record *n*.

Exceptions

Operation	Condition	Action
Delete	no current record	no action
Back	no current record	no action
Replace	no current record	no action
Advance	no current record	first record becomes current record
Delete	current record is last record	previous record becomes current record
Advance	current record is last record	no action
Back	current record is first record	no current record

11.3 *Operational Specifications*

Operational specifications *implement* the data abstraction in a high-level language and ignore efficiency issues. This implementation is not to be regarded as a model of the real implementation but only as a model of the data abstraction. In the following specification a file is represented as an array (of indefinite length) of records.

```
File: array [1.. ] of record;
FileLength: integer;
Current: integer;

NewFile:
    FileLength = 0;
    Current = 0;

Insert(NewRecord):
        for j from FileLength to Current+1 by −1 loop
            File[j+1] = File[j];
            end loop;
        File[Current+1] = NewRecord;
        FileLength = FileLength + 1;
        Current = Current + 1;
```

Replace(NewRecord):
    if Current ≠ 0 *then*
        File[Current] = NewRecord;

Delete:
    if Current ≠ 0 *then*
        for j *from* Current *to* FileLength − 1 *loop*
            File[j] = File[j + 1];
        end loop;
        FileLength = FileLength − 1;
        if Current ⟩ FileLength *then*
            Current = FileLength;

Advance:
    if Current ≠ FileLength *then*
        Current = Current + 1;

Back:
    if Current ≠ 0 *then*
        Current = Current − 1;

Copy(m,n):
    ...

11.4 *Logical Specifications*

Logical specifications use input and output assertions written in predicate calculus to describe the conditions before and after execution of statements, procedures, and programs. If the input assertion is true before execution of the program, then the output assertion is desired to be true after the execution of the program. Program variables are normally used to represent input and output values. In this specification the variable File is a flexible array of records (indexed by one) and Current is an index into File representing the current record (as in the last specification). Similarly, FileLength represents the current number of records in the file. As in the last specification the variables File, Current, and FileLength should be considered as an abstract model of the edited file. $File_0$ and $Current_0$ are the values of the variables before execution of any editor command. The input assertion is the same for all editor commands and is thus labeled as an invariant assertion, so only the output assertions are given for each command.

File:array [1..] of record;
FileLength:integer;
Current:integer;
NewRecord:record   —parameter to Insert and Replace

Invariant Assertion: $0 \leq$ Current $\leq$ FileLength

Output Assertions

NewFile:

    Current$=0 \wedge$ FileLength$=0$

Insert:

    Current $=$ Current$_0 \wedge$ FileLength $=$ FileLength$_0+1$

        $\wedge$ ($\forall$ j) ((j$\langle$Current $\rightarrow$ File(j) $=$ File$_0$(j))

            $\wedge$ (j$=$Current $\rightarrow$ File(j)$=$NewRecord)

            $\wedge$ (j$\rangle$Current $\rightarrow$ File(j) $=$ File$_0$(j-1)))

Replace:

    Current $=$ Current$_0 \wedge$ FileLength $=$ FileLength$_0$

        $\wedge$ ($\forall$ j) ((j $=$ Current $\rightarrow$ File(j)$=$NewRecord)

           $\wedge$ (j $\neq$ Current $\rightarrow$ File(j) $=$ File$_0$(j)))

Delete:

    (Current $=$ Current$_0 = 0 \wedge$ File $=$ File$_0$

     $\wedge$ FileLength $=$ FileLength$_0$)

  $\vee$ (((Current$_0 =$ FileLength $\wedge$ Current $=$ Current$_0 - 1$)

           $\vee$ (Current$_0 \neq$ FileLength$_0 \wedge$ Current $=$ Current$_0$))

    $\wedge$ FileLength $=$ FileLength$_0-1$

    $\wedge$ ($\forall$ j) ((j$\langle$ Current$_0 \rightarrow$ File(j)$=$ File$_0$ (j))

           $\wedge$ (j$\geq$ Current$_0 \rightarrow$ File(j)$=$ File$_0$(j$+1$))))

Advance:

    File$=$ File$_0 \wedge$ Filelength $=$ FileLength$_0$

        $\wedge$ (Current$=$ Current$_0 =$ FileLength$_0$

         $\vee$ (Current$_0 \neq$ FileLength$_0 \wedge$ Current$=$ Current$_0 +1$))

Back:

    File$=$ File$_0 \wedge$ FileLength $=$ FileLength$_0 \wedge$ (Current$=$ Current$_0 =0$

        $\vee$ (Current$_0 \neq 0 \wedge$ Current$=$ Current$_0-1$)

Copy (m,n):

$\quad$ File = File$_0$ $\wedge$ FileLength = FileLength$_0$ $\wedge$ Current = Current$_0$

$\quad$ $\wedge$ (n$\rangle$FileLength$_0$ $\vee$ Current$_0$ +m $\rangle$ FileLength$_0$ $\vee$ Current$_0$ = 0)

$\quad$ $\vee$ (n$\leq$ FileLength$_0$ $\wedge$ Current$_0$+m$\leq$ FileLength$_0$ $\wedge$ Current$_0$ $\neq$0

$\qquad$ $\wedge$ FileLength = FileLength$_0$+m

$\qquad$ $\wedge$ (Current = Current$_0$ $\wedge$ n$\geq$Current

$\qquad\qquad$ $\vee$ Current = Current$_0$+m $\wedge$ n$\langle$Current)

$\qquad$ $\wedge$ ($\forall$j)((j$\leq$n $\rightarrow$ File(j) = File$_0$(j))

$\qquad\qquad$ $\wedge$ (n$\langle$j$\leq$n+m $\rightarrow$ File(j) = File$_0$(Current+j−n+1))

$\qquad\qquad$ $\wedge$ (j$\rangle$n+m $\rightarrow$ File (j) = File$_0$(j+m))))

11.5 *Functional Specifications*

Functional specifications describe the behavior of functions by constructing a mathematical function that precisely describes input and output relationships. Unlike operational specifications, which describe a specific method to *compute* the output from the input, functional specifications only need to describe the output in terms of the input. Functional specifications use traditional mathematical constructions such as sets, functions, and sequences for representing objects. A program is viewed as a function from input to output and is described as such. Lambda calculus is used to denote functions, and the expression

$\quad a \rightarrow b, c$

means "if *a* then *b* else *c*." The set of all (continuous) functions from set *A* to set *B* is represented by "[*A*→*B*]", cartesian product by "*A* × *B*," and tuples and sequences are represented by angle-bracketed lists of values separated by semicolons (e.g., $\langle a; b \rangle \in A \times B$). In the editor specification, each command is viewed as a function with the file as an explicit parameter. The FILES set is a two-tuple with the first element indicating the current record and the second element a function from natural numbers to RECORDS, which may be a record or *void*.

$\quad$ N = set of all natural numbers
$\quad$ RECORDS = set of all records plus *void*
$\quad$ FILES = N × [N → RECORDS]

$\quad$ m,n,j,p $\in$ N
$\quad$ f $\in$ [N → RECORDS]
$\quad$ r $\in$ RECORDS

$\quad$ NewFile: → FILES
$\quad$ NewFile = $\langle$0, λj.*void*$\rangle$

Replace: RECORDS × FILES → FILES
Replace(r,⟨p; f⟩) = ⟨p; λj.(p=0) → f(j), (p=j)→r, f(j)⟩

Insert: RECORDS × FILES → FILES
Insert(r,⟨p; f⟩) = ⟨p+1;λj.(j≤p) → f(j), (j=p+1)→r, f(j−1)⟩

Delete: FILES → FILES
Delete(⟨p; f⟩) = (p=0) → ⟨p; f⟩, ⟨(f(p+1)=*void*)→p−1,p;
      λj.(j⟨p)→f(j),f(j+1)⟩

Advance: FILES → FILES
Advance(⟨p; f⟩) = ⟨(f(p+1)=*void*) → p, p+1 ; f⟩

Back: FILES → FILES
Back(⟨p; f⟩) = ⟨(p=0) → p, p−1; f⟩

Copy: N × N × FILES → FILES
Copy(m,n,⟨p; f⟩) = (f(n)=*void* or f(p+m−1)=*void*) → ⟨p; f⟩,
             ⟨(n⟨p) → p+n, p;
             λj.(j⟨n) → f(j), (n⟨j≤n+m)→f(p+j−n+1),f(j+m)⟩

11.6 *Algebraic Specifications*

Our next specification is the algebraic approach, which is described in much more detail in Chapter 13. The algebraic approach views data types as algebras, and to specify a type one writes down the axioms that describe the algebra. It is convenient to find a canonical form to help write the axioms. The canonical form is a set of expressions that specify all possible values of the data type without duplication. One canonical form for the text editor example is

    Back(… Back(Insert(r_m,…Insert(r_1,NewFile)…)

where r_1, r_2,…, r_m is the sequence of records making up the file, and the number of Backs indicate the current record (from the last record). One additional *hidden* operation is needed to specify this data type, called M. M can be considered as a way of viewing a file as two parts. The first part consists of all records preceding the current record plus the current record. The second part consists of all records following the current record (in reverse order). Another canonical form of a file is thus

    M(Insert(r_n,Insert(r_{n-1},…, Insert(r_1, NewFile)…),
      Insert(r_{n+1}, Insert(r_{n+2},…, Insert(r_m, NewFile)…)

where the file is the sequence $r_1, r_2, ..., r_m$ and the current record is r_n with $0 \le n \le m$. Note that the axioms for the Copy operator have been left as an exercise for those readers who feel that the use of algebraic axioms is simple.

Data Types

FILES = File data type
RECORDS = Record data type
N = Number data type

Operators

NewFile:	$\rightarrow$ FILES
Insert:	RECORDS $\times$ FILES $\rightarrow$ FILES
Replace:	RECORDS $\times$ FILES $\rightarrow$ FILES
Delete:	FILES $\rightarrow$ FILES
Advance:	FILES $\rightarrow$ FILES
Back:	FILES $\rightarrow$ FILES
Copy:	N $\times$ N $\times$ FILES $\rightarrow$ FILES
M:	FILES $\times$ FILES $\rightarrow$ FILES

Axioms

NewFile = M(NewFile,NewFile)

Insert(r,M(x,y)) = M(Insert(r,x),y)

Replace(r,M(Insert(s,x),y)) = M(Insert(r,x),y)
Replace(r,M(NewFile,y)) = M(NewFile,y)

Delete(M(Insert(r,x),y)) = M(x,y)
Delete(M(NewFile,y)) = M(NewFile,y)

Advance(M(x,Insert(r,y))) = M(Insert(r,x),y)
Advance(M(x,NewFile)) = M(x,NewFile)

Back(M(Insert(r,x),y)) = M(x,Insert(r,y))
Back(M(NewFile,y)) = M(NewFile,y)

11.7 Comparison of Specification Methods

Comparing specifications is not easy since it is partly based on subjective criteria. Comparisons of semantic formalisms have been made by Marcotty et al. (1976) and Donahue (1976). Except for English, each of the specification methods imposes a particular viewpoint. English specifications are easy to write because they are adaptable to a wide range of viewpoints and various levels of detail. This flexibility makes English a versatile way of communicating objectives; English fails only when one wants to be precise.

The remaining specifications force a certain perspective on users. Operational specifications describe everything in terms of data structures and algorithms. This approach usually involves more details than one would like. Assertions allow a wide range of views in describing particular objects or data structures. Most often, program variables and data types are used, because it is easier to verify the program. Assertions force the user to look at the entire program from an unusual perspective. The program is viewed as an object, about which assertions are made. The specifications state facts about the program behavior.

Functional specifications also allow a wide range of description. For example, an array can be viewed as a set of ordered pairs, a sequence, or a function. The functional specification forces the viewpoint that a program is a mathematical function. The algebraic approach forces the perspective of a formal system involving axioms and expressions. Axioms are viewed as rewriting rules that manipulate trees of operators. With this perspective, values of new data types are viewed strictly as classes of expressions (or parse trees of operators).

In summary, the four formal methods view programs in very different ways. Operational specifications look at programs as algorithms. Logical specifications look at programs by making assertions about the input and output. Functional specifications look at programs as mathematical functions. And algebraic specifications look at programs as algebras described by axioms.

A specification is complete if the output of a program or function can be determined from the specification for all legitimate inputs. A specification is consistent (unambiguous) if it specifies a unique output for each input of the program. Although completeness and consistency are properties of a particular specification, the specification language has a major impact on the ease with which complete and consistent specifications can be obtained and on how easy it is to determine whether a certain specification is complete or consistent.

Unless English specifications are carefully written it is practically impossible to determine whether they are complete. Their ambiguous nature and the human tendency to read more into a sentence than is written make it unlikely that English will ever be able to give easily recognizable complete specifications. For example, in the editor specifications there is a list of exceptions, which are really not exceptions to the operators, but rather additions to complete the specifications of the operators. If an exception were missing the specification would be incomplete. What is the liklihood that the missing exception would be easily found? It would be discovered when a thorough analysis is made of the editor specifications. A few exceptions have been purposely omitted to illustrate this point. These exceptions can be easily found by examining the functional specification of Copy, but not by simply examining just the English specification. Usually English (or any natural language) is unsuitable for presenting complete specifications. For the same reasons, consistency is equally difficult to determine. If, for example, additional exceptions were added that conflicted with the general operator rules or the other exceptions, which would take precedence?

An operational definition provides an algorithmic way of determining the results of a program or function. Just as with real programs, an operational specification is usually complete and consistent because there is only one way to interpret a program. Occasionally one may find an operational specification that does have holes in it because of *execution errors*, such as division by zero, or logic errors that lead to infinite loops and thus do not provide any answer. In the operational specification of the editor, suppose the array of records did have an upper bound. What would happen if the upper bound was exceeded and subscript-out-of-range errors occurred? We should have to conclude that the operational specification was incomplete.

Logical specifications are notorious for being incomplete (for example, see Gerhart and Yelowitz, 1976). The classic example is the sorted array specification that only asserts that the resulting array is in ascending sequence. It is incomplete because it does not specify the relationship between the output array and the original unsorted input array. It is easy to see some of the reasons why assertions cause problems. Consider the assertion "$(P(x)$ and $A(x))$ or $B(x)$," where predicates A and B specify the output values and predicate P specifies some condition. The intent is that A should occur when P is true and B otherwise. However, the way it is written, B could always occur. The correct assertion is "$(P(x)$ and $A(x))$ or (not $P(x)$ and $B(x))$." It's too easy to forget to add "not $P(x)$." Inconsistent assertions seldom occur, but when they do the result is that the output assertion is always false, a condition for which no program can be written.

Unlike the logical method, the functional method specifies the output values directly in terms of the input values, rather than indirectly with assertions. Like operational specifications, the functional specifications are unlikely to produce inconsistent specifications. Additionally, functional specifications are unlikely to be incomplete because one specifies the output for an arbitrary input value. For example, the sorted array assertion example forgot about the input values, something that would not happen in either operational or functional specifications.

Determining the completeness of an algebraic specification in general is difficult (Guttag, 1975). Trying to describe the algebraic axioms for the set data type is a good example. One can keep coming up with more axioms describing sets and after a while one is unsure when no more axioms are needed. The method commonly used to aid in the completion of a set of axioms is to think of some canonical form of all objects (using just constructor operators) and then define axioms that will reduce all expressions with other operators to canonical forms. Inconsistency occurs when axioms lead to the result that two objects are equivalent when they should have been different. This problem is sometimes detected when "true" becomes equivalent to "false" in the Boolean data type.

Exercises

1. Consider the editor example. Add the operations "top," which moves to the first record of a file, and "exchange," which swaps the current record with the next record. Extend the five specifications to include these two operations. Compare the five additions that you made; which specifications were easy to write?

2. The English specification is incomplete. List those things that are missing from the English specification. Missing information from the Copy operator is suggested by the following questions. What if there are fewer than n records in the file? What if there are fewer than m records after the current record? Does the current record change after a Copy command? Is the file one-indexed or zero-indexed?

Mathematics of Data Types

In Chapter 1 we investigated the definition of a data type using a mix of English and mathematics. But a better and more precise definition is necessary so that questions involving type checking, polymorphism, specification, and correctness issues can be discussed consistently. As with most disciplines, a mathematical foundation provides the right descriptive tools that allow a rigorous definition of data types. Such a foundation should provide insight into the darker corners of data types, such as clarifying the syntactic and semantic issues involved in polymorphism, type checking, and correctness. Many mathematical models have been proposed for data types. In this book we examine in detail the most common approach, sometimes called an *algebraic* approach. It can be characterized as *operator-driven* since it places an emphasis on the operators of a type. An alternative approach is based on *domains*, which simply means a set. This second approach can be characterized as *value-driven* because it is most concerned with the issue of the set of values of a data type. Operations on the values are considered a secondary issue. Despite the different starting points, both approaches tend to end at the same place, namely that a data type is an *algebra*—a set of values and a set of operations on those values.

12.1 Algebras and Data Types

Before developing the mathematics of the algebraic approach, we will give an intuitive outline of the approach. The algebraic approach is oriented around the operations of a data type, so we will first examine the operations and then the values. Operations are denoted by operator symbols and include zero-ary operators called constants. Given a collection of operator symbols, we can construct the set of all possible expressions, called the word algebra. The word algebra defines the scope or extent of all possible values of the data type. The word algebra gives us the syntax of data types. To describe the semantics, we merely need to describe which expressions have the same value. This is done by specifying a congruence relation on the word algebra.

12.2 Signatures: The Syntax of Data Types

A *sort* is a name of a data type. The algebraic approach distinguishes between the sort (which is a name or symbol) and a data type (which is an algebra). *Operators*, perhaps more properly called *operation symbols*, are symbols used to represent operations. The *arity* of an operator specifies the sorts of all the operands and the sort of the value returned by the operator. *Constants* are operators with no operands, that is, constants are zero-ary operators. The notation used for specifying the arity of an operator σ with n operands of sorts s_1, s_2, s_n and returning a value of sort s is

$$\sigma: s_1 \times s_2 \times \ldots \times s_n \to s$$

The notation is intended to suggest that the operation represented by σ is a function, but remember that the operator σ is a symbol, not a function. Arity is considered a syntactic notion associated with a symbol rather than a semantic notion associated with a function.

Let S be a set of sorts. An *S-sorted signature* (or simply *signature* when S is understood or unimportant) is a set of operators with arities using sorts only from S. An example of a signature with $S = \{\text{int}\}$ with constants 0 and 1 and binary operators + and * is:

```
0      : → int
1      : → int
+      : int × int → int
*      : int × int → int
```

This is called a 1-sorted signature because there is only one sort. Many-sorted signatures are more typical in computer science. For example, consider the following more realistic signature using sorts int and bool:

```
true       : → bool
false      : → bool
0          : → int
1          : → int
+          : int × int → int
*          : int × int → int
⟩          : int × int → bool
ifthenelse: bool × int × int → int
```

The last operator has three operands, not all of the same sort.

An alternative and more visual description of signatures is the signature diagram. Circles represent sorts and multitailed arcs represent the arity of operators. Unfortunately, signature diagrams do not convey the order of the operands. The signature diagram of the previous signature is given in Figure 12.1.

When using such familiar examples, it is tempting to put too much meaning into a signature. It is tempting to think of the sort "int" as representing the integers, the operator "1" as representing one and the operator

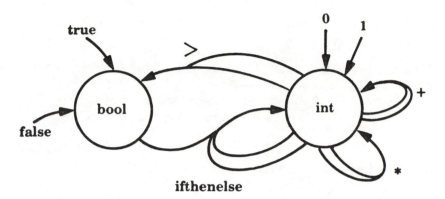

FIGURE 12.1 Signature diagram.

"+" as representing addition. But a signature only describes operators and arities, not operations or values of a type. A signature describes the syntax of data types, not their semantics.

In formulating a mathematical foundation for data types, it is sometimes convenient to ignore certain anomalous examples. For example, some operations (such as maximum and minimum) may take a variable number of arguments, or operations may return more than one value, perhaps by side-effects, such as the pop operation, which changes the stack and returns the top value. A signature does not account for these examples directly. They can be described indirectly, in the first case by either thinking of max(a,b,c) as an abbreviation for max(a,max(b,c)) or thinking of max as taking a single argument that is a list of integers. In the second case, the pop operation can be split into two operations, one for each of the different values returned.

12.3 Terms

Expressions constructed from operators are called *terms*. Constants form terms by themselves. All other operators have operands which are also terms. The formal notation for terms is defined as follows:

For constant $\sigma: \to s$, the expression "σ" is a term.

For operator $\sigma: s_1 \times s_2 \times \ldots \times s_n \to s$
  and terms t_i of sorts s_i (for $1 \le i \le n$),
  the expression "$\sigma(t_1,\ldots,t_n)$" is a term.

Examples of terms from the previous signature are

1
+(0,1)
ifthenelse($\rangle$(0,1), +(1,1),1)

Note that "+($\rangle$(0,0),0)" and "ifthenelse(0,0,0)" are *not* terms, since the definition of term includes type checking.

A grammar that will generate all terms can be easily constructed from a signature. Each sort is replaced with a nonterminal. Each operator,

$\qquad \sigma: s_1 \times \dots \times s_n \to s \qquad$ (with $n\rangle 0$),

is replaced with the production

$\qquad s \to \sigma(\ s_1,\dots,\ s_n)$

and each constant "$\sigma: \to s$" is replaced with the production

$\qquad s \to \sigma$

The grammar formed from the previous example signature is thus:

bool	$\to$ true
bool	$\to$ false
int	$\to$ 0
int	$\to$ 1
int	$\to$ +(int,int)
int	$\to$ *(int,int)
bool	$\to$ $\rangle$(int,int)
int	$\to$ ifthenelse(bool,int,int)

Note that without constants there can be no terms.

Because the formal notation for terms is not always readable, we will often resort to informal notation without any fanfare. For example, the + operator is usually an infix operator and so it is easier to read and write as "(0+1)" instead of "+(0,1)". Likewise, "if true then 0 else 1" is more conventional than "ifthenelse(true,0,1)". We will take other syntactic liberties, such as dropping parentheses to the point of causing possible ambiguity, for example writing "0+1*0" instead of "(0+(1*0))". Note that "0+0+0" is ambiguous since 0 and + are just syntactic symbols and the expression can be parsed in two ways, possibly resulting in two different meanings (e.g., associativity is a property of operations, not operators). In such cases we rely on traditional precedence rules to resolve any ambiguities. We are most interested in the syntactic structure of a term, not the syntactic sugar. In all cases we assume an unambiguous parse of an informally written term. Terms should be thought of as parse trees rather than strings of symbols.

Let Σ be any S-sorted signature. The set of all terms of sort s will be denoted as *terms*(s,Σ). This is the language generated by the grammar with

s as the start symbol. This set of terms, the set of all expressions with sort s, is sometimes called the Herbrand universe. It plays a prominent role in algebraic specifications. When the signature is understood we use the abbreviation *terms(s)* to denote the set of all terms of sort s.

12.4 Polymorphic Types

We are often interested in a whole class of types with similar operations. For example, we may consider the three types *set of integers*, *set of characters*, and *set of sets of integers* as instances of the polymorphic type, set(Z), pronounced "set of Z." To simplify the mathematics in this chapter, we adopt the simple syntactic view of polymorphism. So the specification of polymorphic types is like that of nonpolymorphic types. The following is an example of a signature for the *set* polymorphic type:

emptyset	$: \rightarrow \text{set}(Z)$
insert	$: Z \times \text{set}(Z) \rightarrow \text{set}(Z)$
union	$: \text{set}(Z) \times \text{set}(Z) \rightarrow \text{set}(Z)$
member	$: Z \times \text{set}(Z) \rightarrow \text{bool}$

Each operator symbol is ambiguous (or overloaded) since it may represent any of several operators. If the ambiguity cannot be resolved from context, a subscript will be added to the operator, for example, emptyset$_{\text{int}}$ is a constant of sort *set(int)*.

12.5 Algebras: The Semantics of Data Types

Let Σ be an S-sorted signature. Then a Σ-*algebra* α is a family of sets

$$A = \{ A_s \mid s \in S \}$$

and a set of operations

$$\{ \sigma_\alpha \mid \sigma \in \Sigma \}$$

such that if $\sigma: s_1 \times \ldots \times s_n \rightarrow s$ then

$$\sigma_\alpha: A_{s_1} \times \ldots \times A_{s_n} \rightarrow A_s$$

A_s is called the *carrier* for sort s. Observe that σ is an operator and σ_α is an operation. The operator σ is used, for example, to construct terms of sort s from terms of sort s_1 through s_n, whereas σ_A is a function from sets A_{s_1} thru A_{s_n} to the set A_s . Although we shall refine our concept of data type later in this section, we can initially think of each A_s as the set of values of type s.

To simplify the example below we use only a 1-sorted signature. Let the signature Σ be the simple one we have used before:

```
0      : → int
1      : → int
+      : int × int → int
*      : int × int → int
```

Next, consider the following six Σ-algebras.

1. The carrier is {0,1,2,3,...}, where the operator 0 represents the number 0, 1 represents the number 1, + represents addition, and * represents multiplication.

2. The carrier is the set of real numbers, 0 represents zero, 1 represents one, + represents addition, and * represents multiplication.

3. The carrier is terms(int), (i.e., the Herbrand universe), 0 represents the term "0", 1 represents "1", the operator + represents the concatenation of the strings "+(", first operand, ",", second operand, and ")". Similarly, if x and y are the operands, * represents "*(x,y)".

4. The carrier is {0,1}, 0 represents the number 0, 1 represents the number 1, + represents addition modulo 2, and * represents multiplication.

5. The carrier is {0}, 0 and 1 both represent the number 0, + represents addition, and * represents multiplication.

6. The carrier is {a,b}* (i.e., the set of all strings consisting of a's and b's), 0 represents "a", 1 represents "b", and + and * both represent concatenation.

All six of the above algebras are potential data type candidates for *int*, with the first being the conventional meaning of the symbols we are using. The second is a much larger carrier for the same signature. The third is what a parser or symbolic evaluator night use. The fourth is equivalent to a Boolean algebra, where the symbols might be more appropriately replaced with *false*, *true*, *and*, and *or*. The fifth is a trivial algebra and the sixth is quite arbitrary.

We wish to investigate the relationship between the carrier of sort s of a Σ-algebra and the set of terms(s) for sort s. There is a natural one-to-one correspondence between terms(int) and the carrier of algebra 3 above, simply because they are the same set. Algebra 3 is an example of a special algebra variously called the *free algebra generated by* Σ, an initial Σ-algebra, and the Σ-*word algebra*. So what we really wish to investigate is the relationship between algebra 3 and the others listed above.

Relationships between algebras are succinctly expressed by homomorphisms. We will consider the 1-sorted case; the definition is easily extended to the many-sorted case A *homomorphism* from Σ-algebra α to Σ-algebra β with carriers A and B is a mapping $h:A \to B$ such that all operations (in Σ) are preserved. Constants are preserved if, for each constant σ,

$$h(\sigma_\alpha) = \sigma_\beta.$$

Nonzero-ary operators are preserved if, for each operator σ, and values $v_1 ,..., v_n$ in A,

$$h(\sigma_\alpha (v_1 ,..., v_n)) = \sigma_\beta (h(v_1),...,h(v_n)).$$

One can think of the structure of an algebra as being determined by the operators. A homomorphism preserves the structure of an algebra, and explicitly shows how the structure of one algebra is mapped onto the structure of another algebra. An *isomorphism* is a homomorphism that is one-to-one and onto. Isomorphic algebras have identical structures, but the values of the carriers may have different names. We will often consider isomorphic algebras as being the same, and speak of isomorphism classes of algebras rather than a specific algebra.

Σ-word algebras are important because for any Σ-algebra α, there exists exactly one homomorphism from the word algebra to α. There exists a natural mapping $h_{\alpha,s}$: terms (s) $\rightarrow A_s$ for each sort s (subscripts on h will be dropped when α and s are understood). This unique homomorphism is

for constant σ,
$\quad h(\sigma) = \sigma_\alpha$

for operator σ: $s_1 \times ... \times s_n \rightarrow s$, and terms $t_1 ,..., t_n$ of sorts $s_1 ,..., s_n$,
$\quad h(\sigma(t_1 ,..., t_n)) = \sigma_\alpha (h(t_1),...,h(t_n))$

A value v of a Σ-algebra is called *reachable* if there exists a term t in the word algebra such that

$$h(t) = v$$

where h is the word algebra homomorphism. An *unreachable* value is one that cannot be expressed using the operators of Σ. Only the positive integral values of algebra 2 are reachable; all other elements of algebra 2 are unreachable. All elements of algebras 1, 3, 4, 5, and 6 are reachable. Σ-algebras with unreachable values are not useful in data type applications because the unreachable values are inaccessible to the programmer. So we will exclude Σ-algebras with unreachable elements (or at least ignore the unreachable elements of such an algebra). If we remove the unreachable elements of algebra 2, we get algebra 1.

Two terms x and y are called *equivalent* with respect to a Σ-algebra α with carrier A if and only if $h(x) = h(y)$, where h is the word algebra homomorphism. Equivalent terms imply that the corresponding value in A can be expressed either as x or y. The terms "1+0" and "0+1" are equivalent with respect to algebras 1, 2, 4, and 5, but not for 3 and 6. Note that all terms are equivalent with respect to the trivial algebra 5, but no two different terms in algebra 3 are equivalent. Any two terms that are equivalent with respect to algebra 1 are equivalent with respect to algebra 2.

An equivalence relation is reflexive, symmetric, and transitive. A *congruence relation* is an equivalence relation with the property that (a given set of) operators preserve the relation, i.e., whenever x_i is equivalent to y_i (for $1 \le i \le n$), then $\sigma(x_1, \ldots, x_n)$ is equivalent to $\sigma(y_1, \ldots, y_n)$. Let R be any congruence relation on a 1-sorted Σ-algebra α with carrier A (R is congruent with respect to the operators of Σ). Then the congruence class containing the element x will be denoted

$$[x] = \{ x' \mid R(x,x') \}.$$

Two elements are called *congruent* if they are in the same congruence class. A congruence relation can be viewed as a set of disjoint subsets whose union is A, which is $\{ [x] \mid x \in \{ [x] \mid x \in A \}$ and operations defined as:

> for constant σ,
> $$\sigma_{\alpha/R} = [\sigma_\alpha]$$

> for operator σ: $s_1 \times \ldots \times s_n \to s$, and values $x_1, \ldots, x_n$
> $$\sigma_{\alpha/R}([x_1], \ldots, [x_n]) = [\sigma_\alpha(x_1, \ldots, x_n)]$$

The congruence property of R guarantees that $\sigma_{\alpha/R}$ is well defined. Congruence relations and quotient algebras can be extended in a natural way to the many-sorted case.

The relation "x and y are equivalent terms with respect to Σ-algebra α" is a congruence relation on the set of all terms. The quotient algebra generated by this relation is isomorphic to α. So an alternative method to looking for some Σ-algebra is to look for some congruence relation on the word algebra.

Quotient algebras can be cumbersome to use because the elements are congruence classes. It is more convenient to use a particular element of a congruence class to represent the entire congruence class. A *canonical form* is any subset C of terms(s) such that no two elements of C are in the same congruence class, and every term t in terms(s) is equivalent to some term in C. A *canonical term algebra* uses a canonical form as its carrier. The operations are defined by the natural isomorphism $h(x) = [x]$. The sets $\{0,1\}$ and $\{1,1+1\}$ are canonical forms for algebra 4. The set $\{0, 1, 1+1, 1+(1+1), 1+(1+(1+1)), \ldots \}$ is a canonical form for algebra 1 and 2. The only canonical form for algebra 3 is terms(int) and any singleton set is a canonical form for algebra 5.

We can now state the main thesis of this section: A data type of signature Σ is an isomorphism class of Σ-algebras without unreachable values. Thus, the following are equivalent ways of representing a data type:

1. any Σ-algebra without unreachable values,
2. any congruence relation on the Σ-word algebra,
3. any quotient algebra of the Σ-word algebra,
4. any canonical term algebra.

A canonical form does not necessarily identify a unique data type; an example is given in the next chapter. Canonical forms with appropriate operations make up canonical term algebras that do represent exactly one data type. However, a data type may be represented by more than one canonical term algebra or Σ-algebra. Only, numbers 2 and 3 above represent data types uniquely; that is, each data type is represented by only one congruence relation (or quotient algebra).

Algebras do not fully reflect the properties that we associate with data types. Some of the more important differences are errors, side-effects, and nondeterminism. There are two common approaches to the problem of errors (such as zero division or subscript out of range). One is to introduce error elements in algebras, and the other is to allow operations to be partial functions. Both approaches have been tried, for example, Goguen et al. (1978) add error elements to each sort and provide techniques for writing axioms. Extending operations to partial functions appears easier and more suited for computer science applications, and this approach has been proposed by Majster (1979) and by Broy and Wirsing (1982). Wirsing et al. (1983) persuasively argue that partial functions simplify specifications. They claim that the "necessity to associate a (well-defined) object with every term—even if a term does not make any sense at all—makes specifications lengthy and often obscures the basic algebraic structure."

The algebraic approach also assumes value-oriented data types, thus excluding side-effects. No one has seriously tried to overcome this problem because variable-oriented data types can usually be cast into value-oriented data types without much difficulty. This conversion may, however, require a slight adjustment to the set of operators. Operators with multiple output values are turned into a collection of operators, one for each output value. Nondeterministic operations also cannot be accommodated since an operation returns a fixed value, given its operands. For example, consider a set operation *get* that returns an element of a set that is chosen at random or that is simply implementation dependent. Such an operation cannot be specified in the algebraic framework.

At this point it would be appropriate to give example data types using the algebraic approach. However, the algebraic approach was developed with algebraic specifications as a natural way of expressing data types, so we defer examples to the next chapter.

Exercises

1. Consider the six Σ-algebras of section 12.5. For which algebras are the following terms equivalent?

$1+0$	and	$1+1+1$
$(1+1)+0$	and	$1+(1+0)$

2. Show that Σ-algebra 2 minus the unreachable values is isomorphic to Σ-algebra 1.

3. What are some canonical forms for algebra 6?

4. How might a history sensitive operation be incorporated into the algebraic (or domain) approach? A history sensitive operation is one that computes the return value based on not only the current value of the operand but also previous values passed to the operation. For example, many pseudo random number generators use a static local variable that changes at each call, and that is used to compute the value returned.

5. Given a set of types and polymorphic types one could construct a signature of types (perhaps called a *meta-signature*?). Each nonpolymorphic type is a constant and each polymorphic type is a nonzero-ary operator. For example, consider the types integer, bool, set(Z), and mappings from X to Y, then the type signature is:

int	: → type
bool	: → type
seti	: type → type
mapping	: type × type → type

Construct a signature for the types of Pascal (or your favorite language).

Further Reading

Solutions to recursive domain equations were first solved by Scott in a number of papers (1970, 1976) and presented by Stoy (1977) and Tennent (1976). Domain construction has been primarily used for defining the semantics of programming languages. The algebraic approach in this book is based on the initial algebra approach developed by the ADJ group (Goguen and Thatcher, 1974; Goguen et al. 1975, 1978). Alternative approaches have developed, such as *final algebras* by Wand (1979), and Kamin (1980), also called *terminal algebras* by Hornung and Raulefs (1980).

Algebraic Specifications

In this chapter we introduce a specification technique called *algebraic axioms*, or *axioms* for short. The axioms will specify congruence relations on the word algebra. As was shown in the previous chapter, a congruence relation on the word algebra represents a data type.

13.1 Simple Axioms

A *simple axiom* is a pair of terms x and y of the same sort. The axiom is expressed as

$$x = y$$

To avoid confusion we use the symbol "$\equiv$" to mean that two terms are identically equal (character by character). A congruence relation *satisfies* a set R of axioms if, for each simple axiom $x = y$ in R, x and y are congruent. There may be many congruence relations that satisfy an axiom set. Different viewpoints of algebraic specifications diverge on this point. One viewpoint is that an axiom set should specify the entire class of congruence relations satisfying the axiom set. Another viewpoint is that the axiom set should specify only the smallest such congruence relation that satisfies the axiom set. In this book we adopt the latter viewpoint.

A congruence relation A is *smaller* than congruence relation B if every congruence class of A is contained in some congruence class of B. Thinking of relations as sets of pairs, A is smaller than B simply means that A is a subset of B. The smallest congruence relation satisfying a set R of axioms is called the congruence relation *generated* by R. Since the simple axiom set R can also be thought of as a set of pairs, we can say that R generates the smallest congruence relation containing R. The smallest congruence relation containing R is unique and always exists. The notation

$$x \simeq_R y$$

is used to mean that terms x and y are congruent in the congruence relation generated by R. As usual, the subscript will be dropped when R can be determined from context. We also call x and y *equivalent terms*. We shall also use the notation

$$[x] = \{ y \mid x \simeq y \}$$

to mean the congruence class that term x belongs to. The following inductive definition of $\simeq$ is useful because it shows how to prove terms equivalent with respect to an axiom set R.

$x \simeq y$ if and only if any of the following holds:

Basis: $x = y$ (a simple axiom in R)
Reflexive: $x \equiv y$ (x and y are the same term)
Symmetric: $y \simeq x$
Transitive: There exists a z, such that $x \simeq z$ and $z \simeq y$
Congruence: For some operator σ, $x \equiv \sigma(x_1, ..., x_n)$ and $y \equiv \sigma(y_1, ..., y_n)$
                and for all $0 \leq i \leq n$, $x_i \simeq y_i$

Consider the next signature with constant 0 and unary operator S,

$$0: \rightarrow N$$
$$S: N \rightarrow N$$

and the following axiom sets:

$$R_0 = \{\}$$
$$R_1 = \{0 = 0\}$$
$$R_2 = \{0 = S0\}$$
$$R_3 = \{0 = SS0\}$$
$$R_4 = \{S0 = SS0\}$$

The congruence classes generated by the five axiom sets are:

R_0, R_1 $\{0\}, \{S0\}, \{SS0\}, ...$
R_2 $\{0, S0, SS0, ...\}$
R_3 $\{0, SS0, SSSS0, ...\}, \{S0, SSS0, SSSSS0, ...\}$
R_4 $\{0\}, \{S0, SS0, SSS0, ...\}$

R_0 and R_1 describe the word algebra, because no two different terms are equivalent. R_2 describes the trivial one-element algebra; all terms are equivalent. By the basis $0 \simeq S0$, then by congruence $S0 \simeq SS0$, and by transitivity $0 \simeq SS0$. This process can continue indefinitely $(0 \simeq S0 \simeq SS0 \simeq SSS0 \simeq ...)$. R_3 describes an algebra like the two-element Boolean algebra with the complement operator represented by S. R_4 also describes the two-element Boolean algebra but with S representing a constant function. The set $\{0, S0\}$ is a canonical form for both R_3 and R_4. Note therefore that identical canonical forms do not imply identical congruence relations.

It turns out that any data type with a signature consisting only of a single constant and a single unary operator can be defined with a single simple axiom. Some data types with more complicated signatures cannot be described so easily. Most useful data types require an infinite number of simple axioms. We therefore introduce a more powerful form of axiom.

13.2 Axioms with Variables

A *variable* of sort s is a symbol distinct from all operators. If v_i is a variable of sort s_i (for $1 \leq i \leq n$), then a *term with variables* is any term in which zero or more subterms of sort s_i have been replaced with variable v_i. The notation

$t(v_1, ..., v_n)$

means a term with variables v_1 through v_n; and

$t(t_1, ..., t_n)$

means the same term with every variable v_i replaced with term t_i (where the sort of v_i is the same sort as t_i).

An *axiom* is a pair of terms with variables. As with simple axioms, the equals symbol is used to separate the two terms. A simple axiom is an axiom with zero variables. Every axiom can be expressed with a possibly infinite number of simple axioms obtained by substituting all possible terms of the appropriate sort for variables. For example, the axiom

$r(v_1, ..., v_n) = s(v_1, ..., v_n)$

means the same as the axiom set

$\{ r(t_1, ..., t_n) = s(t_1, ..., t_n) \mid t_i \in \text{terms(sort of } v_i) \}$

We normally use lower-case letters (and occasionally identifiers) for variables. The sort of a variable can usually be determined from context. For easy reference, we will consider the axioms of an axiom set to be ordered and numbered from one in the order of appearance in the axiom set. Consider the signature

$0: \rightarrow N$
$S: N \rightarrow N$
$+: N \times N \rightarrow N$

and the axiom sets

$R_5 = \{ x+0=x, \quad x+Sy=S(x+y) \}$
$R_6 = \{ 0+x=x, \quad Sy+x=S(y+x) \}$
$R_7 = \{ 0+x=x, \quad x+0=x, \quad Sx+Sy=x+y \}$
$R_8 = \{ SSx=x, \quad x+0=0, \quad x+S0=x \}$

R_5 and R_6 specify the same data type, the integers—with the number zero represented by operator 0, successor by S, and addition by +. The successor operation adds one to a number. To show that $SS0+S0 \approx SSS0$, first note that by substituting SS0 for x and 0 for y in axiom 2 of R_5, we obtain the simple axiom $SS0 + S0 = S(SS0 + 0)$, and by substituting $SS0$ for x in the first axiom, we get the axiom $SS0 + 0 = SS0$. Using the property of congruence one can make the appropriate substitution. We can summarize the proof as follows:

$$
\begin{aligned}
SS0 + S0 &\simeq S(SS0 + 0) && \text{by axiom 2} \\
&\simeq S(SS0) && \text{by axiom 1} \\
&\equiv SSS0
\end{aligned}
$$

Using R_6, the proof would be

$$
\begin{aligned}
SS0 + S0 &\simeq S(S0 + S0) && \text{by axiom 2} \\
&\simeq SS(0 + S0) && \text{by axiom 2} \\
&\simeq SS(S0) && \text{by axiom 1} \\
&\equiv SSS0
\end{aligned}
$$

Showing equivalence of terms by rewriting or reducing terms with axioms has led to alternative names for axioms, such as *rewrite rules*, *reduction rules*, and *equations*.

The algebraic structure of the integers leads one to the obvious canonical form $C = \{0, S0, SS0, \ldots\}$ for both R_5 and R_6. To prove that C is a canonical form we show first that all terms are equivalent to one of the canonical terms and second that no two different canonical terms are equivalent. By induction on the axioms, we can show that any term with a $+$ operator can be rewritten or reduced to a term without a $+$ operator. We can also show that the axioms preserve the number of S operators in a term, and that since every two different canonical terms have a different number of S operators, no two canonical terms can be equivalent.

R_7 also describes the integers, but the operator $+$ represents difference rather than sum. Showing C is a canonical form for R_7 is a bit more difficult since the third axiom does not preserve the number of S operators. R_8 describes a two-element Boolean algebra where 0 represents false, S represents complement, and $+$ represents the Boolean *and* operation. Alternatively one can think of R_8 as describing the two-element Boolean algebra where 0 represents true, S represents complement, and $+$ represents the Boolean *or* operation. These two Boolean algebras are isomorphic and thus both are plausible interpretations of R_8.

13.3 Hidden Operators

We now ask the next obvious question: whether a finite number of axioms is sufficiently powerful to describe all data types. Majster was one of the first to investigate this problem. She used the traversable stack example to conclude that finite axiom sets are not powerful enough. This result initiated a long history of correspondence conducted in *SIGPLAN Notices*. The toy stack is a simplified version of the traversable stack (Thatcher et al. 1979). The following is an infinite axiom set specification of the toy stack.

$0: \rightarrow T$ *empty stack*
$E: \rightarrow T$ *error*
$P: T \rightarrow T$ *push*
$D: T \rightarrow T$ *down—look at next value in stack*

$R_9 = \{ DE=E, PE=E, PDx=E \} \cup \{ D^n P^k 0 = E \mid n \rangle k \}$

where D^n is a shorthand notation for DDDD... n times. The set of congruence classes generated by R_9 is $\{ \{ D^n P^k 0 \} \mid n \leq k \} \cup \{\{E,D0,DE,PE,...\}\}$ and thus a natural canonical form is $\{ D^n P^k 0 \mid n \leq k \} \cup \{E\}$.

There is no finite axiom set for the toy stack; see Thatcher et al. (1979) for a proof. This stumbling block is removed with hidden operators.

A hidden operator is a new operator added to the signature for the sole purpose of specification. It is hidden or inaccessible to the user of the data type. The signature of the data type is unchanged for all practical purposes (except for the practical purpose of specification). With hidden operators one can define with a finite number of axioms any computable data type (Guttag, 1980). For example, the toy stack can be specified with one hidden operator that we call H. In the following specification and future ones, hidden operators will be marked with asterisks.

    $0: \rightarrow T$
    $E: \rightarrow T$
    $P: T \rightarrow T$
    $D: T \rightarrow T$
* $H: T \rightarrow T$

$R_{10} = \{$ $DE=E, PE=E, HE=E, D0=E,$
               $PDx=E, PHx=E,$
               $DHx=HDx,$
               $DP0=H0,$
               $DPPx=HPx \}$

With hidden operators comes the need to clarify some definitions. Given a signature Σ, a superset $\Sigma' = \Sigma \cup \{$hidden operators$\}$, and a set of axioms R for Σ', the congruence relation generated by R will be restricted to the set of congruence classes

$A = \{ [t] \mid t \in \text{terms}(\Sigma',s) \}$

rather than

$A' = \{ [t] \mid t \in \text{terms}(\Sigma',s) \}$

The congruence class $[t]$ is defined as before:

$[t] = \{ t' \mid t' \simeq t \}$

There may not be a difference between A and A' but when there is one, it means there exists a congruence class in A' where every term has at least one hidden operator. Thus, this congruence class is *unreachable* and is not considered a value of the data type.

13.4 Conditional Axioms

Some formulations of algebraic axioms use yet another kind of axiom. Two common forms of conditional axioms are:

$p = $ if q then r else s
$(q) => p=r$

where p, r and s are terms of the same sort and q is a Boolean term. The *if then else* construction is not an operator in this formulation, but a construct that means that p is equivalent to r if q is true, otherwise p is equivalent to s. The meaning of the second form of conditional axiom is that p is equivalent to r if q is true. Both of the above conditional forms can be easily duplicated with the ifthenelse operator. If the ifthenelse operator is not available, then it can be added as a hidden operator. The second form is achieved with the axiom

$p = $ ifthenelse(q,r,p)

or as the more readable version

$p = $ if q then r else p

Whenever necessary we will assume the possible hidden operator ifthenelse for each sort Z. The axioms for ifthenelse are:

$R_{11} = \{$
    if true then x else $y = x$,
    if false then x else $y = y \}$

13.5 Extensions and Enrichments

An *algebraic specification* contains five parts:

1. the name of the specification,
2. a list of sorts,
3. a signature,
4. a list of variables and their sorts,
5. a list of axioms.

A specification describes a set of data types. The congruence relations generated by the axioms for each sort specify data types. A specification of the Boolean data type will illustrate the format that we have adopted.

Name: FirstExample
Sorts: Bool
Operators:

true:	$\rightarrow$ Bool
false:	$\rightarrow$ Bool
ifthenelse:	Bool $\times$ Bool $\times$ Bool $\rightarrow$ Bool
not:	Bool $\rightarrow$ Bool
and:	Bool $\times$ Bool $\rightarrow$ Bool
or:	Bool $\times$ Bool $\rightarrow$ Bool

Variables:

x,y:	Bool

Axioms:

if true then x else $y = x$
if false then x else $y = y$
not x = if x then false else true
x and y = if x then y else false
x or y = if x then true else y

In a programming environment, data types are usually constructed with consideration of their relationships with other data types. Boolean and integer data types are commonly assumed to exist and to provide predicates and numeric operations. For example, in constructing a string data type, comparison operators require a Boolean type, and the *length* operator may return a number. Because it is inconvenient to copy the entire specification for the Boolean type every time it is needed in some other specification, the concept of *extension* is introduced.

An *extension* of a previously defined specification T is a new specification T' that in addition to containing all the previously defined sorts, operators, and axioms of T, also contains new sorts, operators, and axioms, with the property that all types of T are unchanged in T'. This property is called *protection* and is precisely defined later. An *enrichment* is an extension in which no new sorts are added. Extensions and enrichments use the same format as algebraic specifications but they refer by name to the old specification on which each is built and they explicitly list only the new sorts, operators, and axioms. The format of such a specification is:

Name: *name* (extends | enriches) *list of names*
Sorts: *list of new sorts*
Operators:
　　　　list of new operators and their arities

Variables:
>   *list of variables and their sorts*

Axioms:
>   *list of new axioms*

The list of names following one of the keywords *extends* or *enriches* specifies the names of specifications that contain all the old sorts, operators, and axioms. The sorts section is deleted from enrichment specifications. The variables section will usually be deleted if the sort of a variable can be easily determined from context. Every specification can be considered as an extension of the empty specification. Here is the simplest Boolean specification with only two operators:

Name: SimpleBoolean
Sorts: Bool
Operators:
>   true: → Bool
>   false: → Bool

Axioms: none

The unique canonical form is clearly {true,false}. Next are examples of a simple enrichment and extension of SimpleBoolean.

Name: SimpleBoolean
Name: EnrichedBoolean enriches SimpleBoolean
Operators:
>   ifthenelse: Bool × Bool × Bool → Bool

Axioms:
>   if true then x else $y = x$
>   if false then x else $y = y$

Name: SimpleInt extends Boolean
Sorts: Int
Operators:
>   0:   → Int
>   S: Int → Int
>   ≤:   Int × Int → Bool

Axioms:
> $0 \leq x$ = true
> $Sx \leq 0$ = false
> $Sx \leq Sy$ $= x \leq y$

Because there are no axioms that rewrite terms of sort Int, the canonical form for Int is terms(Int), which is {0,S0,SS0,...}.

13.6 Protection, Completeness, and Consistency

The terms *completeness, consistency,* and *protection* need precise definitions. We want to protect old types by requiring that extensions do not alter the old types. Let T be a specification of a set of data types with signature Σ and axiom set A, and let T' be another specification with signature Σ', a superset of Σ, and axiom set A', a superset of A. For some sort s, let R be the congruence relation generated by A and R' the congruence relation generated by A'. If every congruence class in R' contains a term of some congruence class of R, then T' is called *s-complete with respect to* T. Intuitively, it means that s did not get any new values going from T to T'. If for every pair of noncongruent terms x and y found in R, x and y are not congruent in R', then T' is called *s-consistent with respect to* T. Intuitively it means that distinct values of s in T are still distinct values in T'. If all sorts s in T are s-complete in T', then T' is called *complete with respect to* T (Guttag, 1975, calls this *sufficiently complete* and Wand, 1979, calls this Λ-*full*). If all sorts s in T are s-consistent then T' is called *consistent with respect to* T (Wand, 1979, calls this Λ-*faithful*). If T' is both consistent and complete with respect to T, then T is *protected* in T' and T' is a legal *extension* of T.

Completeness assures us that no new values (of old types) are created by extension, and consistency assures us that unique values have not merged into one value by the extension. Incompleteness implies that we need more (or stronger) axioms, and inconsistency implies that we need fewer (or weaker) axioms. One way to show that a sort s is both complete and consistent is to show that it has the same canonical form in T' as in T.

To show that SimpleBoolean is indeed protected in EnrichedBoolean, we need to show that {true,false} is a canonical form for sort Bool in EnrichedBoolean. By induction, any term involving the operator *ifthenelse* can be rewritten without the *ifthenelse* operator because the first operand can be reduced to either *true* or *false*. It remains to be shown that *true* is not equivalent to *false*. This is typically the harder half of this kind of proof.

13.7 Derived Operators

A *derived operator* is one that can be defined as a term with variables. For example, the Boolean operations *complement, and,* and *or* can be defined in terms of the *ifthenelse* operator. A derived operator σ can be defined with exactly one nonrecursive axiom of the form

$$\sigma(x_1,\ldots,x_n) = t(x_1,\ldots,x_n)$$

Such derived operators never cause incompleteness or inconsistency. Derived operators can be considered as a term abbreviation, and thus they do not alter a canonical form. Here is an example of an enriched type using only derived operators.

Name: Boolean enriches EnrichedBoolean
Operators:

not:	Bool → Bool
and:	Bool × Bool → Bool
or:	Bool × Bool → Bool

Axioms:

not x	= if x then false else true
x and y	= if x then y else false
x or y	= if x then true else y

The integers with the standard arithmetic operations constitute another useful data type:

Name: Integer enriches SimpleInt, Boolean
Operators:

+:	Int × Int → Int
*:	Int × Int → Int
**:	Int × Int → Int
=:	Int × Int → Int
≠:	Int × Int → Int
≥:	Int × Int → Int
⟨:	Int × Int → Int
⟩:	Int × Int → Int
1:	→ Int
2:	→ Int

Axioms:

$$0+x = x \qquad Sy+x = S(x+y)$$
$$0*x = 0 \qquad Sy*x = x+y*x$$
$$x**0 = 1 \qquad x**Sy = x*x**y$$

$$(x=y) \quad = x \leq y \text{ and } y \leq x$$
$$(x \neq y) \quad = \text{not } x=y$$
$$(x \geq y) \quad = y \leq x \text{ and } x \neq y$$
$$(x \rangle y) \quad = \text{not } x \leq y$$
$$(x \langle y) \quad = \text{not } x \geq y$$

$$1 = S0$$
$$2 = S1$$

Note that all of the above comparison operators and constants are derived operators, and that each arithmetic operator is defined recursively on the canonical form determined from SimpleInt.

The Boolean and integer examples have been constructed in stages. The Boolean specification is equivalent to the FirstExample specification. The purpose of the stage is to easily prove the correctness of the specifications. In the simple initial stages of Bool and Int, the canonical forms are

easy to determine and verify with respect to our intuitive notions of the
Boolean and integer values. In these initial stages, we look for the simplest
set of operations that will generate all the values of a data type. In
SimpleInt we could have deferred the definition of ≤ to Integer. The operations in the early stages are usually called *constructor* operations because
they construct all the values of a data type. They are useful for determining
suitable canonical forms.

Once the constructor operations have been identified, the remaining
operations can be defined in a straightforward manner. Derived operations
are the easiest. Other operations can be visually checked for completeness
by verifying that any term with the operator can be reduced to one without. The operands of the operator can be assumed to be in canonical form
(since we usually use inductive proofs). Consistency is more difficult, as
usual.

13.8 *Parameterized Data Types and Set(Z)*

We now consider the specification of parameterized types using the set
example. Using the methods previously discussed, the definition of set of
Int is straightforward. We wish, however, to specify set of Z for any type Z.
Z is called a type parameter and we may assume that certain operations
come with the type. In the following example we require that Z has an
equality operator, therefore set of Z is defined only for types that have the
equality operator. A type parameter must be protected like any other previously defined operator. The sorts section of the specification must be
enhanced to include parameterized sorts and their operations.

    Name: set extends Boolean
    Sorts: set(Z with eq: Z × Z → Bool)
    Operators:
            emptyset: → set(Z)
            insert: Z × set(Z) → set(Z)
            delete: Z × set(Z) → set(Z)
            member: Z × set(Z) → Bool
            union: set(Z) × set(Z) → set(Z)
            intersect: set(Z) × set(Z) → set(Z)
            subset: set(Z) × set(Z) → Bool
            seteq: set(Z) × set(Z) → Bool

    Axioms:
      1.   insert(x,insert(y,s)) =   if eq(x,y)
                                        then insert(x,s)
                                        else insert(y,insert(x,s))

2. $\quad$ delete(x,emptyset) $=$ $\quad$ emptyset
3. $\quad$ delete(x,insert(y,s)) $=$ $\quad$ if eq(x,y)
$\qquad\qquad\qquad\qquad\qquad$ then delete(x,s)
$\qquad\qquad\qquad\qquad\qquad$ else insert(y,delete(x,s))

4. $\quad$ member(x,emptyset) $=$ false
5. $\quad$ member(x,insert(y,s)) $=$ if eq(x,y)
$\qquad\qquad\qquad\qquad\qquad$ then true
$\qquad\qquad\qquad\qquad\qquad$ else member(x,s)

6. $\quad$ union(s,emptyset) $=$ $\quad$ s
7. $\quad$ union(s,insert(x,t)) $=$ $\quad$ insert(x,union(s,t))

8. $\quad$ intersect(s,emptyset) $=$ emptyset
9. $\quad$ intersect(s,insert(x,t)) $=$ $\quad$ if member(x,s)
$\qquad\qquad\qquad\qquad\qquad$ then insert(x,intersect(s,t))
$\qquad\qquad\qquad\qquad\qquad$ else intersect(s,t)

10. $\quad$ subset(emptyset,s) $=$ $\quad$ true
11. $\quad$ subset(insert(x,s),t) $=$ $\quad$ if member(x,t)
$\qquad\qquad\qquad\qquad\qquad$ then subset(s,t)
$\qquad\qquad\qquad\qquad\qquad$ else false

12. $\quad$ seteq(s,t) $=$ subset(s,t) and subset(t,s)

Two *ifthenelse* operators are used in the above axioms. One of them is the one defined in EnrichedBoolean and the other is

ifthenelse: Bool $\times$ set(Z) $\times$ set(Z) $\rightarrow$ set(Z)

As mentioned at the end of the previous section, the *ifthenelse* operators will be used whenever convenient. Their use implies the two appropriate axioms.

The constructors of the set data type are *emptyset* and *insert*. All other operators (except the derived operator *seteq*) have two axioms, one to take care of the emptyset case, and the other to take care of the insert operator. Thus each term of sort set(Z) can be reduced to a term with only *insert* and *emptyset* operators.

It is harder to describe a canonical form for set(Z) than for Bool or Int. The set

$\{$ insert(z_1,...insert(z_n, emptyset)...) $\mid n \geq 0$ $\}$

is not a canonical form because, for example,

insert(x,insert(x,emptyset)) $\simeq$ insert(x,emptyset)

Even the set

{ insert(z_1,...insert(z_n, emptyset)...) | $n \geq = 0$ and for all i,j with $i \neq j$,
   not eq(z_i, z_j) }

is not a canonical form, since

   insert(x,insert(y,emptyset)) $\simeq$ insert(y,insert(x,emptyset))

If the elements of Z can be ordered then the set

{ insert(z_1,...insert(z_n, emptyset)...) | $n \geq 0$ and $z_1 \langle ... \langle z_n$ }

is a canonical form for set(Z). A complicated canonical form makes checking for the completeness and consistency of each operator difficult.
Suppose the *then* part of axiom 3 were "then s" rather than "then
delete(x,s)". This at first may seem like an innocent change, but it would
make the specification Bool-inconsistent.

true
$\simeq$ member(x,insert(x,emptyset))   by axiom 5
$\simeq$ member(x,delete(x,insert(x,insert(x,emptyset))))   by axiom 3*
$\simeq$ member(x,delete(x,insert(x,emptyset)))   by axiom 1
$\simeq$ member(x,emptyset)   by axiom 3*
$\simeq$ false   by axiom 4

13.9   Stack(Z) and Errors

This example is a first attempt to describe a stack of Z. It is not Z-complete
or Bool-complete.

Name: UnfinishedStack extends Boolean
Sorts: stack(Z)
Operators:
   emptystack: $\to$ stack(Z)
   push: Z $\times$ stack(Z) $\to$ stack(Z)
   pop: stack(Z) $\to$ stack(Z)
   top: stack(Z) $\to$ Z
   empty?:   stack(Z) $\to$ Bool
Axioms:
1.   pop(push(z,s)) = s
2.   top(push(z,s)) = z
3.   empty?(emptystack) = true
4.   empty?(push(z,s)) = false

---

* By the modified version of axiom 3:
   delete(x,insert(y,s)) = if eq(x,y) then s else insert(y,delete(x,s)).

Before analysing UnfinishedStack, imagine what a canonical form might be, based on your intuitive notion of a stack. All stacks can be created with the emptystack and push operators. Thus a reasonable canonical form could be:

$$C = \{ \text{push}(z_1, \dots \text{push}(z_n, \text{emptystack})\dots) \mid n \geq = 0 \}$$

However, expressions with the pop operator cannot always be reduced to expressions involving just emptystack and push operators, in particular pop(emptystack). So a canonical form for stack(Z) of UnfinishedStack is

$$C \cup \{ \text{pop}(\dots\text{pop}(\text{emptystack}) \dots) \mid \text{for 1 or more pops} \}$$

This does not leave one with a comfortable feeling about stacks. There are a couple of things we can do to fix this situation. First, we can let pop(emptystack) be an error and add this error to our intuitive canonical form, thus making

$$C' = C \cup \{\text{stack-error}\}$$

This reasonable and logical resolution leads to the new axiom:

5.   pop(emptystack) = stack-error

But now complications begin, because we must decide what push(z,stack-error), top(stack-error), and empty?(stack-error) should return. It seems we must also add an error value to each of the sorts Bool and Z and add the new axioms:

6.   top(stack-error) = z-error
7.   pop(stack-error) = stack-error
8.   empty?(stack-error) = Bool-error
9.   push(z,stack-error) = stack-error

But alas, these axioms are neither Bool-consistent nor Z-consistent!

Bool-error	$\simeq$ empty?(error)	by axiom 8
	$\simeq$ empty?(push(z,error))	by axiom 9
	$\simeq$ false	by axiom 4
z	$\simeq$ top(push(z,stack-error))	by axiom 2
	$\simeq$ top(stack-error)	by axiom 9
	$\simeq$ top(push(x,stack-error))	by axiom 9
	$\simeq x$	by axiom 2

These are a few of the problems encountered when pursuing the issue of errors. Goguen et al. (1978) give solutions to these problems and present methods for incorporating errors in algebraic specifications. An alternative approach to errors in specifications is to generalize the idea of operations to partial functions (Guttag et al., 1978; Majster, 1979; Kamin and Archer, 1984). Errors can then be incorporated into specifications without the problems we encountered above.

Another but less pleasing approach to the problem is to design data types without errors. To do this one must define what the pop and top operations do on an emptystack. We can let pop(emptystack) be emptystack but what about top(emptystack)? To define this value, we make emptystack a unary operator that specifies a value from Z that is to be used like an error value. This nonstandard stack is now easily specified as:

Name: Nonstandard-stack extends Boolean
Sorts: stack(Z)
Operators:

emptystack:	Z → stack(Z)
push:	Z × stack(Z) → stack(Z)
pop:	stack(Z) → stack(Z)
top:	stack(Z) → Z
empty?:	stack(Z) → Bool

Axioms:
1. $pop(emptystack(z)) = emptystack(z)$
2. $pop(push(z,s)) = s$
3. $top(emptystack(z)) = z$
4. $top(push(z,s)) = z$
5. $empty?(emptystack(z)) = true$
6. $empty?(push(z,s)) = false$

13.10 The Lambda Calculus Specification

As the last example in this section, we present an algebraic specification of the lambda calculus. This example is particularly appropriate since the lambda calculus is a favorite language for studying type issues and it also illustrates the power of the algebraic specification method. The grammar for the lambda calculus is simple:

expression → identifier
expression → (expression expression)
expression → (λ identifier . expression)

Lambda calculus expressions are constructed from identifiers, application of a function to an argument, and abstraction. There are three conversion rules of the lambda calculus.

α If w is not free in M then $(\lambda v.M) = (\lambda w.sub(M,v,w))$
β $((\lambda x.M)N) = sub(M,x,N)$
η If x is not free in M, then $(\lambda x.(M\ x)) = M$

where $sub(a,b,c)$ means to substitute c for all free occurrences of b in expression a. The algebraic specification first specifies the domain of identifiers (similar to the definition of integers), and provides three operators, "var," "app," and "abs," for constructing expressions. Two hidden operators, "sub" and "notfree," represent substitution and bound identifiers. The algebraic specification of the lambda calculus follows:

```
Name: Lambda-Calculus extends Boolean
Sorts: Exp, Id
Operators:
        firstid:        → Id
        nextid:         Id → Id
        eq:             Id × Id → Bool
        var:            Id → Exp
        app:            Exp × Exp → Exp
        abs:            Id × Exp → Exp
   *    sub:            Exp × Id × Exp → Exp
   *    notfree:        Id × Exp → Bool
```

Axioms:

$abs(v,M) = $ if $notfree(w,M)$ -- α *conversion*
                then $abs(w,sub(M,v,var(w)))$
                else $abs(v,M)$

$app(abs(x,M),N) = sub(M,x,N)$ -- β *conversion*

$abs(x,app(M,var(x))) = $ -- η *conversion*
                if $notfree(x,M)$
                then M
                else $abs(x,app(M,var(x)))$

$sub(var(y),x,E)\ \ = $ if $eq(x,y)$ then E else $var(y)$
$sub(app(M,N),x,E) = app(sub(M,x,E),sub(N,x,E))$
$sub(abs(y,M),x,E) = $ if $eq(x,y)$
                    then $abs(y,M)$
                    else if $notfree(y,E)$
                    then $abs(y,sub(M,x,E))$
                    else $sub(abs(y,M),x,E)$

$notfree(x,var(y))$ $= $ not $eq(x,y)$
$notfree(x,app(M,N))$ $= notfree(x,M)$ and $notfree(x,N)$
$notfree(x,abs(y,M))$ $= eq(x,y)$ or $notfree(x,M)$

$eq(x,x) = $ true
$eq(firstid,nextid(x)) = $ false
$eq(nextid(x),firstid) = $ false
$eq(nextid(x),nextid(y)) = eq(x,y)$

13.11 *Initial and Final Algebras*

The approach to data types presented in this and the previous chapter is based on initial algebras developed by the ADJ group (Goguen, Thatcher,

Wagner, and Wright). An algebra A is initial in a class of algebras if for every algebra X in the class there exists a unique homomorphism from A to X. For any signature Σ, the Σ word algebra is initial for all algebras with Σ as the signature. This means that there exists a unique mapping of terms to the values of any Σ-algebra. This is a powerful concept since it means that one needs only to identify such an algebra and the mapping of terms to elements of the algebra comes free. In the context of algebraic specifications, the smallest congruence relation generated by a set of axioms gives an algebra that is initial among all algebras that satisfy the axioms. This initial algebra is obtained by assuming that terms represent different values unless those terms can be proven equivalent by the axioms. Consider the following specification:

Name: Example extends Boolean
Sorts: X
Operators:

empty:	$\rightarrow$ X
add:	X $\rightarrow$ X
isempty:	X $\rightarrow$ Bool

Axioms:

isempty(empty) = true
isempty(add(s)) = false

Because no X term can be proven equivalent to any other X term, the initial algebra approach assumes that all X terms represent different values. Thus, the term "add(empty)" is a different value from "add(add(empty))".

An alternative viewpoint is based on observability concepts proposed by Giarratana et al. (1976) and further developed by Wand (1979), Hornung and Raulefs (1980), and Kamin (1980). The major idea is that terms are *abstractly identical* if they cannot be distinguishable by the operations of the data type. In the above example, the terms "add(empty)" and "empty" are distinguishable by the operation "isempty." In the first case "isempty" will return false and in the other it will return true. However the terms "add(empty)" and "add(add(empty))" cannot be distinguished because there is no operation or sequence of operations whose output will tell us the difference. Note that the observability concept must use previously defined data types in which we know the values. The Boolean type is sufficient and we assume that true is distinguishable from false. Thus two terms x and y of sort s are abstractly identical if and only if there does not exist a Boolean term $t(v)$ with a single variable v of sort s such that

$t(x)$ = true
$t(y)$ = false

Otherwise the two terms are considered abstractly different. Whereas the initial algebra approach assumes that all terms that cannot be proven equivalent must therefore be different, the final algebra approach assumes only that abstractly different terms are indeed different. The difference is the treatment of abstractly identical terms that are not equivalent (for example, "add(empty)" and "add(add(empty))"). The initial algebra approach assumes they are different values. The final algebra approach assumes they are the same value. For many data type specifications, the initial and final algebras are the same. In the above example, they are the same if we add the axiom:

$$add(add(s)) = add(s)$$

An algebra A is a *final algebra* in a class of algebras if there exists a homomorphism from every algebra in the class to A. The final algebra specified by the final algebra approach is the final algebra in the class of algebras that satisfy the axioms and at the same time protect all old data types (i.e., preserve previously existing algebras).

A compromise or rather more generous interpretation of algebraic specifications is to consider any algebra that may lie between the final and initial algebras. This approach is equivalent to saying that no assumption is made about abstractly identical terms that are not equivalent. Such terms may or may not represent the same element of the data type. With such an interpretation, the data type no longer represents an isomorphism class.

Exercises

1. Show that the set $C = \{0, S0\}$ is a canonical form for axiom set R_8.

2. Show that the set $C = \{0, S0, SS0, ...\}$ is a canonical form for axiom set R_7.

3. Show that the following specifications are not extensions by showing that they are either not SimpleBoolean-complete or not SimpleBoolean-consistent or both.

Name: Exer1 enriches SimpleBoolean
Operators:
    →:   Bool × Bool → Bool
Axioms:
    true→false = false
    x→true = true
Name: Exer2 enriches SimpleBoolean
Operators:
    →:   Bool × Bool → Bool
Axioms:
    x→x = true
    true→x = false
    false→x = true

Name: Exer3 enriches SimpleBoolean
Operators:
    →:   Bool × Bool → Bool
Axioms:
    $x→x$ = true
    true$→x$ = false

4. Prove that any data type with a signature with a single constant and a single unary operator can be expressed with a single simple axiom.

5. Write an algebraic specification for sequence(Z) with unary operator seq(Z) which creates a one element sequence consisting of z, sequence concatenation, "+", and *length(s)*, which returns the length of sequence s.

6. Enrich the specification of the previous exercise with the operation replace(a,b,c) which returns sequence a with the first occurence of sequence b replaced with sequence c. If there is no occurrence of sequence b in sequence a, the replace operator returns sequence a.

7. In the previous chapter, six Σ-algebras were given. Determine the sets of axioms that specify the last five of these algebras.

8. Write an algebraic specification for the rational numbers with operations: 0, 1, +, −, *, /, and a constant E that indicates zero divide error. If E is an operand of any operator, the E value is returned. Find and describe a canonical form for this type.

9. Write an algebraic specification for stack(Z) with errors. First, create a new type ErrBool which has three values: true, false, and BoolError. Second, let Z-error be a constant of type Z. Third, let all operations on error values return an error value of the appropriate sort.

10. Consider the algebraic specification for arrays (an example from Wand, 1979).

Name: IntArrays extends Integer
Sorts:. A
Operators:
        empty: → A
        val: A × Int → Int
        alt: A × Int × Int → A
Axioms:
        val(empty,x) = 0
        val(alt(a,x,y),z) =   if ($x=z$)
                              then y
                              else val(a,z)

Give some examples of abstractly identical terms that are not equivalent. Is the initial or final algebra more appropriate for this data type?

What axioms are needed to make the initial and final algebras the same? (Note that adding such axioms changes the initial algebra, but not the final algebra.)

11. Show that all abstractly identical terms in the set algebraic specification are also equivalent (thus showing that the final and initial algebras are the same). Let Nset be exactly like the set algebraic specification excluding the first axiom. Show that the final and initial algebras of Nset are different. Show that the final algebra specified by Nset is isomorphic to the initial algebra specified by set.

Further Reading

The algebraic material of this chapter is largely derived from the work of the ADJ group, in particular from Goguen et al. (1978). Algebraic specifications were independently developed by Zilles (1974), Goguen et al. (1975), and Guttag (1975). Earlier work on axiomatic approaches to data types includes Hoare (1972a) and Standish (1973). Kamin (1979) attempts to standardize the terminology.

There are many semantic formalisms for languages that are nicely surveyed by Pagan (1981). Just as a data type can be considered a simple programming language, so a programming language can be considered as a complicated data type. This leads to the use of algebraic specifications to define programming languages (Wand, 1980; Broy and Wirsing, 1980; Cleaveland, 1980).

There are many fertile areas of research and applications of algebraic specifications, including executable specifications such as Affirm (Musser, 1979) and OBJ (Goguen and Tardo, 1979; Goguen, 1984), and equational programming (Hoffmann and O'Donnell, 1982, 1984). The completeness issue is discussed by Thiel (1984) and Jouannaud and Kirchner (1984).

For more details about the lambda calculus and models see Stoy (1977) for an introduction and Wadsworth (1976) or Barendregt (1981) for complete details.

Bibliography

Addyman, A.M. (1980), "A Draft Proposal for Pascal," *SIGPLAN Notices* **15**, 4, pp. 1–66.

Albano, A. (1983), "Type Hierarchies and Semantic Data Models," *Proceedings of the SIGPLAN '83 Symposium on Programming Language Issues in Software Systems, SIGPLAN Notices* **18**, 6, pp. 178–186.

Allen, J. (1978), *Anatomy of LISP,* McGraw-Hill, New York.

Anderson, E.R., F.C.Belz, and E.K.Blum (1976), "SEMANOL(73): A Metalanguage for Programming the Semantics of Programming Languages," *Acta Informatica* **6**, pp. 109–131.

Backus, John (1978a), "The History of FORTRAN I, II, and III," in *ACM SIGPLAN History of Programming Languages Conference*, June 1978, *SIGPLAN Notices* **13**, 8, pp. 165–180.

Backus, John (1978b), "Can Programming be Liberated from the von Neumann Style? A Functional Style and its Algebra of Programs," *Communications of the ACM* **21**, 8, pp. 613–641.

Baker, T.P. (1982), "A One-Pass Algorithm for Overload Resolution in Ada," *ACM Transactions on Programming Languages and Systems* **4**, 4, pp. 601–614.

Barendregt, H.P. (1981), *The Lambda Calculus: Its Syntax and Semantics,* North-Holland, Amsterdam.

Beech, D. (1970), "A Structural View of PL/I," *Computing Surveys* **2**, 1, pp. 33–64.

Berry, D.M., L.M.Chirica, J.B.Johnston, D.F.Martin, and A. Sorkin (1978), "Time Required for Reference Count Management in Retention Block-Structured Languages," *Int. J. Comput. Inf. Sci.* **7**, 1, pp. 11–64 (part 1); **7**, 2, pp. 91–119 (part 2).

Berry, D.M., and R.L.Schwartz (1979), "Type Equivalence in Strongly Typed Languages: One More Look," *SIGPLAN Notices* **14**, 9, pp. 35–41.

Berry, D.M., and A. Sorkin (1978), "Time Required for Garbage Collection in Retention Block-Structured Languages," *Int. J. Comput. Inf. Sci.* **7**, 4, pp. 361–404.

Bert, D. (1983), "Refinements of Generic Specifications with Algebraic Tools," *Information Processing 83* pp. 815–820.

219

Blum, E.K., and F. Parisi-Presicce (1983), "Implementation of Data Types by Algebraic Methods," *Journal of Computer and System Sciences* **27**, pp. 304–330.

Borning, A.H., and D.H.H.Ingalls (1982), "A Type Declaration and Inference System for Smalltalk," *Conference Record of the Ninth Annual ACM Symposium on Principles of Programming Languages*, pp. 133–141.

Brainerd, W. (editor) (1978), "Fortran 77," *Communications of the ACM* **21**, 10, pp. 806–820.

Broy, M., and M. Wirsing (1980), "Programming Languages as Abstract Data Types," in M. Dauchet (ed.), Les arbres en algèbre et en programmation, 5ème Colloque de Lille, pp. 160–177, *Acta Informatica* **18**, pp. 47–64.

Broy, M., and M. Wirsing (1982), "Partial Abstract Types," *Acta Informatica* **18**, pp. 47–64.

Bruce, K.B., and A. Meyer (1984), "The Semantics of Second Order Polymorphic Lambda Calculus," in *Semantics of Data Types*, edited by G. Kahn, D. B. MacQueen, and G. Plotkin, *Lecture Notes in Computer Science* **173**, Springer-Verlag, pp. 131–144.

Burge, W.H. (1975), *Recursive Programming Techniques*, Addison-Wesley, Reading, Mass.

Burstall, R.M., and J.A.Goguen (1977), "Putting Theories Together to Make Specifications," *Proceedings of the Fifth International Joint Conference on Artificial Intelligence*, August 1977, Cambridge, Mass., pp. 1045–1058.

Burstall, R.M., D.B.MacQueen, and D.T.Sannella (1980), "HOPE: An Experimental Applicative Language," University of Edinburgh, Internal Report CSR-62-80, May 1980.

Burton, F.W., and B.J.Lings (1981), "Abstract Data Types, Subtypes and Data Independence," *The Computer Journal* **24**, 4, pp. 308–311.

Cardelli, L. (1984), "A Semantics of Multiple Inheritance," in *Semantics of Data Types*, edited by G. Kahn, D. B. MacQueen, and G. Plotkin, *Lecture Notes in Computer Science* **173**, Springer-Verlag, pp. 51–68.

Cleaveland, J.C. (1975), "Meaning and Syntactic Redundancy," in *New Directions in Algorithmic Languages*, Inst. de Recherche d'Informatique et d'Automatique, Rocquencourt, 1975, pp. 115–124.

Cleaveland, J.C. (1980), "Programming Languages Considered as Abstract Data Types," *Proceedings ACM 80*, Nashville, Tenn., October 1980.

Cohen, J. (1981), "Garbage Collection of Linked Data Structures," *Computing Surveys* **13**, 3, pp. 341–367.

Cohen, J., and A. Nicolau (1983), "Comparison of Compacting Algorithms for Garbage Collection," *ACM Transactions on Programming Languages and Systems* **5**, 4, pp. 532–553.

Coppo, M. (1983), "On the Semantics of Polymorphism," *Acta Informatica* **20**, 2, pp. 159–170.

Cormack, G.V. (1983), "Extensions to Static Scoping," *Proceedings of the SIGPLAN '83 Symposium on Programming Language Issues in Software Systems,* in *SIGPLAN Notices* **18**, 6, pp. 187–191.

Cousot, P., and R. Cousot (1977), "Static Determination of Dynamic Properties of Generalized Type Unions," *Proceedings of an ACM Conference on Language Design for Reliable Software,* in *SIGPLAN Notices* **12**, 3.

Curry, H.B., and R. Feys (1958), *Combinatory Logic I,* North-Holland, Amsterdam.

Dahl, O.J., and C.A.R.Hoare (1972), "Hierarchical Program Structures," in Dahl et al. (1972).

Dahl, O.J., C.A.R.Hoare, and E.W.Dijkstra (1972), *Structured Programming,* Academic Press, New York.

Dahl, O.J., B. Myhrhaug, and K. Nygaard (1968), *The Simula 67 Common Base Language,* Norwegian Computing Centre, Forskningsveien 1B, Oslo 3.

Damas, L., and R. Milner (1982), "Principal Type-Schemes for Functional Programs," *Conference Record of the Ninth Annual ACM Symposium on Principles of Programming Languages,* pp. 207–212.

Demers, A., J. Donahue, and G. Skinner (1978), "Data Types as Values: Polymorphism, Type-checking, Encapsulation," *Conference Record of the Fifth Annual ACM Symposium on Principles of Programming Languages,* pp. 23–30.

Demers, A.J., and J.E.Donahue (1980a), "Data Types, Parameters and Type Checking," *Conference Record of the Seventh Annual ACM Symposium on Principles of Programming Languages,* pp. 12–23.

Demers, A.J., and J.E.Donahue (1980b), " 'Type-Completeness' as a Language Principle" *Conference Record of the Seventh Annual ACM Symposium on Principles of Programming Languages,* pp. 234–244.

Dewar, R.B.K, A.Grand, Ssu-Cheng Liu, J.T.Schwartz, and E.Schonberg (1979), "Programming by Refinement, as Exemplified by the SETL Representation Sublanguage," *ACM Transactions on Programming Languages and Systems* **1**, 1, pp. 27–49.

Donahue, J.E. (1976), *Complementary Definitions of Programming Language Semantics, Lecture Notes in Computer Science* **42**, Springer-Verlag.

Dungan, D.M., (1979), "Bibliography on Data Types," *SIGPLAN Notices* **14**, 11, pp. 31–59.

Eggert, P.R. (1981), "Detecting Software Errors before Execution," UCLA Computer Science Dept. Report No. CSD-810402, April 1981.

Falkoff, A.D., and K.E.Iverson (1973), "The Design of APL," *IBM Journal of Research and Development* July 1973, pp. 324–334; also in Horowitz (1983), pp. 212–222.

Falkoff, A.D., and K.E.Iverson (1978), "The Evolution of APL," in Wexelblat (1978).

Fleck, A.C. (1978), "Formal Models for String Patterns," in Yeh (1978), pp. 216–240.

Friedman, D.P., and D.S.Wise (1976), "CONS Should Not Evaluate Its Arguments," in *Automata, Languages and Programming*, S. Michaelson, and R. Milner (editors), Edinburgh University Press, Edinburgh.

Gannon, J.D. (1977), "An Experimental Evaluation of Data Type Conventions," *Communications of the ACM* **20**, 8, pp. 584–595.

Gannon, J.D., and J.J.Horning (1975), "Language Design for Programming Reliability," *IEEE Transactions on Software Engineering* **1**, 2, June, 1975.

Ganzinger, H. (1983), "Parameterized Specifications: Parameter Passing and Implementation with Respect to Observability," *ACM Transactions on Programming Languages and Systems* **5**, 3, pp. 318–354.

Gehani, N., and D. Gries (1977), "Some Ideas on Data Types in High Level Languages", *Communications of the ACM* **20**, pp. 414–420.

Gerhart, S.L., and L. Yelowitz (1976), "Observations of Fallibility in Applications of Modern Programming Methodologies," *IEEE Transactions on Software Engineering*, **2**, 3, pp. 195–207.

Geschke, C.M., J.H. Morris Jr. and E.H.Satterwaite (1977), "Early Experience with Mesa," *Communications of the ACM* **20**, 8, pp. 540–553.

Giarratana, V., F. Gimona, and U. Montanari (1976), "Observability Concepts in Abstract Data Type Specifications, in A. Mazurkiewicz (editor), *Lecture Notes in Computer Science* **45**, Springer-Verlag, pp. 576–587.

Goguen, J.A. (1984), "Parameterized Programming," *IEEE Transactions on Software Engineering* **10**, 5, pp. 528–543.

Goguen, J.A., and J.J.Tardo (1979), "An Introduction to OBJ: A Language for Writing and Testing Formal Algebraic Program Specifications," *Proceedings IEEE Specifications of Reliable Software*.

Goguen, J.A., and J.W.Thatcher (1974), "Initial Algebra Semantics," *Proceedings of the 15th IEEE Symposium on Switching and Automata Theory,* New Orleans, October 1974.

Goguen, J.A., J.W.Thatcher, and E.G.Wagner (1978), "An Initial Algebra Approach to the Specification, Correctness, and Implementation of Abstract Data Types," in Yeh (1978), pp. 80–149.

Goguen, J.A., J.W.Thatcher, E.G.Wagner, and J.B.Wright (1975), "Abstract Data Types as Initial Algebras and the Correctness of Data Representations," *Proceedings, Conference on Computer Graphics, Pattern Recognition, and Data Structures*, pp. 89–93.

Goldberg, A., and D. Robson (1983), *Smalltalk-80, The Language and Its Implementation*, Addison-Wesley, New York.

Goodwin, J.W. (1981), "Why Programming Environments Need Dynamic Data Types," *IEEE Transactions on Software Engineering* **7**, 5, Sept. 1981.

Gordon, M.J., A.J.Milner, and C.P.Wadsworth (1979), *Edinburgh LCF, Lecture Notes in Computer Science* **78**, Springer-Verlag.

Gries, D. (editor) (1978), *Programming Methodology: A Collection of Articles by Members of IFIP WG2.3*, Springer-Verlag, New York.

Griswold, R.E. (1982), "The Evaluation of Expressions in Icon," *ACM Transactions on Programming Languages and Systems* **4**, 4, pp. 563–584.

Griswold, R.E. (1983), *ICON Programming Language*, Prentice-Hall, Englewood Cliffs, N.J.

Griswold, R.E., J.F.Poage, and I.P.Polonsky (1971), *The SNOBOL 4 Programming Language* (Second Edition), Prentice-Hall, Englewood Cliffs, N.J.

Gull, W.E., and M.A.Jenkins (1979), "Decisions for 'Type' in APL," *Conference Record of the Sixth Annual ACM Symposium on Principles of Programming Languages*, pp. 190–196.

Guttag, J.V. (1975), "The Specification and Application to Programming of Abstract Data Types," Ph.D. Thesis, University of Toronto, Department of Computer Science, CSRG-59.

Guttag, J.V. (1977), "Abstract Data Types and the Development of Data Structures," *Communications of the ACM* **20**, 6, pp. 396–404.

Guttag, J.V., and J.J.Horning (1983), "An Introduction to the Larch Shared Language," *Information Processing 83*, pp. 809–814.

Guttag, J.V., E.Horowitz, and D.R.Musser (1978), "The Design of Data Type Specifications," in Yeh (1978), pp. 61–80.

Habermann A.N., and D.E.Perry (1983), *Ada for Experienced Programmers*, Addison Wesley, Reading, Mass.

Harland, D.M. (1984), *Polymorphic Programming Languages: Design and Implementation*, Ellis Horwood, Chichester, England.

Harland, D.M., and H.I.E.Gunn (1982), "Another Look at Enumerated Types," *SIGPLAN Notices* **17**, 7, pp. 62–71.

Harle, J. (1983), "The Proposed Standard for BASIC," *SIGPLAN Notices* **18**, 5, pp. 25–40.

Henderson, P. (1980), *Functional Programming: Application and Implementation*, Prentice-Hall, Englewood Cliffs, N.J.

Henderson, P., and J.H. Morris Jr. (1976), "A Lazy Evaluator," *Third ACM Symposium on Principles of Programming Languages*, pp. 95–103.

Hindley, R. (1969), "The Principal Type-Scheme of an Object in Combinatory Logic," *Transactions of the American Mathematical Society* **146**, pp. 29–60.

Hoare, C.A.R. (1972a), "Notes on Data Structuring," in Dahl et al. (1972).

Hoare, C.A.R. (1972b), "Proof of Correctness of Data Representations," *Acta Informatica* **1**, pp. 271–281; also in Gries (1978).

Hoare, C.A.R., and N. Wirth (1973), "An Axiomatic Definition of the Programming Language PASCAL," *Acta Informatica* **2**, pp. 335–355.

Hoffmann, C.M., and M.J.O'Donnell (1982), "Programming with Equations," *ACM Transactions on Programming Languages and Systems* **4**, 1, pp. 83–112.

Hoffmann, C.M., and M.J.O'Donnell (1984), "Implementation of an interpreter for abstract equations," *Conference Record of the Eleventh Annual ACM Symposium on Principles of Programming Languages*, pp. 111–120.

Hornung, G., and P. Raulefs (1980), "Terminal Algebra Semantics and Retractions for Abstract Data Types," in J. DeBakker, and J. Leeuwen (editors), *Lecture Notes in Computer Science* **85**, Springer-Verlag, pp. 310–323.

Horowitz, E. (editor) (1983), *Programming Languages: A Grand Tour*, Computer Science Press, Rockville, Maryland.

Ichbiah, J.D., J.C. Heliard, O. Roubine, J.G.P. Barnes, B. Krieg-Brueckner, B.A. Wichmann (1979), "Rationale for the design of the Ada programming language," *SIGPLAN Notices* **14**, 6, part B.

Jackson, M.A. (1977), "COBOL," in *Software Engineering*, edited by R.H.Perrott, pp. 47–57, Academic Press, New York.

Jensen, K., and N. Wirth (1974), *PASCAL User Manual and Report* (Second Edition), Springer-Verlag, New York and Berlin.

Jouannaud, J.P., and H. Kirchner (1984), "Completion of a Set of Rules Modulo a Set of Equations," *Conference Record of the Eleventh Annual ACM Symposium on Principles of Programming Languages*, pp. 83–92.

Kamin, S. (1979), "Some Definitions for Algebraic Data Type Specifications," *SIGPLAN Notices* **14**, 3.

Kamin, S. (1980), "Final Data Specifications: a New Data Type Specification Method," *Conference Record of the Seventh Annual ACM Symposium on Principles of Programming Languages*, pp. 131–138.

Kamin, S. (1983), "Final Data Types and Their Specification," *ACM Transactions on Programming Languages and Systems* **5**, 1, pp. 97–123.

Kamin, S., and M. Archer (1984), "Partial Implementations of Abstract Data Types: A Dissenting view on Errors," in *Semantics of Data Types*, edited by G. Kahn, D. B. MacQueen, and G. Plotkin, *Lecture Notes in Computer Science* **173**, Springer-Verlag, pp. 317–336.

Kaplan, M.A., and J.D.Ullman (1980), "A Scheme for the Automatic Inference of Variable Types," *Journal of the ACM* **27**, 1.

Karr, M., and D.B.Loveman III (1978), "Incorporation of Units into Programming Languages," *Communications of the ACM* **21**, 5, pp. 385–391.

Kernighan, B.W., and D.M.Ritchie (1978), *The C Programming Language*, Prentice-Hall, Englewood Cliffs, N.J.

Knuth, D.E. (1968), "Semantics of Context-Free Languages," *Mathematical Systems Theory* **2**, pp. 127–145.

Knuth, D.E. (1973), *The Art of Computer Programming, Vol. I: Fundamental Algorithms*, Addison-Wesley, Reading, Mass.

Lampson, B. W., J.J. Horning, R.L. London, J.G. Mitchell, and G.J. Popek (1977), "Report on the Programming Language Euclid," *SIGPLAN Notices* **12**, 2, pp. ii–79.

Leivant, D. (1983a), "Polymorphic type inference," *Conference Record of the Tenth Annual ACM Symposium on Principles of Programming Languages*. pp. 88–98.

Leivant, D. (1983b), "Structural semantics for polymorphic data types," *Conference Record of the Tenth Annual ACM Symposium on Principles of Programming Languages.* pp. 155–166.

Liskov, B., A. Snyder, R. Atkinson, and C.Schaffert (1977), "Abstraction Mechanisms in CLU," *Communications of the ACM* **20**, 8, pp. 564–576.

Lucas, P., P. Lauer, and H. Stigleitner (1968), "Method and Notation for the Formal Definition of Programming Languages," Technical Report 25.087, IBM Laboratory, Vienna.

MacLennan, B.J. (1982), "Values and Objects in Programming Languages," *SIGPLAN Notices* **17**, 12, pp. 70–79.

MacQueen, D.B., G. Plotkin, and R. Sethi (1984), "An Ideal Model for Recursive Polymorphic Types," *Conference Record of the Eleventh Annual ACM Symposium on Principles of Programming Languages,* pp. 165–174.

MacQueen, D.B., and R. Sethi (1982), "A Semantic Model for the Types of Applicative Languages," *Proceedings of 1982 ACM Symposium on LISP and Functional Programming,* pp. 243–252.

Majster, M.E. (1977), "Limits of the 'Algebraic' Specification of Abstract Data Types," *SIGPLAN Notices* **12**, 10, pp. 37–42.

Majster, M.E. (1979), "Treatment of Partial Operations in the Algebraic Specification Technique," *Proceedings of the Specifications of Reliable Software Conference,* April 1979, pp. 190–197.

Marcotty, M., H.F.Ledgard, and G.V.Bochmann, "A Sampler of Formal Definitions," *Computing Surveys* **8**, 2, pp. 191–276.

McCarthy, J. (1960) "Recursive Functions of Symbolic Expressions and Their Computation by Machine, part 1," *Communications of the ACM* **3**, 4, pp. 184–95.

McCarthy, J., and M.Levin (1965), *LISP 1.5 Programmers Manual,* MIT Press, Cambridge, Mass.

McCracken, D.D. (1957), *Digital Computer Programming,* John Wiley & Sons, Inc., New York.

McCracken, N. (1984), "The Typechecking of Programs with Implicit Type Structure," in *Semantics of Data Types,* edited by G. Kahn, D. B. MacQueen, and G. Plotkin, *Lecture Notes in Computer Science* **173**, Springer-Verlag, pp. 301–316.

Meertens, L.G.L.T. (1983), "Incremental Polymorphic Type Checking in 'B'," *Conference Record of the Tenth Annual ACM Symposium on Principles of Programming Languages,* pp. 265–275.

Meyer, A.R. (1982), "What Is A Model of the Lambda Calculus?," *Information and Control* **52**, 1, pp. 87–122.

Miller, T.C. (1979), "Type Checking in an Imperfect World," *Conference Record of the Sixth Annual ACM Symposium on Principles of Programming Languages,* pp. 237–243.

Milner, R. (1978), "A Theory of Type Polymorphism in Programming," *Journal of Computer and System Science* **17**, pp. 348–375.

Mitchell, J. C. (1984), "Coercion and Type Inference," *Conference Record of the Eleventh Annual ACM Symposium on Principles of Programming Languages*, pp. 175–185.

Mitchell, J.G., and B. Wegbreit (1978), "Schemes: A High-level Data Structuring Concept," in Yeh (1978), pp. 150–184.

Moffat, D.V. (1981), "Enumerations in Pascal, Ada, and Beyond," *SIGPLAN Notices* **16**, 2, pp. 77–82.

Morris, J.H. (1973). "Types Are Not Sets," *Conference Record of ACM Symposium on the Principles of Programming Languages*, pp. 120–124, October 1973.

Musser, D.R. (1979), "Abstract Data Type Specification in the AFFIRM System," *Proceedings of the Specifications of Reliable Software Conference*, April 1979.

Naur, P. (editor) (1963), "Revised Report on the Algorithmic Language ALGOL 60," *Communications of the ACM* **6**, 1, pp. 1–20.

Nicholls, J.E. (1975), *The Structure and Design of Programming Languages*, Addison-Wesley, Reading, Mass.

Oyamaguchi, M. (1985), "On the Data Type Extension Problem for Algebraic Specifications," *Theoretical Computer Science* **35**, pp. 329–336.

Pagan, F.G. (1981), *Formal Specification of Programming Languages: A Panoramic Primer*, Prentice-Hall, Englewood Cliffs, N.J.

Popek, G.J., J.J.Horning, B.W.Lampson, J.G.Mitchell, and R.L.London (1977), "Notes on the Design of Euclid," *SIGPLAN Notices* **12**, 3, pp. 11–19; also in Horowitz (1983), pp. 252–260.

Reynolds, J.C. (1970), "GEDANKEN - A Simple, Typeless Language Based on the Principle of Completeness and on the Reference Concept," *Communications of the ACM* **13**, 5, pp. 308–319.

Reynolds, J.C. (1975), "User-Defined Types and Procedural Data Structures as Complementary Approaches to Data Abstraction" in *New Directions in Algorithmic Languages*, Inst. de Recherche d'Informatique et d'Automatique, Rocquencourt, 1975, pp. 157–168; also in Gries (1978).

Reynolds, J.C. (1978), "Syntactic Control of Interference," *Conference Record of the Fifth Annual ACM Symposium on Principles of Programming Languages*, pp. 39–46.

Reynolds, J.C. (1983), "Types, Abstractions and Parametric Polymorphism," *Information Processing 83*, pp. 513–523.

Reynolds, J.C. (1984), "Polymorphism Is Not Set-Theoretic," in *Semantics of Data Types*, edited by G. Kahn, D. B. MacQueen, and G. Plotkin, *Lecture Notes in Computer Science* **173**, Springer-Verlag, pp. 145–156.

Richards, M. (1969), "BCPL: A Tool for Compiler Writing and System Programming," *Proceedings of AFIPS Spring Joint Computer Conference* **34**, pp. 557–66.

Robinson, J.A. (1965), "A Machine-Oriented Logic Based on the Resolution Principle," *Journal of the ACM* **12**, 1, pp. 23–41.

Schonberg, E., J.Schwartz, and M. Sharir (1981), "An Automatic Technique for Selection of Data Representation in SETL Programs," *ACM Transactions on Programming Languages and Systems* **3**, 2.

Scott, D.S. (1970), "Lattice Theory, Data Types, and Semantics," in *Formal Semantics of Programming Languages*, edited by R. Rustin, 2nd Courant Computer Science Symposium, Prentice-Hall (1972).

Scott, D.S. (1976), "Data types as lattices," *SIAM J. on Computing* **5**, 3, pp. 522–586.

Shaw, M. (1976), "Research Directions in Abstract Data Types," *Conference Proceedings on Data: Abstraction, Definition and Structure, SIGPLAN Notices* **8**, 2, pp. 66–68.

Sherman, M. (1984), "Paragon: Novel Uses of Type Hierarchies for Data Abstraction," *Conference Record of the Eleventh Annual ACM Symposium on Principles of Programming Languages*, pp. 208–217.

Standish, T.A. (1973), "Data Structures: An Axiomatic Approach," BBN Report 2639, Bolt Beranek and Newmann, Cambridge, Mass.

Standish, T.A. (1980), *Data Structures Techniques*, Addison-Wesley, Reading, Mass.

Stoy, J.E. (1977), *Denotational Semantics: The Scott-Strachey Approach to Programming Language Theory,* MIT Press, Cambridge, Mass.

Stroustrup, B. (1986), *The C++ Programming Language*, Addison-Wesley, Reading, Mass.

Suzuki, N. (1981), "Inferring Types in Smalltalk," *Conference Record of the Eighth Annual ACM Symposium on Principles of Programming Languages*, ACM.

Taghva, K. (1983), "Constructive Fully Abstract Models of Typed Lambda-Calculi," CSR 159, Computer Science Dept., New Mexico Tech, Socorro, N.M., December 1983.

Tanenbaum, A.S. (1976), "A Tutorial on Algol 68" *Computing Surveys* **8**, 2, pp. 155-190; also in Horowitz (1983), pp. 89–124.

Tenenbaum, A.M. (1974), "Compile Time Type Determination in SETL," *Proceedings of the ACM 1974 Annual Conference*, November 1974.

Tennent, R.D. (1973), "Mathematical Semantics of SNOBOL4," *Conference Record of ACM Symposium on Principles of Programming Languages*, pp. 95–107.

Tennent, R.D. (1976), "The Denotational Semantics of Programming Languages," *Communications of the ACM* **19**, 8, pp. 437–453.

Tennent, R. (1978), "Another Look at Type Compatibility in Pascal," *Software Practice and Experience* **8**, pp. 429–437.

Tennent, R.D. (1981), *Principles of Programming Languages*, Prentice-Hall, Englewood Cliffs, N.J.

Thatcher, J.W., E.G.Wagner, and J.B.Wright (1979), "Data Type Specification: Parameterization and the Power of Specification Techniques," IBM Research Report RC 7757, 34 pages; also in *ACM Transactions on Programming Languages and Systems* **4**, 4, pp. 711–732.

Thiel, J.J. (1984), "Stop Losing Sleep over Incomplete Data Type Specifications," *Conference Record of the Eleventh Annual ACM Symposium on Principles of Programming Languages,* pp. 76–82.

van Wijngaarden, A., B.J. Mailloux, J.E.L. Peck, C.H.A. Koster, M. Sintzoff, C.H. Lindsey, L.G.L.T. Meertens, and R.G. Fisker (editors) (1975), "Revised Report on the Algorithmic Language Algol 68," *Acta Informatica* **5**, pp. 1–236.

Wadsworth, C.P. (1976), "The Relation between Computational and Denotational Properties for Scotts D_∞-Models of the Lambda-Calculus," SIAM Journal on Computing 5, pp. 488–521.

Wampler, S.B., and R.E.Griswold (1983), "The Implementation of Generators and Goal-Directed Evaluation in Icon," *Software Practice and Experience* **13**, pp. 495–518.

Wand, M. (1979), "Final Algebra Semantics and Data Type Extensions," *Journal of Computers and System Sciences* **19**, 1, pp. 27–44.

Wand, M. (1980), "First-Order Identities as a Defining Language," *Acta Informatica* **14**, pp. 337–357.

Wand, M. (1984), "A Types-as-Sets Semantics for Milner-Style Polymorphism," *Conference Record of the Eleventh Annual ACM Symposium on Principles of Programming Languages,* pp. 158–164.

Wasserman, A.I. (editor) (1980), *Tutorial: Programming Language Design,* IEEE Catalog No. EHO 164-4.

Wegbreit, B. (1974), "The Treatment of Data Types in EL1," *Communications of the ACM* **17**, 5, pp. 251–264.

Wegner, P. (1972), "The Vienna Definition Language," *Computing Surveys* **4**, 1, pp. 5–63.

Welsh, J., W.J.Sneeringer, and C.A.R.Hoare (1977), "Ambiguities and Insecurities in Pascal," *Software Practice and Experience* **7**, pp. 685–696.

Wexelblat, R.L. (editor) (1978), *ACM SIGPLAN History of Programming Languages Conference, SIGPLAN Notices* **13**, 8

White, J.R. (1983), "On the Multiple Implementation of Abstract Data Types Within a Computation," *IEEE Transactions on Software Engineering* **9**, 4, pp. 395–410.

Wirsing, M., P. Pepper, H. Partsch, W. Dosch, and M. Broy (1983), "On Hierarchies of Abstract Data Types," *Acta Informatica* **20**, 1, pp. 1–33.

Wirth, N. (1971), "The Programming Language Pascal," *Acta Informatica,* **1**, 1, pp. 35–63.

Wirth, N. (1977), "MODULA: a Language for Modular Multiprogramming," *Software Practice and Experience,"* **7**, pp. 3–35; also in Horowitz (1983).

Wirth, N. (1980), *MODULA-2,* Berichte des Instituts fur Informatik No. 36, ETH, Zurich.

Wulf, W.A., R.L.London, and M.Shaw (1976), "An Introduction to the Construction and Verification of Alphard Programs," *IEEE Transactions on Software Engineering* **2**, 4, pp. 253–265.

Wulf, W.A., D.B.Russell, and A.N.Habermann (1971), "BLISS: A Language for Systems Programming," *Communications of the ACM* **14**, 12, pp. 780–790.

Yeh, R.T. (editor) (1978), *Current Trends in Programming Methodology, Vol. IV, Data Structuring*, Prentice-Hall, Englewood Cliffs, N.J.

Zilles, S.N. (1974), "Algebraic Specification of Data Types," Project MAC Progress Report 11, MIT, Cambridge, Mass., pp. 28–52.

*I*ndex